REBOUNDING FROM SETBACKS

Role Models of Resilience

Emerson Klees

D1514371

Cameo Press, Rochester, New York

Cameo Press
P. O. Box 18131
Rochester, New York 14618

Library of Congress Control Number 2014921715

ISBN 978-1-891046-23-0

Printed in the United States of America
9 8 7 6 5 4 3 2 1

DEDICATION

This book is dedicated to my wife, Patricia, and to Robert, David, and Stephanie, our greatest accomplishments.

OTHER BOOKS BY EMERSON KLEES

Role Models of Human Values Series

One Plus One Equals Three—Pairing Man / Woman Strengths:
    Role Models of Teamwork
Entrepreneurs In History—Success vs. Failure: Entrepreneurial
    Role Models
Staying With It: Role Models of Perseverance
The Drive to Succeed: Role Models of Motivation
The Will to Stay With It: Role Models of Determination
Paul Garrett: Dean of American Winemakers
A Song of the Vine: A Reflection on Life
Emotional Intelligence: People Smart Role Models
Emotional Intelligence: People Smart Role Models II
Emotional Intelligence: People Smart Role Models III

The Moral Navigator: Stories From Around the World

Inspiring Legends and Tales With a Moral I
Inspiring Legends and Tales With a Moral II
Inspiring Legends and Tales With a Moral III

Books About New York State and the Finger Lakes Region

People of the Finger Lakes Region
Legends and Stories of the Finger Lakes Region
The Erie Canal in the Finger Lakes Region
Underground Railroad Tales With Routes Through the Finger Lakes
    Region
More Legends and Stories of the Finger Lakes Region
The Women's Rights Movement and the Finger Lakes Region
Persons, Places, and Things In the Finger Lakes Region [6 lakes]
The Crucible of Ferment, New York's "Psychic Highway"
The Iroquois Confederacy: History and Legends
Rochester Lives
Wineries of the Finger Lakes Region—100 Wineries
Persons, Places, and Things Of the Finger Lakes Region [11 lakes]
Finger Lakes Wineries: A Pictorial History

THE ROLE MODELS OF HUMAN VALUES SERIES

"Example teaches better than precept. It is the best modeler of the character of men and women. To set a lofty example is the richest bequest a man [or woman] can leave behind."

Samuel Smiles

The Role Models of Human Values Series provides examples of role models and of lives worthy of emulation. The human values depicted in this series include perseverance, motivation, determination, and resilience. Role models are presented in biographical sketches of historical figures that describe the environment within which they strived and delineate their personal characteristics.

These profiles illustrate how specific human values helped achievers reach their goals in life. We can learn from these examples in strengthening the human values that are so important to our success and happiness. The Introduction in each book highlights the factors that contributed to these achievers' success.

PREFACE

"Life affords no higher pleasure than that of surmounting difficulties, passing from one step of success to another, forming new wishes and seeing them gratified. He that labors in any great or laudable undertaking has his fatigues first supported by hope and then by joy."

Samuel Johnson

This book provides role models of resilience through profiles of thirty-five individuals who displayed resilience at one phase of their lives or throughout their lifetimes. The thirty-five biographical sketches represent seven areas of endeavor:

Composers / Artists / Playwrights

Reformers / Activists

Luminaries / Notables

Researchers / CEOs / Inventors

Statesmen / Rulers

Soldiers / Sailors / Airmen

Organizers / Planners

Although the subject of this book is resilience, these individuals displayed other strong personal characteristics, including perseverance, motivation, and determination, discussed in other books in the Human Values Series. If we put our daily challenges and problems into perspective alongside those faced by these thirty-five individuals, our concerns pale in comparison. We can then turn our challenges and problems into opportunities and our lives will be richer for it.

TABLE OF CONTENTS

Page No.

INTRODUCTION

"Most of the important things in the world have been accomplished by people who have kept on trying when there seemed to be no hope at all."

Dale Carnegie

Resilience is the ability to rebound from setbacks and failures. Over the course of our lives most of us will encounter significant trauma, such as abuse as a child, domestic violence, an automobile accident in which we or a family member are seriously injured, loss of mobility, an incapacitating disease, or financial ruin. It is estimated that 90% of us will encounter at least one major trauma during our lifetimes.

In *Resilience: The Science of Mastering Life's Greatest Challenges*, Steven Southwick and Dennis Charney observed: "In the physical sciences, materials and objects are termed resilient if they resume their original shape after being bent or stretched. In people, resilience refers to the ability to 'bounce back' after encountering difficulty." Southwick and Charney identified ten "resilience factors":

- realistic optimism
- facing fear
- moral compass
- religion and spirituality
- social support
- resilient role models
- physical fitness
- brain fitness
- cognitive and emotional stability
- meaning and purpose

Southwick and Charney admit that this isn't necessarily a complete list, but they were the resilience factors most often described as crucial, and sometimes even life-threatening, for the individuals interviewed.

The American Psychological Association defines resilience as "the process of adapting well in the face of adversity, trauma, tragedy, threats, and even significant sources of stress—such as family and relationship problems, serious health problems, or workplace and financial stresses."

Adversity can take several forms. One is to be in a situation over which we have no control, such as an unavoidable automobile accident, or having a genetically inherited disease. A second example is the case in which we have exercised poor judgement in making decisions, possibly financial decisions. We feel responsible for the adversity. Thirdly, we may have intentionally taken risks that do not result in our favor. We went into this situation knowing the risks in advance.

In *A Vietnam Experience,* Admiral J. B. Stockdale observed that those who are resilient generally meet failure head on and use it as an opportunity to learn and self-correct. He views resilience from the point of view of history:

> The only way I know to handle failure is to gain
> historical perspective, to think about men who have
> successfully lived with failure in our religious and
> classical past. When we were in prison we remembered
> the book of Ecclesiastes: "I returned and realized that
> the race is not always to the swift nor the battle to the
> strong . . . but time and chance happeneth to them all."
> . . Failure is not the end of everything. A man can always
> pick himself up off the canvas and fight one more
> round. To handle tragedy may, in fact, be the mark
> of an educated man, for one of the principal goals
> of education is to prepare us for failure.

We may have a fear of failure, but the important thing is how we deal with the setback. Some individuals are motivated just to give in. We can learn from the adversity, however, and actually become stronger individuals because of it. Author Shari Cohen noted, "It is easy to give in to failure . . . 'I can't do that again; it didn't work for me the first time' . . . Don't be fooled. The success stories that you read and hear about don't involve people who try things just once. The excuses: 'It was too difficult to attempt again,' or 'Why should I try?'—fall flat on the ears of those opportunity chasers, the ones who strive for achievement."

Some individuals who experienced trauma note that they now enjoy life more and have improved relationships with their friends and family than they had before the adversity. Poet Elizabeth S. Lucas observed: "The forces of fate that bear down on man and threaten to break him also have the capacity to ennoble him."

A young entrepreneur traveled to Silicon Valley to apply to a venture capitalist for money to begin his start-up. The venture capitalist told him that he would rather invest in an entrepreneur who had failed four times than one on his first attempt. The venture capitalist believed that the one who had failed four times knew what not to do.

In *The Resilience Factor,* Karen Reivich and Andrew Shatte identify seven keys to finding our strengths and overcoming life's hurdles:

1. Learning Your ABCs—Know the Facts of a Situation
2. Avoiding Thinking Traps—Do Not Jump to Conclusions
3. Detecting Icebergs—Below the Surface of Consciousness
4. Challenging Beliefs—Realistic Problem Solving
5. Putting in Perspective—Not Every Failure Is a Catastrophe
6. Calming and Focusing—Don't Be Overwhelmed By Stress
7. Real-Time Resilience—Avoid Nonproductive Thoughts

Psychological factors play a large role in our ability to be resilient. Jennifer Pearson and Darlene Kordich Hall, in *Reaching In . . . Reaching Out: Resiliency Guidebook,* provide a list of critical abilities associated with resilience:

• Emotional Regulation—Being in charge of our emotions
• Impulse Control—Deciding to act on desire to take action
• Causal Analysis—Deciding on the cause of a problem
• Realistic Optimism—A positive but realistic outlook
• Empathy—Understanding the feelings and needs of another
• Self-efficacy—Belief that what we do matters
• Reaching out—Ability to take on new opportunities

Overcoming difficulties can make us stronger individuals than we would have been if we had not encountered any adversity. For example, Nelson Mandela thought that the twenty-seven years that he spent in prison helped to develop hidden strengths and to forge personal capabilities that served him in leading South Africa out of apartheid and in becoming the leader of the country.

Franklin Delano Roosevelt went through an extremely debilitating illness, polio, in his early thirties. It appeared that his time in public life was over. He continued to be optimistic and to do everything he could do to utilize the physical strength that remained. His wife, Eleanor, and many historians believe that FDR was a better President of the United States because he had suffered and overcome polio than he would have been had he not had that experience.

QUOTATIONS

"If we had no winter, the spring would not be so pleasant. If [we] did not sometimes taste of adversity, prosperity would not be so welcome."

Charlotte Bronte

"I think one of life's great milestones is when a person can look back and be almost as thankful for the setbacks as for the victories. Gradually, it dawns on us that success and failure are not polar opposites. They are parts of the same picture—the picture of a full life, where you have your ups and your downs. After all, none of us can ever lose unless we have the courage to try. Losing means that at least you were in the race."

Robert Dole

"There are no hopeless situations; there are only people who have grown hopeless about them."

Clare Boothe Luce

"Be of good cheer. Do not think of today's failures, but of the success that may come tomorrow. You have set your-selves a difficult task, but you will find success if you persevere; and you will find joy in overcoming obstacles. Remember, no effort that we make to attain something beautiful is lost."

Helen Keller

"A man is not finished when he is defeated. He is finished when he quits."

Richard Nixon

"What should happen when you make a mistake is this: You take your knocks, you learn your lessons, and then you move on."

Ronald Reagan

CHAPTER 1

COMPOSERS / ARTISTS / PLAYWRIGHTS

"There is no failure except in no longer trying."

Elbert Hubbard, *The Note Book,* 1927

RICHARD RODGERS (1902-1979) Composer of Popular Music

"Of all the writers whose songs are considered and examined . . . those of Rodgers show the highest degree of consistent excellence, inventiveness and sophistication . . . After spending weeks playing his songs, I am more impressed and respectful; I am astonished."

Composer Alec Wilder

Richard Rodgers composed the music for over 1,000 popular songs, of which over 200 were notable hits, and about 100 have become popular classics. He also wrote thirty-five stage productions, including sixteen that were major successes. Two of them established box-office records. The musicals for which he is known include *A Connecticut Yankee, On Your Toes, The Boys from Syracuse, Pal Joey, Oklahoma, Carousel, South Pacific,* and *The King and I.* His most popular songs include "Some Enchanted Evening," and "You'll Never Walk Alone." Also, he composed music for television and Hollywood films. Rodgers was influenced by composers Victor Herbert and Jerome Kern.

Of Rodgers, Ira Gershwin observed: "I am sure that musicologists, present and future, will have to agree that Rodgers is not only one of our most successful composers of theater music but also one of exquisite taste and resourcefulness, and as a composer-showman, one of integrity and courage." Leonard Bernstein considered Rodgers the most imitated songwriter of our time, and noted: "He has established new levels of taste, distinction, simplicity in the best sense, and inventiveness."

Rodgers's first lyricist partner was Lorenz (Larry) Hart, whom he knew from his years at Columbia University. Later, Oscar Hammerstein II wrote the lyrics for his music. In working with Hart, Rodgers usually composed the music first and then Hart wrote the lyrics. It was the reverse with Hammerstein, who usually wrote the lyrics and then Rodgers composed the music. Occasionally, the composer and the lyricist worked together in an ongoing joint effort.

Rodgers was born on June 28, 1902, into a prosperous German Jewish family in Queens, New York City. He was the son of Mamie Levy Rodgers and Dr. William Abrahams Rodgers, a prominent physician. Rodgers began playing the piano by ear at the age of six and was influenced in his early years by the Broadway operettas his parents took him to see. He attended summer camp at Camp Wigwam in Harrison, Maine, where he composed his first songs at the age of fourteen.

Rodgers was introduced to Hart by mutual friend Philip Leavitt when Rodgers was in high school and Hart had dropped out of Columbia College at the age of twenty-three. Rodgers decided to work with Hart even though he was known to be difficult and unreliable. Later, Rodgers noted that "In one afternoon, I acquired a career, a partner, a best friend, and a source of permanent irritation."

In 1919, Rodgers decided to attend Columbia College, mainly because it put on varsity shows with student talent. Hart had participated in these shows and had maintained his contacts at the college. Rodgers and Hart worked together on two plays at Columbia.

Rodgers's and Hart's first play on Broadway was *Poor Little Rich Girl* that opened on July 28, 1920, and ran for 119 performances. Only half the score was by Rodgers, the other half was by Sigmund Romberg. After this modest success, it was five years before their work appeared in the professional theatre. They took any small music job that was available.

Rodgers was discouraged with his lack of success and with the courses at Columbia in which he had no interest, such as history and mathematics. He wanted to concentrate on music and considered transferring to the Institute of Musical Art, which is now Juilliard. He spoke with his father about his plans and his father was beginning to question his son's choice of music as a career, a field in which he did not seem to be experiencing much success. His two years at the Institute opened new opportunities for Rodgers.

William Rodgers was concerned about his son, who was now twenty-two years old and living on an allowance provided by his father. He could see no possibility of his son earning a living from music. William consulted a lawyer friend who suggested that he give Richard a little more time. What William did not know was that Richard himself was beginning to question his preparation for the future.

Rodgers decided to find a job in business. A friend referred him to a manufacturer of children's underwear. Rodgers was offered $50.00 a week to sell its products and promised a more responsible position if he proved to be successful. Rodgers discussed the position with his father and told him he was tired of living on an allowance and that he wanted to begin to earn his own living.

Fortunately, before Rodgers could accept the job, he received a call from the lawyer friend of his father who had met with some young actors from the Theatre Guild planning a sophisticated revue. They were looking for a composer and a lyricist. The revue, *The Garrick Gaieties,* was scheduled for only two performances— a matinee and an evening at the Garrick Theatre on May 17, 1925. Rodgers and Hart were chosen for the job.

The revue was a series of parodies and comedy sketches that included two very popular Rodgers and Hart tunes: "Manhattan" and "Sentimental Me." The critics were enthralled. Alexander Woollcott called it "fresh and spirited and engaging." Robert Benchley described it as "the most civilized play in town." Four additional performances were scheduled in early June. The revue began regular performances on June 8 and ran for twenty-five weeks. For the first time, Rodgers and Hart earned a regular income.

The next success of Rogers and Hart was *Dearest Enemy,* which included the hit song "Here in My Arms." It ran for just under a year and helped to bring attention to the composer and lyricist. They were much in demand, and in 1926, they had five shows on Broadway, including *The Girl Friend,* which ran for over 400 performances, and *The Melody Man.*

Rodgers and Hart followed with *Peggy-Ann,* an unorthodox play that nevertheless was popular with the critics—Robert Benchley and Dorothy Parker thought that it was the best musical they had seen. It ran for almost a year before moving to London.

Their next musical, *A Connecticut Yankee,* was their most successful to date. It included a song they had written earlier, "My Heart Stood Still," a song popularized in England by the Prince of Wales, who sang it in public." Thou Swell" also gained popularity. In 1925, Rodgers was ready to give up song writing and accept a job in business. One year later, he was the fair-haired boy of Broadway.

17

Larry Hart continued to be difficult to work with. He was undisciplined and irresponsible. Although Rodgers was younger than Hart, he functioned as his older brother. Rodgers referred to Hart as "the sweetest little guy in the world." Rodgers observed of Hart's writing of lyrics: "He hated doing it and loved it when it was done." In 1929, Rodgers and Hart wrote *Spring Is Here*, which introduced the hit "With a Song in My Heart."

On March 5, 1930, Richard Rodgers married Dorothy Feiner, whom he had known since she was seven years old. Their fathers were friends, and Rodgers and Dorothy's brother, Ben, were also friends. They knew that they were meant for each other from the time she was sixteen. They honeymooned in Europe. In London, they were honored guests at a dinner party given by Lord and Lady Louis Mountbatten.

In the early 1930s, Rodgers and Hart spent four years in Hollywood making movies. When they returned to New York, they found that they had almost been forgotten. Their musical *On Your Toes* was one of their early successes on their return to Broadway. This was the first musical in which Rodgers and Hart wrote the book, in addition to the music and lyrics. They began to fully integrate the text and the music, and, to some extent, to tell a story. The ballet "Slaughter on Tenth Avenue" was an important element of *On Your Toes*.

Babes in Arms, which opened in 1937, was the first musical in which Rogers and Hart wrote the entire book without any outside assistance. It contained "Where or When," My Funny Valentine," "Johnny One Note." and "I Wish I were in Love Again." Its sophisticated "The Lady Is a Tramp" had a new rhythmic energy. One of the last musicals in which Rodgers and Hart collaborated was *Pal Joey*, which opened to mixed reviews from the critics. It was rereleased in 1952 for a 542 performance run on Broadway. It became a very popular musical.

The gulf between Rodgers and Hart widened. The disciplined Rodgers had more difficulty dealing with Hart's drinking. Hart had always been concerned with his short stature and his lack of success with women. Toward the end, he paid no attention to his appearance and people would cross the street to avoid speaking with him. When the end came, it came suddenly, surprising many of his friends. He died in 1943.

Rodgers began to collaborate with Oscar Hammerstein II as his lyricist. Rodgers and Hammerstein had both attended Columbia College and worked on variety shows. Hammerstein was older than Rodgers; he was Hart's age. Hammerstein, like Rodgers, had an inauspicious start—four failures in three years before he collaborated on a successful Broadway show.

Rodgers's and Hammerstein's first collaboration was the immensely successful *Oklahoma* in 1943. In the opinion of Cole Porter: "The most profound change in forty years of musical comedy has been—Rodgers and Hammerstein." The songs, "Oklahoma" and "Oh, What a Beautiful Morning", were two of the most popular songs in a musical rich in good songs. *Oklahoma!* ran for 2,248 performances over five years and nine weeks, the longest run of any Broadway play to date.

Two of Hammerstein's earliest successes were *Rose Marie* and *The Desert Song,* both of which he wrote for Rudolf Friml. The greatest of his early works were the lyrics for *Showboat,* which he wrote with Jerome Kern. It was produced by Florenz Ziegfeld in 1927.

State Fair was one of the best scores that Rodgers wrote for motion pictures. "It Might As Well Be Spring" won the Academy Award for best song.

The next big Rodgers and Hammerstein hit was *Carousel,* which featured "June Is Bustin' Out All Over," "If I Loved You," and "You'll Never Walk Alone." The next Rodgers and Hammerstein successes included *South Pacific* and *The King and I,* which had 1,246 performances on Broadway over three years.

Rodgers and Hammerstein won a special Pulitzer Prize for *Oklahoma!* in 1944. Their musicals earned them 35 Tony Awards, 15 Academy Awards, two Pulitzer Prizes, two Grammy Awards and two Emmy Awards. Rodgers is a member of the American Theatre Hall of Fame. He died of a heart attack at the age of 77 in 1979. He had survived cancer of the jaw, a laryngectomy, and an earlier heart attack.

FREDERICK DELIUS (1862-1934) Rebounded from Illness to Compose

"I think that the most stupid thing one can do is to spend one's life doing something one hates, or in which he has no interest; in other words, it is a wasted life. I do not believe in sacrificing the big things in life to anyone or anything. Everything depends on your perseverance. One never knows how far one can go . . . One's talent develops like muscles that you are constantly training. Trust more in hard work than inspiration."

Frederick Delius

The music of English composer Frederick Delius is delicate and reserved, perhaps too delicate to be widely appreciated; nevertheless, he is considered one of the masters of music of the early twentieth century. He composed over ninety works, including six operas, four concertos, five pieces of chamber music, and many songs. His work is not widely presented.

Delius's choral works include *A Mass of Life*, *Sea Drift*, *A Song of the High Hills*, and *Requiem*. Examples of orchestral works are *Over the Hills and Far Away, Paris: The Song of a Great City, Life's Dance, Brigg Fair,* and two exquisite pieces for small orchestra, *Summer Night on the River* and *On Hearing the First Cuckoo in Spring*.

In the Introduction to *Frederick Delius* by Peter Warlock, Norman O'Neill compares the man, who continued to compose after going blind and becoming paralyzed, with his music: "Delius's music is so tender. The man Delius was not tender but purposeful and projective. The legend that has grown out of his paralyzed blindness is entirely at variance with the trapper of dreams himself. The man Delius was totally unlike his music, the one displaying a most purposeful character, the other a vivid nebulosity of dreams."

Frederick Delius, the second son of Julius and Elise Krönig Delius, was born on January 29, 1862, in Bradford, England. Julius Delius was a successful wool merchant with an international business. He took his children to Manchester to hear the Hallé Orchestra and to the Theatre Royal in Leeds to attend the opera. He was a patron of the Hallé Orchestra and willingly paid for music lessons for his children. Young Frederick chose the violin as his first instrument and also played the piano. His mother encouraged him to improvise when he played.

Delius was educated at the Bradford Grammar School and the International School in Isleworth, London. He studied Latin, Greek, geography, mathematics, natural history, physics, and social science. He wasn't much of a scholar. Going to school in London provided him with access to concerts at Covent Garden and St. James Hall, where he discovered Wagner, Grieg, and Berlioz. Upon Frederick's graduation from the International School, his father expected him to go into the family business.

Delius went to work for Delius and Company in Bradford but spent all of his spare hours on music. He traveled to London to hear works by Chopin, Grieg, and Wagner. He was sent to Chemnitz, Germany, and to Norköpping, Sweden, as a unpaid apprentice to learn all aspects of the wool industry. While in Sweden, he took hiking trips to Norway, where he learned Norwegian and was introduced to Ibsen's plays.

Delius was doing what his father wanted him to do; however, he was not doing it well, and he was certainly not enjoying it. Julius was disappointed with reports about his son's performance as an apprentice. Young Frederick had wandered off from the workplace and had attended concerts in Germany and Sweden. Next, Delius was sent to St. Etienne, France, with little money to spend on concerts. He failed there and again as an assistant office manager back home in Bradford. He wanted to attend the Leipzig Music Conservatory, but his father refused to pay his tuition.

Delius saw a poster in Bradford advertising farmland with orange groves in Florida. He told his father that he would like to become an orange grower. His father reluctantly agreed to lease a Florida orange and grapefruit plantation with an option to buy for Delius to manage. Delius and a friend traveled to Solano Grove, which was about forty miles south of Jacksonville. The rundown plantation was cared for by the Anderson family, African-Americans who had worked for the previous owner.

Delius was more fascinated by the Negro music, including hymns and spirituals, than by the challenge of growing oranges and grapefruit. The instruments used were banjos, cowbells, log drums, and seed pods. He was moved by the music, which was about slavery and separation; he entered into, in his words, "a state of illumination" and realized that the only future for him was music. He began to compose music in his head similar to what he had heard at the Anderson home.

On a trip to Jacksonville, Delius met Thomas Ward, organist at the Catholic cathedral in St. Augustine, who gave music lessons in Jacksonville. Ward offered to teach him the basics of harmony and counterpoint and loaned him Hector Berlioz's book on orchestration. Ward moved to Solano Grove to give music lessons to Delius on a rented piano. Delius wanted to capture the Negro music. The only other composer to attempt this was Louis Gottschalk, who had written pieces based on New Orleans music.

When his father found out that Delius was concentrating on music and paying no attention to orange growing, he cut off his allowance. His older brother, Ernest, who had failed at sheep farming in New Zealand, showed up at Solano Grove, and Delius turned over the plantation to him. Delius moved to Jacksonville and gave music lessons. He had many eager students, but he accepted a better opportunity, teaching music at Roanoke Female College in Danville, Virginia.

One of Delius's sponsors at the Roanoke Female College wrote to his father about his success in teaching music and asked him to reconsider sending his son to a music conservatory. Julius Delius gave in and agreed to pay for an eighteen month course in music theory at the Leipzig Conservatory. Delius received instruction in performing with musical instruments, but he did not receive substantial instruction on composing.

Delius composed *Florida*, which was based on the music he had heard there. His professors were not comfortable with his unconventional passages and did not encourage him. However, he had met Edvard Grieg on a hiking trip to Norway; Grieg was very supportive and encouraged him to compose according to his own lights.

Delius moved to Paris to compose while living on a miniscule allowance from his father. He worked on *Magic Fountain*, a opera about the search for the fountain of youth in Florida by a Spaniard named Solano with the help of a Seminole Indian princess. It was not successful, but an earlier work, *On the Heights*, about the composer's memories of Norway's mountains, enjoyed a limited success. He worked to improve *Magic Fountain*, as well as *On the Heights*.

In 1896, Delius composed an African-American folk opera, *Koanga*, which was about an African prince captured by slave traders. The storyline was about planters and overseers on plantations and in the fields, a subject Delius knew from his time in Florida. The instrumentation was for banjos, bones, and fiddles. While working on *Koanga*, he met a young artist, Helen Sophie Emilie Rosen, who went by her childhood name, Jelka. She loved his music and encouraged him to continue his work on *Koanga*. She fell in love with him, but it took him a long time to realize that he was in love with her.

Jelka painted in the garden of an old rundown house in Grez, a hamlet forty miles south of Paris. Delius found it to be a peaceful place in which to compose. His compositions were not selling well. His New York agent told him that his harmonies were too complicated, his melodies were not memorable, and the discords were not appreciated.

Delius finally realized that he was in love with Jelka. He missed her when she left Grez; he realized that he couldn't live without her. They were married on September 23, 1903. He was forty-one; she was thirty-five. Jelka gave up her career in art and devoted the rest of her life to Delius; she did everything that she could, including financial and administrative tasks, to allow her husband to concentrate on composing.

A Norwegian playwright, Gunnar Heiberg, wrote a political satire, *The Council of the People*, and asked Delius to write the accompanying music. Since *The Council of the People* was mocking and satirical, Delius wrote the background music, *Norwegian Suite*, in the same tone. Delius conducted its premiére in Oslo. The audience booed, hissed, and eventually cursed at Heiberg's mockery of the Norwegian parliament.

When they reached the point of Delius's parody of the Norwegian anthem in a minor key, the audience gasped, stomped their feet and rushed the conductor and the orchestra. A pistol was waved, and a shot rang out. The conductor and playwright ran out of the theater's rear exit to the Grand Hotel next door, while the police dealt with the crowd outside.

An elderly gentleman with white sideburns looked at them quizzically until Delius explained what had happened. The gentleman said, "I am sorry for the affront Norway has offered a distinguished visitor, Herr Delius. You must remember we are barbarians up here. Allow me to apologize. I am Henrik Ibsen." When the crowd had settled down, Delius returned to his own hotel, only to be told that he was not allowed to stay there.

In 1913, the premiére of Igor Stravinsky's *Le Sacre du Printemps* at the Theatre des Champs Elysées in Paris caused a near riot. The audience hissed, shouted, and whistled at what they viewed as a affront to traditional music. Pandemonium reigned, but nobody shot at the conductor. Fortunately for Delius, the pistol used to shoot at him was loaded with blanks.

A young German conductor, Fritz Cassirer, offered to conduct Delius's symphony *Appalachia* in London. Delius, who had just met Sir Thomas Beecham, asked if Cassirer could use Beecham's orchestra. Beecham agreed and then sat in the audience and was captivated by Delius's music. Beecham became the most active promoter in England of Delius's work, which was popular in Germany but not in England. The famous conductor included at least one Delius work every year in his programs and, occasionally, used his fortune to pay for performances.

Beecham was known for his conducting ability and his sense of humor. One evening he was conducting an opera in which everything that could go wrong, did. Musicians missed their cues, singers sang off key, and props fell onto the stage. Finally, a young elephant, which was part of the opera story, defecated on the stage. Beecham looked at the odoriferous pile, halted the orchestra, turned around to face the audience and said: "The critics have spoken." He resumed conducting the opera after the stage was cleaned.

Delius worked so hard that it began to affect his health. He was exhausted and did not feel well. In the fall of 1910, Jelka took him to a sanitarium in Germany. Slowly, he began to regain his health. Percy Grainger visited him and suggested that he write music for smaller orchestras that would be less expensive to produce. The results of this suggestion were *On Hearing the First Cuckoo in Spring* and *Summer Night on the River*.

In the spring of 1915, Delius had problems with his eyesight and began to wear thick glasses. The fingers on his right had stiffened. One morning while composing *Hassan*, an Arabian nights story, at the piano, the pen fell out of his hand. With difficulty, he picked up the pen with his left hand, but his right hand could not grip the pen. He was listless, and his legs were weak. A homeopathic doctor in the area told him that it was a "lameness that would pass off."

By the summer of 1922, Delius needed two canes to walk. On some days, he could only see large objects that were close to him. Two years later, he had to use a wheelchair. He tried hydrotherapy, electric shock treatments, and hypnotism, but no treatment improved his condition for long. Eventually, he had to be carried everywhere he went by a male nurse, and he virtually lost his sight. His condition slowed his composing, but it did not stop it.

Jelka helped Delius finish *Hassan*; however, she was a painter, not a musician. She was not familiar with orchestration; she made many mistakes, and the score had many erasures. Finishing the work was painful to Jelka as well as to Delius. Obviously, he could not continue to compose music in this fashion. In between working on his own compositions, Percy Grainger helped Delius when he could.

In May 1928, a young Yorkshireman, Eric Fenby, offered clerical help to Delius in composing his music. After several months, they evolved a productive way of working together. Delius became a news item. He was referred to as the "blind composer" and the "crippled genius." Fenby described life at Grez: "There was nothing of the sickly, morbid, blind composer as known by popular fiction here, but a man with a heart like a lion, and a spirit that was as untamable as it was stern."

In January 1929, King George presented Delius with the Order of the Companion of Honor. Delius was proud of the recognition. In the fall of 1929, Sir Thomas Beecham convinced Delius to come to London to hear his music performed in a series of six concerts. Delius was overwhelmed by the fervor of his fans in England. Beecham had prepared well for the concerts, and the concerts were standing room only. Delius was asked to speak after one of the concerts: "Ladies and gentlemen. Thank you for the very fine reception you have given me. It was wholly unexpected. I also wish to thank

Sir Thomas Beecham for the inspired manner in which he played my music. This festival has been the time of my life. Again I thank you."

Delius, Jelka, and Fenby returned to Grez, where Delius worked on a sonata. The pressure of working with an elderly person who was ill was taking a toll on Fenby. He was on the verge of a nervous breakdown. He told Delius that he had to go home to England, at least briefly. Fenby returned to Grez early in 1931 to help Delius with his work on *Irmelin*, an opera about a princess who fell in love with a prince who searched for a magic river and a wandering troubadour.

In January 1933, Delius began to sleep during much of the day. In May 1934, Jelka had cancer surgery, and Fenby returned to help the nurse care for Delius. Jelka returned from the hospital the following month and was home in Grez on June 10, 1934, when Delius died. The British Broadcasting Corporation released a news bulletin: "We regret to announce the passing of Mr. Frederick Delius, Companion of Honor," accompanied by the playing of "The Walk to a Paradise Garden" from *A Village Romeo and Juliet*. A newspaper headline announced: "MUSIC'S BLIND HERO IS DEAD; HIS SOUL GOES MARCHING ON."

ANTON CHEKHOV (1860-1904) Medical Doctor and Playwright

"Medicine is my lawful wife, and literature is my mistress. When I tire of the one, I spend the night with the other. As long as it does not become a regular habit, it is not humdrum and neither of them suffers from my infidelity. If I did not have my medical pursuits, I should find it difficult to devote my random thoughts and spare time to literature."

Anton Chekhov

Anton Chekhov, who created a new style of literature, was the first in a series of talented writers who flourished in Russia late in the late nineteenth and early twentieth centuries. Tolstoy observed: "One cannot compare Chekhov as an artist with any of the previous writers, Turgenev, Dostoevsky, or myself. Like the impressionists, Chekhov possesses his own peculiar style."

Chekhov's early works in the 1880s were mainly humorous short stories. Although his work became increasingly more mature and complex, his early writing indicated his superior talent and his regard for his fellow man. In *Makers of the Modern World*, Louis Untermeyer commented:

> It is one of literature's paradoxes that Anton Pavlovich Chekhov, who loved the comic element in life and who was known to most of his countrymen as the author of countless humorous short stories, is celebrated today as a writer who founded a new literature of unresolved suspensions, subdued in tone and minor in key, expressive of man's sense of unhappy isolation and his failure to understand his fellow man.

Chekhov, whose goal was "making the reader think," said, "When I write, I stake everything on the reader and count on him to supply for himself whatever elements may be lacking from my story." His life and his illness, tuberculosis, are reflected in many of his works, particularly in the plays that he wrote later in his life.

Anton Chekhov was born on January 17, 1860, in Taganrog, a port on the Sea of Azov. His artistic father, Pavel, was a marginally successful shopkeeper, religious zealot, and strict disciplinarian who beat his five sons regularly. Pavel's father had been born a slave but had worked hard to purchase his freedom. Chekhov's mother, Eugenia, was a warm person with a happy disposition whose father, a cloth merchant, had ensured that she received some education. She and the Chekhov children's nurse were accomplished storytellers.

Chekhov's older brothers, Alexander and Nicholas, drank and generally avoided obligations of any kind. Young Chekhov, who from the age of eight worked in the family store, became the one who assumed family responsibilities as he grew older. He was a "nice, easy-going fellow," a handsome youth with a way with women. From an early age, he was a great storyteller and mimic; also, he was accomplished in improvisation.

As a youth, Chekhov loved the theater and went to plays whenever he could. His teachers liked him, but he wasn't an exceptional student. He and his classmates started a magazine, and his first literary efforts, a drama and a vaudeville sketch, were done while he attended school in Taganrog. When Chekhov was sixteen, his father's business failed and he left Taganrog to avoid his creditors. The family joined Pavel in Moscow, except for Anton, who remained in Taganrog to finish his schooling. He lived with friends of the family and earned his keep by tutoring.

Chekhov became seriously ill by taking an ice-cold bath after a long, hot walk. This illness permanently weakened him and probably increased his susceptibility to the tuberculosis that would haunt him as a adult. The young man living away from his family was treated by a kind German physician, Dr. Strümpf. This illness and the care provided by Dr. Strümpf were factors in his deciding to become a doctor himself.

In August 1879, Chekhov joined his family in Moscow. Although he loved Moscow in his adult years, his first impressions weren't favorable. The poverty in which he found his family probably contributed to his early impressions. His father worked six long days a week in a store. Chekhov's two older brothers had moved out of the family apartment. He became the economic and disciplinary support for his two younger brothers and his sister. His younger brother, Michael, said, "His will became the dominant one."

Over the next seven years, Chekhov earned money to help support the family by writing for humor magazines. He used a pseudonym when writing potboilers, principally parodies and satires, to earn money for the family. At the age of nineteen, he passed the examination for medical school on his second attempt and won a scholarship.

Chekhov never regretted his career choice of medicine. He felt that his knowledge of science made him question the unknown and helped to give him a real direction in life. His colleagues believed that his ability to make scientific observations was a major influence on his literary works.

Chekhov applied himself to medical school, which was very demanding, and to writing. He was a prolific writer whose stories became more critical and satiric as he grew older. By the age of twenty-seven, concurrently with medical school, internship, and three years of private practice, he had written 600 short stories. The stressful life that he lived contributed to his contracting tuberculosis in his mid-twenties. He recognized the symptoms but downplayed its seriousness to his family and to himself. He could not afford the time or the cost of extended treatment.

Chekhov's medical practice grew slowly, and occasionally he was bored. His close friend and mentor, Suvorin, gave him valuable advice about his writing that helped him change his style. His friend, a self-made man who was twenty-five years his senior, impressed upon him his responsibility as a literary artist. He advised Chekhov "to respect his talent, and to publish only truly finished stories."

Chekhov enjoyed pursuing two careers. Suvorin encouraged him to give up his medical practice to write full time. He responded in a letter to Suvorin: "You advise me not to hunt two hares at once, and not even to think about my medical profession. Why not? I feel more cheerful and satisfied when I realize that I have two things to do instead of one."

Chekhov wrote an unsuccessful novel, in which he attempted to enlighten rather than to entertain. His next effort was a play about a man of the 1880s, *Ivanov*, which received both critical and popular acclaim. Also, he was awarded the Pushkin Prize for a collection of short stories. Although he was now a successful writer, he had difficulty believing that the popularity of his literary works would last. He continued to drive himself, partly because he still bore the financial responsibility for his family.

In 1888, Chekhov wrote a second play, *The Wood Spirit*, which was unsuccessful. This failure reinforced his belief that he was not a playwright; he did not attempt another play for seven years.

Chekhov was a humanitarian in his home region. He donated 10,000 rubles for the construction of model schools at Melikhovo, Novoselki, and Talezh. He contributed many books to the school in his hometown, Taganrog—eight large consignments in one two-year period. One year, he sent 319 books by French authors to Taganrog from Nice. He really couldn't afford to do this, but he did it anyway because he was aware of the critical need.

During the summer of 1892, Chekhov was unable to pursue his literary work. As a medical doctor, he was asked to prepare for an expected cholera epidemic. The Melikhovo district had experienced a severe epidemic in 1848, and the anticipated one was expected to be at least as serious. Medical facilities in the region were limited, and it was difficult to transport patients elsewhere because of the poor roads.

In 1895, Chekhov wrote his third play, *The Sea Gull*. His friends didn't like it, and the patrons at the Alexandrinski Theater in St. Petersburg, who had expected a comedy, booed loudly at the première and called it "decadent." It was a dismal failure, partly because the producer had not understood Chekhov's intentions for the play.

Two years later, Vladimir Nemirovich-Danchenko and Konstantin Stanislavski, co-founders of the Moscow Art Theater, resurrected the play. Audiences and the critics gave it an overwhelming response.

Drama critic Brooks Atkinson of the *New York Times* wrote a perceptive review of *The Sea Gull:* "Beyond and behind the surface, Chekhov has caught the great truths of life—the carelessness, selfishness, and weariness of civilized existence—the candid truth of human society, comic in its inadequate grasp of the fundamentals of social living, tragic in its consequences."

Chekhov rewrote his play, *The Wood Spirit*, and renamed it *Uncle Vanya*. The Moscow Art Theater produced it; it was a resounding success. In the play, Chekhov describes a "slice of life," leaving the audience to imagine what had preceded those events and what followed them. In *The Personal Papers of Anton Chekhov*, he wrote, "The artist should be not the judge of his characters, but only an unbiased witness . . . My business is merely to report . . . to be able to distinguish important and unimportant statements, to be able to illuminate the characters and speak their language . . . to transmit the conversation exactly as I hear it and let the jury—that is, the readers—estimate its value."

Chekhov spent most of his time in Yalta, where the climate was more favorable for his health than Moscow. However, he came to love Moscow and the Moscow Art Theater that produced his plays. Olga Knipper, one of the leading actresses of the Moscow Art Theater, had been romantically interested in Chekhov for several years. In October 1898, Chekhov wrote to Suvorin from Yalta:

> Before my departure I attended the rehearsals of *Tsar Fedor Ioannovich*. I was moved by the intelligence which marked the performance. Real art was on the stage . . . Irena [Olga Knipper] I think excellent. Her voice, the elevation of her character, her sincerity are so wonderful that I enjoy the mere recollection of it . . . Best of all is Irena! If I had stayed in Moscow I should have fallen in love with that Irena.

Olga pursued him for two years and, finally, proposed to him. On April 18, 1901, he wrote to her: "If you promise to me that not a soul in Moscow shall know about our wedding before it has taken place, I will marry you on the very day of my arrival. Somehow I dread the ceremony, the congratulations, the champagne glass in my hand, and a vague smile on my face." On May 25, 1901, Chekhov and Olga Knipper were married.

In 1900, Chekhov had been elected to the belles-lettres division of the Russian Academy. His good friend and fellow author, Maxim Gorki, was expelled from the Academy in 1902 for his political beliefs. Chekhov resigned from the Academy that year to protest his friend's expulsion.

In 1900-01, Chekhov wrote *Three Sisters*, considered the

gloomiest of his plays. He conceived this play and his last play, *The Cherry Orchard*, as comedies; however, audiences looked upon them as bleak plays depicting Russian life. Upon reading *Three Sisters* for the first time, the actors and actresses were confused by it. They viewed it as a scheme, not a completed play. To them, it was composed of hints and intimations, not well-delineated roles.

Olga played the second of the sisters, Masha. *Three Sisters* is intended as a dialog between the author and Masha in the distance. This play, perhaps his most nostalgic, is a drama of restlessness and strain in the provinces; however, it also provides glimpses into the future. Although initially less successful than *The Seagull* and *Uncle Vanya,* it had more performances than his earlier plays.

In 1903-04, Chekhov wrote *The Cherry Orchard*, subtitled *A Comedy*. His health was declining rapidly; in considerable physical pain, he could write only a few lines a day. He intended the play to be a comedy using irony, but the producer portrayed it as the tense drama of the replacement of old criteria by new standards as a fading upper class gave way to increasing materialism. The advertising referred to it as a drama. The première performance, an overwhelming success, was on January 17, 1904.

In early 1904, Chekhov's condition became acute. His wife, the joy of his later years, was always at his bedside. She observed, "Growing weaker in body but stronger in spirit, he took a perfectly simple, wise, and beautiful attitude to his bodily dissolution, because he said, 'God has put a bacillus in me.'" In June, Chekhov and his wife traveled to a sanatorium at Badenweiler in the Black Forest of Germany. He told his friends that he was going away to "peg out."

On July 2, Chekhov awakened in the middle of the night with difficulty breathing. He became delirious and talked about Russia and her people. He regained consciousness and was given a glass of champagne to stimulate his heart. He said, "Ich sterbe" (I am dying) and died. He was buried in Moscow alongside his father. Chekhov said, "Everything I have written will be forgotten in a few years. But the paths I have traced will remain intact and secure, and there lies my only merit." As usual, he underestimated himself. His works have been influential, and he is remembered as one of the great modern playwrights.

After Chekhov's death, Maxim Gorki wrote a moving memoir about his friend:

> I have never known a man feel the importance of work as a foundation of civilization as profoundly and completely as Anton Chekhov. It was apparent in the everyday details of his personal life, in his choice of themes, and in that noble love of things which, free from any desire to acquire them, never tires of admiring in them the creations of the human mind.

PIERRE-AUGUSTE RENOIR (1841-1919) Artist Who Overcame Arthritis

"Courage and perseverance have a magic talisman, before which difficulties disappear and obstacles vanish into the air."

John Quincy Adams

Pierre-Auguste Renoir was born at Limoges on February 25, 1841. In 1845, his father, a struggling tailor, moved the family to Paris. Renoir displayed an inclination toward art at an early age by his frequent doodling; however, he also showed a talent in music. His singing in the choir on Sundays at the Eglise Saint-Roch impressed choirmaster Charles Gounod. Renoir's practical father decided that the field for his son was ceramics, the principal industry of Limoges. The father reasoned that his son had enough artistic ability to become a successful painter on porcelain. At the age of thirteen, Renoir began his apprenticeship as a porcelain painter in Paris.

Renoir began by painting bouquets and figures on dishware that was shipped to customers in the Far East. His preference for luminous colors began at this time. He worked in a factory located within walking distance of the Louvre, where he spent many of his lunch hours. He was introduced to sculpture at the Louvre. He was particularly impressed by *Fontaine des Innocents* by Jean Goujon. In addition to his use of bright, contrasting colors, Renoir's choice of the subject of sensuous, full-bodied women began at this time.

From 1862 to 1864, Renoir enrolled in courses at the Ecole des Beaux-Arts. Concurrently, he studied at Gleyre's studio, where he met Monet and Sisley. Gleyre, who was considered one of the premier teachers of art in Paris, looked at Renoir's work and remarked, "You are, I presume, dabbling in paint to amuse yourself."

Renoir responded, "Of course, when it ceases to amuse me, I will stop painting." He never lost his interest in painting, and he painted a wide range of subjects, including floral still lifes, sun-filled landscapes, family groups, and nudes. The painting style of Diaz influenced him most at this stage of his development.

Renoir and his friends enjoyed painting in the forest of Fontainebleau, where members of the Barbizon School, including

Corot, Diaz, Millet, and Rousseau, went to paint. In the forest, Renoir met Diaz, who looked at Renoir's painting and commented, "Not badly drawn, but why the devil do you paint so dark?" Diaz suggested that the young painter stop using black altogether, and he referred Renoir to his own color dealer. Meeting Diaz was a turning point in Renoir's career. Later, Renoir was influenced by Courbet, Manet, and, to some extent, Delacroix.

When he was twenty-four, two of Renoir's paintings were accepted by the Salon, and, by the age of thirty-three, he participated in the Societe Anonyme des Artistes, Peintres, Sculpteurs et Graveurs, with Cezanne, Degas, Monet, and Pissarro. The society's first two exhibitions received negative reviews in the press. In particular, Cezanne and Renoir were targeted for derision. Critic Albert Wolff wrote that Renoir's painting of a woman looked like "a mass of flesh in the process of decomposition with green and violet spots which denote the state of complete putrefaction of a corpse." Manet told Monet, "Renoir has no talent at all. You, who are his friend, should tell him kindly to give up painting." Manet was the painter most respected by Renoir and his friends. Renoir considered Manet "the standard-bearer of the group, but only because his work was the first to get down to that simplicity we were all out to master."

It was one of Monet's paintings, *Impression: Sunrise*, that was the origin of the name of the group of painters who painted in a new, vague style. They became known as "Impressionists" and thought: "Treating a subject in terms of the tone and not of the subject itself is what distinguishes the Impressionists from other painters." They considered themselves to be reinterpreting reality.

In *The History of Impressionism*, John Rewald observed, "They succeeded in blurring the outlines of objects and merging them with the surroundings. This method permitted the introduction of one color into the area of another without degrading or losing it, thus enriching the color effects. Moreover, this technique of vivid strokes seemed best suited to their efforts at rapidly changing aspects."

In 1873, Renoir met Paul Durand-Ruel, the first dealer who was serious about marketing his paintings. Later, Ambroise Vollard became both a promoter of Renoir's paintings and a close friend.

During the summers of 1879 and 1880, Renoir painted along the banks of the Seine River. He completed *Oarsmen at Chatou* at this time and sketched *Luncheon of the Boating Party.* The model he found most attractive was Aline Charigot, the young woman with a small puppy in the left foreground of the boating party painting. She became his wife as well as his model; they had a long and happy marriage. One of their three sons, Jean, became a renowned film director.

When Renoir entered his forties, he began to distance himself from the Impressionists. He thought that they weren't paying enough attention to composition. He wanted to change the way that he used colors, which he thought had become too soft, and to use bolder structures that would be "solid and enduring."

Renoir traveled to Algeria, Pompeii, Rome, and Florence to absorb, to observe, and to learn about stronger designs and hotter colors. He reflected, "Nothing can be taken for granted. The sections of an orange, the leaves of a tree, the petals of a flower are never identical. It would seem that beauty derives its charm from this diversity."

Renoir's art went through a "Harsh Period" in the 1880s, when his paintings were cold and severe. *Afternoon at Wargemont,* which he painted in 1884, was an early example. Two works from 1887, *Girl with a Cow* and *A Ewe and Girls Playing Shuttlecock,* represent the apex of this period. The Harsh Period was followed by an "Iridescent Period" characterized by colors that glowed and had a mellower texture than his earlier works. *Bather Seated on a Rock* and *Girls at the Edge of the Sea* are representative of this period.

In 1897 at Essoyes, Renoir fell from a bicycle and broke his right arm. His broken arm was placed in a plaster cast, but, since he was ambidextrous, he continued to paint with his left hand. He told his friend Vollard that he was probably the only artist who painted as well with his left hand as his right. Pain in his right shoulder continued after the cast was removed.

Renoir told his friends at a Christmas party in Paris of his lingering pain from the fracture. Degas mentioned that attacks of rheumatism and arthritis can result from a fracture. He said it in a light vein, and no one at the party, including Renoir, took him seriously. Renoir's son, Jean, thought that his father's onset of rheumatism and arthritis dated from the fall in which he broke his arm.

Renoir's joint problems began with twinges in his arms and legs on damp winter days and while painting at the seaside during the summer. His first severe bout with arthritis and rheumatism occurred in December 1898. He couldn't move his right arm, and he was in too much pain to paint. He intended to paint as long as he was able, but, from this time onward, his family and friends knew that he was going to struggle with his ailments. His ankles became swollen; his fingers curled up, and his hands were stiff.

Renoir looked for a warmer climate, hoping that his symptoms would lessen. He investigated the area around Nice. He wrote to his dealer, Durand-Ruel, "I am properly caught. The doctor here foresees that I will have at least eighteen months of it before I'm really cured. You can imagine my hollow laughter." Renoir knew that his ailments were with him for the rest of his life. He visited the spas at Acqui, north of Genoa, and at Saint Laurent-les-Bains, the first two of his many attempts at relief by taking the waters. He got only temporary relief from these visits.

In 1900, Renoir's name appeared on the honors list as a Chevalier of the Legion of Honor. This honor put a strain on his friendship with Monet. Monet had been offered the same award but had turned it down because it had come twenty years too late.

In 1901, facial paralysis that Renoir had experienced earlier returned. The optic nerve in his left eye was partially paralyzed, causing that eye to stare. His fingers continued to curl, and his hands became twisted. He had to walk with a cane because of swelling in the joints of his feet. Chronic pain disrupted his sleep; nevertheless, he continued painting.

Renoir's third and fourth attempts to obtain relief at spas were at Aix-les-Bains and at Bourbonne-les-Bains, where he obtained limited relief. Even with his impediments, his production of quality work continued. In 1904, he painted *La Boulangere*, a nude study of one of the family servants. He was also productive in 1905 and 1906, although the deformity in his limbs was worsening.

Renoir had become famous, and many people wanted to visit him and to interview him. He reduced the number of visitors and began to live a lonely existence. He had outlived many of the friends, including Cezanne, Pissarro, and Sisley, who had called upon him regularly over the years.

In 1908, Renoir moved into the last phase of his painting, usually referred to as his "Red Period." He concentrated on the use of red of every shade in his paintings. He observed, "I arrange my subject the way I want it, then I go ahead and paint like a child. I want a red to be sonorous like a bell; if it doesn't turn out that way I apply more reds or other colors until I do get it. I am no cleverer than that. I have no rules and no methods; anyone can look at my materials and watch my painting—he will see that I have no secrets." He considered art to have two requisite qualities: "It must be indescribable and inimitable."

In early 1912, Renoir's rheumatism affected him to the extent that he couldn't climb the stairs to his studio. He traveled to Nice to take advantage of the warmer climate. En route, he had an attack that paralyzed him—not only his face, but also his hands and feet. He completed his trip to Nice in an ambulance. His wife wrote to Durand-Duel, "My husband is a little better. He is beginning to be able to move his arms but the legs remain just the same. It is impossible for him to stand up, but he is much less discouraged than he was. He is getting used to his immobility, but it is really heartbreaking to see him in this state."

In late summer that year, Renoir had foot, hand, and knee operations. He was confined to a wheelchair; he would never walk again. He had to be carried up to his studio every day. His motivation never flagged. He commented: "Now I'll have to paint all the time. Ah, but I'm a lucky beggar all the same; I can still paint." Durand-Ruel visited him and observed, "Renoir is in the same sad state, but his strength of character is simply amazing, he can neither walk nor lift himself from his chair. Two people have to carry him everywhere. What torture! Yet in spite of all this he shows the same sunny humor and happiness when he is able to paint."

Renoir's left hand became so twisted with arthritis that he could no longer hold the palette. He placed the palette either on the ledge of the easel or on his knee. His friend, Albert Andre, noticed that "When he got in front of the easel again he was transfigured. He whistled, hummed the songs his models taught him. He had this habit, when wheeling himself up and down before the canvas, of staring at the picture, then looking down at his left hand to try to find the same tone on the palette. He always seemed astonished not to find it there."

Finally, Renoir could no longer hold the brush in his right hand. Most biographers note that the brush had to be taped to his hand by plaster strips. However, his son, Jean, who was also his biographer, wrote that "the truth is that his deformed hands were still strong enough to hold a brush and were as precise as a compass, but the rubbing of the handle affected his parchment-like skin, and he used to protect it with a piece of linen. These skin irritations, added to his muscular pains, were an ordeal."

The principal change that this reduced capability brought to Renoir's painting was his inability or unwillingness to change brushes during a sitting. He had to rely on frequently dipping his brush in spirits when he wanted to change colors. The loss of the feeling of the brush in his hand was a serious handicap to him.

In 1914, Renoir's two older sons enlisted to fight in World War I and were seriously wounded in action in the following year. Also in that year, eight years before the discovery of insulin, his wife was diagnosed with diabetes. She visited her wounded sons and became very ill when she returned to Paris. She died soon afterward.

Renoir continued to paint, but he took rest periods more frequently. However, at the age of seventy-five, he was transformed by a new model, sixteen year old Andrée from Nice. She had red hair, a full figure, and a happy nature. Most importantly to Renoir, her skin reflected light better than any of his models. He made over 100 paintings and sketches of Andrée.

Renoir's painting over the last three years of his life was a display of pure will; he painted up until his last days. He died of pneumonia on December 3, 1919, at the age of seventy-eight. Toward the end of his life, Matisse asked him, "Why do you still have to work? Why continue to torture yourself?" Renoir replied, "The pain passes, but the pleasure—the creation of beauty—remains."

LUDWIG VAN BEETHOVEN (1770-1827) Overcame Deafness to Compose

"The man who succeeds above his fellows is the one who, early in life, clearly discerns his object, and towards that habitually directs his powers. Even genius itself is but fine observation strengthened by fixity of purpose. Every man who observes vigilantly and resolves steadfastly grows unconsciously into genius."

Edward G. Bulwer-Lytton

Ludwig van Beethoven was born on December 16, 1770, in Bonn, Germany. His father, Johann van Beethoven, was a tenor at the court of the Elector of Cologne. Ludwig was a child prodigy. He composed his first three sonatas before the age of four and published his first musical works at the age of thirteen.

Johann taught his son to play the piano and the violin; he was a tough taskmaster. He observed his son's gifts early and ensured that Ludwig worked hard at his musical studies. When his son was nine, Johann realized that he had taught him all that he knew. Ludwig then studied with the court organist, Van den Eeden, and his successor, Christian Gottlob Neefe. By the age of twelve, Ludwig was the deputy organist. His formal schooling in the common school ended the following year.

In 1787, the Elector sent young Beethoven to Vienna to take lessons from Mozart. After hearing Beethoven play several of his own compositions, the master commented to his friends, "Pay attention to him; he will make a noise in the world some day or other." One of Beethoven's early sponsors was Count Waldstein, a friend of the Elector. Waldstein was immortalized in 1803 when Beethoven dedicated his *Opus 33, The Waldstein Sonata,* to him.

In 1792, Beethoven returned to Vienna to study with Haydn, who had succeeded Mozart as the foremost Viennese composer. Beethoven studied with Haydn for just under a year before launching his own career. Beethoven lived in Vienna, which was then considered the music capital of the world, for the rest of his life. He was a highly regarded pianist and teacher before he became widely known as a composer.

In his late twenties, Beethoven began to hear humming in his ears. He couldn't hear all of the high notes, and the lower volume passages in music and parts of conversations were inaudible to him. For a while, he didn't tell any of his friends about his hearing problem; if they noticed anything, they thought he was absorbed in his thoughts or just not listening to what they were saying.

Beethoven went to two doctors who told him not to expect any notable improvement in his hearing, and he was filled with hopelessness. He took the advice of a third doctor to move to a quiet place where he could be away from the noises of the city. He rented a house at Heiligenstadt, a Vienna suburb, where he could be near the peace of woods and meadows, but close enough to the city that his friends could visit him. The composer was actively writing music at this time and frequently worked on three or four compositions simultaneously; he had the ability to move back and forth among several ongoing works. The summer of 1802 was a landmark time for Beethoven; he had to accept the fact that his loss of hearing was making him different from other people, and that he wasn't going to be able to communicate as he had in the past.

Beethoven spent an introspective summer in the country, but it was a productive one. He wrote sections of *Piano Sonatas, Opus 31*, and *Violin Sonatas, Opus 30*, and most notably, his *Second Symphony*. The *Second Symphony* reflects the quiet of the woods and the meadows and indicates a new willingness to heighten the character of each instrument.

However, Beethoven finally had to face reality and return to society. In Vienna, he resumed his normal activities of giving lessons, playing the piano, and accepting invitations to social events. His social companions didn't know the extent of his hearing problem. To them, he seemed outwardly stronger. He displayed an extraordinary resilience and bounced back with a forcefulness that became the theme of his next work, the *Eroica Symphony*. His major effort, upon completion of the *Eroica Symphony,* was the *Fifth Symphony*, with its strong beginning that came to signify the dot-dot-dot-dash Morse code for the V for victory symbol of the Allied forces in World War II.

A duality can be found in the alternating movements within Beethoven's compositions and, in his symphonies, an alternation between a peaceful theme and a driving, forceful theme. Beginning with the *Second Symphony*, the even-numbered symphonies are placid and calm and are styled in the traditional, classical mold. The odd-numbered symphonies are more robust, grand, and creative in pushing the boundaries that existed at the time. The *Pastoral Symphony* followed the *Fifth Symphony* and has more of a rural, peaceful theme.

In 1812, Beethoven composed the *Seventh Symphony* and *Eighth Symphony,* another contrasting pair in the same pattern. The popular *Ninth Symphony,* which wasn't completed until 1824 when Beethoven was totally deaf, took its place with the odd-numbered symphonies with their daring, forceful style. After completing the *Ninth Symphony*, he switched his efforts to the composition of quartets for the remainder of his life.

Beethoven contracted pneumonia during the winter of 1826-27 and died on March 26, 1827. His death scene was dramatic. Anselm Huttenbrenner, a merchant of music supplies, and Beethoven's sister-in-law, Frau Johann van Beethoven, maintained a vigil at his bedside when he died. As described by John Burk in *The Life and Works of Beethoven,* Huttenbrenner wrote the following description of Beethoven's death:

> Frau van Beethoven and I only were in the death chamber during the last moments of Beethoven's life. After Beethoven had lain unconscious, the death rattle in his throat, from three o'clock in the afternoon until past five, there came a flash of lightning accompanied by a violent clap of thunder which garishly lit the death chamber.

> After this unexpected phenomenon of nature, which startled me greatly, Beethoven opened his eyes, lifted his right hand and looked up for several seconds with his fist clenched, and a very serious, threatening expression as if he wanted to say: "Powers of evil, I defy you! Away with you! God is with me!" When he let the raised hand sink to the bed, his eyes closed half-way. Not another breath, not a heartbeat more!

Beethoven was an innovative composer who introduced many lasting changes. He both broadened and lengthened the symphony, and he increased the size of the orchestra required to perform it. He elevated the piano to first place among musical instruments. One of the most important of his accomplishments was his changing the style of music from the Classical style to the Romantic style.

Among the composers influenced by Beethoven were Brahms, Schubert, Tchaikovsky, and Wagner, as well as Berlioz, Mahler, and Strauss. He not only persevered with his composing after he lost his hearing, but some of his greatest works were created when he was totally deaf.

CHAPTER 2

REFORMERS / ACTIVISTS

"We are all faced with a series of great opportunities disguised as insoluble problems."

John Gardner

MARTIN LUTHER KING, JR. (1929-1968) U.S. Civil Rights Activist

"A final victory is an accumulation of many short-term encounters. To lightly dismiss a success because it does not usher in a complete order of justice is to fail to comprehend the process of achieving full victory."

Martin Luther King, Jr.

On February 25, 1948, Martin Luther King, Jr., was ordained a minister and became assistant pastor of Ebenezer Baptist Church in Atlanta, his father's church. After graduating from Morehouse College, King enrolled at Crozer Seminary. While at Crozer, King attended a lecture by the president of Howard University, who had just returned from a visit to India. He talked about the role of Mohandas Gandhi in freeing India from British rule by using non-violent means. He also discussed civil disobedience and passive resistance and made a profound impression on young King.

King thought what he had heard "was so profound and fascinating that I left the meeting and bought a half dozen books on Gandhi's life and works." Later, he wrote in his book *Stride Toward Freedom*, "Not until I entered Crozer Theological Seminary . . . did I begin a serious intellectual quest for a method to eliminate social evil."

In 1951, King graduated first in his class from Crozer. He gave the valedictory address at commencement, won the Plafker Award as the most outstanding student, and received a fellowship to Boston University's School of Theology. In Boston, King met Coretta Scott, a voice student at the New England Conservatory of Music. They were married by Martin Luther King, Sr., on June 18, 1953.

King knew what he was going to do with his life. He explained his goal to his wife: "I'm going to be pastor of a church, a large Baptist church in the South . . . I'm going to live in the South because that's where I'm needed."

In April 1954, the Dexter Avenue Baptist Church in Montgomery, Alabama, offered King the position of pastor. He and Coretta moved to Montgomery in August when she graduated from the conservatory. King continued to work on his doctoral dissertation and received his Ph.D. in Theology on June 5, 1955.

On December 1, 1955, an incident of national significance occurred in Montgomery. Rosa Parks, an African-American seamstress at a local department store, was riding home on a public bus after a busy work day. The bus driver asked her to give up her seat to a white passenger who had just boarded the bus. She was sitting in the first row of the African-American section of the bus, one row behind the white section; her feet hurt and she was carrying packages, so she refused to move. The driver asked her again to move. She responded again, firmly, "No."

The driver called the police; Parks was taken to the police station where she was booked for a violation of a city bus ordinance. She called E. D. Nixon, a member the National Association for the Advancement of Colored People (N.A.A.C.P.) to request bail. Nixon cheered when he heard that Rosa had been charged with violating the local bus segregation law. The N.A.A.C.P. was looking for a test case to challenge the blatantly unfair ordinance as far as the U.S. Supreme Court, if necessary. Nixon suggested a boycott of the city bus service using car pools. The boycott was virtually 100 percent successful on the first day.

Rosa Parks was found guilty and fined; the N.A.A.C.P. had their case. A new organization, the Montgomery Improvement Association (M.I.A.) was established to direct the boycott, and King was elected president. This surprised him, since he was new to the city and only 26 years old. He expected an older person to be nominated, but he willingly accepted the position.

Early in the boycott, King gave a rousing speech at a rally at the Holt Street Baptist Church. He said to the gathering, "If we protest courageously, and yet with dignity and Christian love, when the history books are written in the future, somebody will have to say, 'There lived a race of people, of black people, of people who had the moral courage to stand up for their rights. And thereby they injected a new meaning into the veins of history and civilization.'"

King received many life-threatening phone calls—as many as 30 to 40 calls a night. One evening he became depressed; he thought that he could no longer cope with his burden. He said later, "At that moment I experienced the presence of the Divine as I had never experienced Him before." He heard an inner voice that directed him to "Stand up for righteousness, stand up for truth, and God will be at your side forever."

On January 30, 1956, King spoke at an M.I.A. meeting at the First Baptist Church. Coretta was home with their daughter, Yolanda, when they heard something hit the front porch. They moved quickly from the front room to the back of the house as a bomb exploded; it destroyed part of the front porch and sent shards of glass all over the room they had just left.

King hurried home from the meeting. A crowd of African Americans, armed with clubs, knives, and guns, gathered in front of their home ready to retaliate for the bombing. He dispersed them by telling them to put away their weapons and to pursue a path of non-violence. He said, "I want you to love your enemies. Be good to them. This is what we must live by. We must meet hate with love."

The city government tried to stop the boycott by enforcing a little-known law banning boycotts. Almost 100 M.I.A. members were charged, and King was the first one to be tried. He was found guilty; his sentence was a $500 fine or 386 days of hard labor. His attorney appealed the decision.

The city passed an injunction to stop the use of carpools by declaring them a public nuisance. King was in court in November when he was told that the U.S. Supreme Court had ruled that Alabama's State and local bus segregation laws were unconstitutional.

King was gaining national attention. In February 1957, he became a national celebrity when his picture was on the cover of *Time* magazine and the cover article was about him. King was now viewed as the leader of 16 million African Americans.

A bill was sent to Congress to establish a civil rights commission to investigate violations of African-American rights, including their right to vote. The bill became the Civil Rights Act of 1957.

In early 1957, King and other African-American clergymen and leaders met to found the Southern Christian Leadership Conference (S.C.L.C.). King was elected president. He wrote the book that Harper and Brothers asked him to write, *Stride Toward Freedom*, a combination of an autobiography and a description of the Montgomery boycott.

Activity in the civil rights movement increased. On February 1, 1960, four African-American students from North Carolina

Agricultural and Technical State University in Greensboro occupied stools at a segregated lunch counter at a Woolworth store. They weren't waited on, so they opened their books on the counter and began to study.

On the following day, six times their number engaged in a sit-in at the same Woolworth store. Within a week and a half, sit-ins occurred in South Carolina, Virginia, and other areas of North Carolina. By year-end, over 125 Southern towns had desegregated their lunch counters. The Student Non-violent Coordinating Committee (S.N.C.C.) grew out of the lunch-counter sit-ins.

Older adults continued what the students had started, and on October 19, 1960, King and 35 other African Americans were arrested in Rich's department store in Atlanta for trespassing when the waiters in the Magnolia Room refused to wait on them. Mayor William Hartsfield didn't like keeping King in the Fulton County jail; nevertheless, all except King were released promptly.

King had been arrested earlier in DeKalb County, Georgia, for driving with an expired license, fined, and placed on probation for a year. Fulton County officials complied with DeKalb County's request to turn King over to them. He was found guilty of violating his parole, denied bail, and sentenced to four months of hard labor at the State penitentiary at Reidsville, a prison for hardened criminals.

On October 25, Coretta received a call from Senator and presidential candidate John F. Kennedy, who offered his help in releasing her husband. Robert Kennedy, who managed his brother's presidential campaign, called the judge who sentenced King and expressed his thoughts about the injustice to King. He was released on bail within three days of JFK's call to Coretta.

On December 13, 1961, King spoke in Albany, Georgia, at a rally for an ongoing voter registration campaign sponsored by the S.N.C.C. Late the following day, he led a march to the City Hall. He and the other marchers were jailed for obstructing traffic, released within two days, and jailed again when they refused to pay a fine. Again, they were released after a short stay.

The S.C.L.C. chose Birmingham, Alabama, as the next target for a civil rights demonstration because of its history of segregation. The S.C.L.C. issued a demand to integrate public facilities and hire blacks for positions for which they hadn't been hired previously.

The Commissioner of Public Safety arrested and jailed 20 African Americans engaged in sit-ins in department stores. The following day, King led a group of 50 marchers on city hall. King was jailed again and subjected to abusive treatment.

Coretta called President Kennedy, and Kennedy talked to Birmingham officials about King's release. While in jail, King wrote his 6,400-word "Letter from Birmingham Jail." He wrote it in the margins of newspapers and on toilet paper and smuggled it out of jail. It was published as a pamphlet by the American Friends Service Committee and later published in a magazine with a circulation of a million copies. After eight days, King was released on bail and recruited more marchers.

On May 2, over 1,000 marchers were greeted with high-pressure fire hoses that knocked them to the ground and into walls. Marchers were also attacked by snarling German shepherd police dogs. President Kennedy sent troops to Birmingham to assist in maintaining order.

On August 28, 1963, a high point of King's role as leader of the civil rights movement in the United States occurred on the mall between the Washington Monument and the Lincoln Memorial in Washington, D.C. A march on Washington was led by African-American civil rights organizers to demonstrate the widespread support for the recently introduced civil rights legislation. Organizers anticipated a crowd of 100,000; however, the size of the crowd approached 250,000.

At 3:00 p.m., the last speaker of the rally was introduced, a man referred to as "the moral leader of the nation." King began to give his prepared speech, but the responsiveness of the crowd, which clapped in cadence with his speech, caused him to set aside the prepared text and speak extemporaneously from his heart—drawing on previous speeches he had given. The result was his famous "I have a dream" speech:

> • I have a dream that one day on the red hills of Georgia the sons of former slaves and the sons of former slave owners will be able to sit down together at the table of brotherhood. . . .
>
> .

- I have a dream that my four little children will one day live in a nation where they will not be judged by the color of their skin, but by the content of their character. . . .

- And when we allow freedom to ring, when we let it ring from every State and city, we will be able to speed up that day when all of God's children—black men and white men, Jews and gentiles, Catholics and Protestants—will be able to join hands and to sing in the words of the old Negro spiritual, "Free at last, free at last, thank God almighty, we are free at last."

After the rally, President Kennedy invited the leaders of the march to the White House, where he promised his support in moving the civil rights legislation through Congress.

President Kennedy was assassinated on November 22, 1963. Fortunately, his successor, President Lyndon Johnson, was also a supporter of the civil rights movement, and the legislation was passed within a year. Enforcement of that legislation took much longer. *Time* magazine designated King "Man of the Year" for 1963.

On July 2, 1964, President Johnson signed the Civil Rights Act, authorizing the integration of public facilities and public schools. Civil rights leaders were invited to the White House for the signing ceremony in the East Room.

In October 1964, the Norwegian Parliament selected King for the Nobel Peace Prize. At 35, he was the youngest recipient to date of one of the most prestigious honors in the world, awarded for contributions to international peace.

The civil rights leaders were pleased with the passage of the Civil Rights Act and pushed for a Voting Rights Act. In some areas of the deep South, blacks were terrorized at polling places.

The S.C.L.C. chose Selma, Alabama, where only 383 of 15,000 African Americans were registered to vote, as the site for voting rights activity. The sheriff arrested 226 African Americans merely for attempting to register to vote. On March 7, 1965, the S.C.L.C. marched from Brown Chapel to the Edmund Pettus bridge over the Alabama River, where they were attacked by the sheriff's troopers. Almost 80 of the 600 marchers were treated for broken ribs and collar bones, fractured skulls, head cuts, and many other injuries on what was called "Bloody Sunday."

These incidents motivated President Johnson to push for voting rights. He stated that "This time, on this issue, there must be no delay, no hesitation, and no compromise with our purpose." African Americans were entitled to "the full blessing of American life," and "their cause must be our cause, too." Everyone must strive to "overcome the crippling legacy of bigotry and injustice. And . . . we shall . . . overcome." On August 6, 1965, the Voting Rights Act was signed into law by President Johnson.

King and his followers next turned their attention to the economic inequality faced by African Americans. Initially, their efforts were concentrated in Chicago. However, when the striking garbage collectors of Memphis requested King's help, he went to Tennessee for a rally on April 3, 1968.

On April 4, King was joined at the Lorraine Motel by his brother, A. D., and several friends. Just after 6:00 p.m., King stood on the balcony outside room 306 with Hosea Williams, Jesse Jackson, and Ralph Abernathy. As they prepared to leave to go to dinner, King was shot in the neck and lower right side of his face by a single bullet fired by James Earl Ray from a rooming house across the street.

King died at about 7:00 p.m. His body was returned to Atlanta for his funeral at the Ebenezer Baptist Church on April 9, 1968. Over 60,000 people attended the funeral service, 800 inside the church and the rest outside, who listened to the service on loudspeakers. He was buried in South View Cemetery in Atlanta, where his paternal grandfather was buried. The epitaph on his crypt is "Free at last, free at last. Thank God Almighty, I'm free at last." During the course of his struggle, he said, "If you are cut down in a movement that is designed to save the soul of a nation, then no other death could be as redemptive."

THOMAS GARRETT (1789-1871) Underground Railroad Leader

> "In life's small things be resolute and great.
> To keep thy muscle trained: know'st thou when Fate
> Thy measure takes, or when she'll say to thee
> I find thee worthy; do this deed for me."

James Russell Lowell

Thomas Garrett, who helped over 2,900 slaves escape to the North, was highly regarded by his peers. Abolitionist William Lloyd Garrison expressed his feelings upon Garrett's death in a letter to one of his sons: "In view of his singularly beneficent life, there is no cause for sorrow, but [I would like] to express the estimation in which I held him, as one of the best men who ever walked the earth, and one of the most beloved among my numerous friends and co-workers in the cause of the oppressed and downtrodden race, now happily rejoicing in their heavenly wrought deliverance."

Thomas Garrett, one of eleven children of Thomas and Sarah Price Garrett, was born in Upper Darby, Pennsylvania, on August 21, 1789. Thomas, Sr., operated mills and was a scythe- and tool-maker. Young Thomas worked in his father's businesses.

Garrett's motivation to spend a lifetime supporting antislavery causes began when he was twenty-four years old and was still living at home with his parents. He had returned home one day to find his mother and sisters distressed. Two men had come to the house and kidnapped an African-American woman who worked for the family.

Garrett pursued their wagon, following marks made by a broken wheel. He tracked them to the Navy Yard and then to Kensington, where the men had stopped at a roadside tavern. He found the kidnapped woman in the kitchen of the tavern and returned with her to Upper Darby.

During the time he was pursuing the kidnappers and while riding home, Garrett thought about the wrongs of the slavery system. It was wrong that men thought that they had a right to enter a home and carry off a woman against her will. He made a resolution to aid oppressed slaves in any way that he could.

On October 14, 1813, Garrett married Mary Sharpless of Birmingham, Pennsylvania. She was his partner in Underground Railroad work. In 1822, they moved to Wilmington, Delaware, a thriving town with plenty of opportunity for an ambitious young man. Garrett opened an iron, steel, and coal business. He had early difficulties, which were described by James A. McGowan in *Station Master on the Underground Railroad*:

> A rival house in the iron business sought to run him off the track by reducing the price of iron to cost, but Friend Thomas, nothing daunted, employed a man to take his place in the store, tied on his leather apron, took to his hammer and anvil and in the prosecution of the trade learned from his father prepared to support his family with his own hands as long as the run lasted. Thus, by the sweat of his brow, he foiled the purpose of his rival and laid the foundation of what after many reverses became one of the permanent business houses of the city.

Locally, Garrett was looked upon with suspicion; his house was under constant surveillance by the police, who realized that it was a station on the Underground Railroad. He was not bothered by this lack of popularity or by adverse opinion because he knew that the Lord approved of his activities. Garrett believed in doing his duty. He thought that a man's duty is shown to him and that duty, once recognized, was an obligation. His approach to life was summarized by Geoffrey Hubbard a century later, "Every Quaker defines his position fully and clearly by his life."

Garrett had a powerful physique and considerable personal bravery. He had no fear of the proslavery supporters who attempted to bully him. An example of his fearlessness was his response to a supporter of slavery who told Garrett that if he ever came to his town, he would shoot him. Garrett responded, "Well, I think of going that way before long, and I will call upon thee." He called upon the man as he had promised. Garrett said, "How does thee do friend? Here I am, thee can shoot me if thee likes." He was not shot.

Men confronted Garrett flourishing pistols and bowie knives. He pushed them aside and told them that only cowards resorted to such measures. On one occasion, two men were overheard planning to kill him, as noted by biographer James A. McGowan:

> He was warned, but having a meeting to attend that night, he went out as usual. In the street two men leaped upon him, but his brawny hands caught them by the backs of their necks and brought them up standing. He shook them well and looked them over, then said, "I think you look hungry. Come in and I will give you supper." He forced them into his house and his wife prepared a warm supper, while Friend Thomas chaffed them about their adventure, and turned the enmity into friendship.

On another occasion, Garrett boarded a train in Wilmington to prevent an African-American woman from being carried off to the deep South. Several Southerners attempted unsuccessfully to throw him off the train. At one point, a reward of $10,000 was offered for him in Maryland. He wrote to the parties offering the reward and told them that this was not enough. For $20,000, he would turn himself in.

In 1848, eight African Americans—a man, his wife, and six children—ran away from a plantation on the eastern shore of Maryland. Except for two of the children who had been born in slavery, they were free. They sought refuge at the home of a wealthy Quaker in Middletown, Delaware. Unfortunately, they had been followed. They were arrested and sent to jail in New Castle. The Sheriff and his daughter, who were antislavery supporters, notified Garrett of their plight.

Garrett visited them in jail in New Castle and returned to Wilmington. The following day, he and U.S. Senator Wales presented Judge Boothe with a writ of *habeas corpus*. Judge Boothe decided that there was no evidence to hold them, and, in the absence of evidence, "the presumption was always in favor of freedom." He discharged them. Garrett said, "Here is this woman with a babe at her breast, and the child suffering from a white swelling on its leg; is there any impropriety in my getting a carriage and helping them over to Wilmington?" Judge Boothe responded, "Certainly not."

Six weeks later, the slaveholders filed a suit against Garrett in New Castle for helping fugitive slaves escape. The trial, presided over by Judge Hall and Chief Justice Taney in May 1848, lasted three days. Garrett's friends suspected that the jury had been stacked against him. He was convicted, and every dollar of his property was taken from him. He responded, "Now, Judge, I do not think that I have always done my duty, being fearful of losing what little I possessed; but now that you have relieved me, I will go home and put another story on my house, so that I can accommodate more of God's poor."

Garrett's friends helped him in his time of difficulty. He was almost 60 years old, but he made the addition to his house and increased his support of escaped slaves. His activities were aided by donations from friends in England. He continued to work to help the slaves until President Abraham Lincoln freed them in 1863 by signing the Emancipation Proclamation.

Thomas Garrett died on January 25, 1871. During his lifetime, he had helped just under 3,000 slaves on their journey to the North. Not one of these slaves was captured on the road to freedom.

Throughout his life, Garrett believed in social responsibility: "I should have done violence to my convictions of duty, had I not made use of all the lawful means in my power to liberate those people, and assist them to become men and women, rather than leave them in the condition of chattels."

SUSAN B. ANTHONY (1820-1906) Women's Rights Organizer

"Susan B. Anthony became one of the most unconventional women of the nineteenth century. Her life of confrontational political leadership on behalf of her sex provokes a question: If not from personal anguish and rebellion, if not with high political questions, how did a common woman arise and, in Anthony's case, become the most dramatic and charismatic of feminist rebels—known by many as the 'Napoleon' of nineteenth century feminism?"

Kathleen Barry, *Susan B. Anthony:
A Biography of a Singular Feminist*

Two weeks after the first Women's Rights Convention on July 19 and 20, 1848, in Seneca Falls, New York, a second women's rights convention was held in Rochester. Susan B. Anthony was working in Canajoharie, New York, as the girls' headmistress of the Canajoharie Academy and didn't attend either convention; however, her father, mother, and sister attended the Rochester convention and signed petitions in support of the resolutions.

Within two years, Anthony was not only informed about the subject of women's rights, but also had discussed the subject with the abolitionists Frederick Douglass and William Lloyd Garrison, who were promoting the women's rights cause. Her interest in the Women's Rights Movement was sparked by meeting Elizabeth Cady Stanton in 1851 in Seneca Falls, after an antislavery meeting.

It was the beginning of a friendship and a working relationship that was to last for over half a century. Anthony's attention to detail and organizational skills were a perfect match with Cady Stanton's strengths as a philosopher and policy-maker.

In 1852, Anthony attended her first women's rights convention, the third National Women's Rights Convention. Cady Stanton did not attend, because she was at home awaiting the birth of her fifth child. However, she sent a letter for Anthony to read to the convention. Two thousand delegates attended, including Lucretia Mott, James Mott, and Lucy Stone.

The working relationship between Anthony and Cady Stanton was demonstrated by the way they prepared a speech for Stanton to give to the New York State Legislature in February 1854. They addressed the right of women to earn and keep their own wages and the right of women to own property in their name. Cady Stanton was willing to give the speech; however, with her large, young family, she didn't have enough time to prepare it. She sent a plea for help to Anthony, and they arranged to collaborate. Anthony and a lawyer friend would research the laws including discriminating statements against women, if Cady Stanton would write and present the speech.

Cady Stanton's perception of their working relationship is observed by Elizabeth Griffith in *In Her Own Right:*

> In thought and sympathy we were one, and in the division of labor we exactly complemented each other. In writing, we did better work together than either of us could have done alone. I am the better writer, she the better critic. She supplied the facts and statistics, I the philosophy and rhetoric and together we have made arguments that have stood unshaken through the storms of 30 long years. Our speeches may be considered the united product of two brains.

Cady Stanton's speech at Albany provided examples of the ways in which women were discriminated against and the means by which the law could be changed to address the discrimination. Anthony obtained 6,000 signatures on the petitions for women's property and wage reform and 4,000 signatures on the petition in support of women's right to vote. Changes to the laws on women's property and wage reform wouldn't come for another six years in New York. When the changes came, Cady Stanton and Anthony knew that they had played a key role in making those changes.

The Fifteenth Amendment to the Constitution, which was adopted in 1870, includes a statement that "the right of citizens of the United States to vote shall not be denied . . . on account of race, color, or previous condition of servitude." The suffragists wanted the phrase "or sex" to be included in the Fifteenth Amendment. However, the phrase wasn't included, so women began to test the interpretation of their rights as citizens implied by the Fifteenth

Amendment. Anthony wasn't the first woman to test this interpretation of the Amendment, but she certainly received more news coverage than any other woman.

On November 1, 1872, Anthony attempted to register to vote. The election judges told her that, according to New York State law, she wouldn't be permitted to register. Anthony quoted to them from the amendments to the Constitution and insisted that she, as a citizen, had the right to vote. She was permitted to register, and she voted in the general election on November 5. She received wide newspaper coverage, including articles in the *Chicago Tribune* and the *New York Times*. She realized that she may have broken the law, and that she might be liable for a $500 fine. On November 18, a marshal came to Anthony's home and arrested her.

Anthony was arraigned, and her bond was set at $500. She refused to pay it, so her lawyer, Henry Selden, who didn't want to see his client go to jail, paid her bail. Unfortunately, by posting the bail for her, he had, inadvertently, prevented her from appealing to higher courts—potentially as high as the Supreme Court; posting bail indicated that she wasn't contesting the lawfulness of her arrest. Anthony made many speeches describing her circumstances, including speeches in Monroe County, where her case was to be tried. The trial was moved to Ontario County, south of Rochester, which was considered a more neutral venue.

On June 17, 1873, Anthony's trial began in Canandaigua, the county seat of Ontario County. The judge selected to try her case was Judge Ward Hunt, an inexperienced judge recently appointed to the bench. Selden conducted a skillful defense, pointing out that Anthony sincerely believed that she had been given the right to vote by the the Fourteenth and Fifteenth Amendments. Judge Hunt refused to let her speak in her own defense.

Judge Hunt stated that it didn't matter what Anthony's beliefs were; she had broken the law. He took a note from his pocket, turned toward the jury, and read from it. The note concluded with the statement, "If I am right in this, the result must be a verdict . . . of guilty and I therefore direct that you find a verdict of guilty." An incensed Selden reminded the judge that he didn't have the right to provide that type of instruction to the jury and demanded that the jury be asked for their verdict. Judge Hunt ignored Selden, instructed the court clerk to record the verdict, and dismissed the jury.

This blatant injustice was widely covered by the press. Many who disapproved of Anthony's voting now sided with her because of this unjust treatment in the courtroom. Judge Hunt's actions were politically motivated. His mentor was Roscoe Conkling, U.S. Senator from New York and a known foe of the Women's Rights Movement. Selden requested a new trial on the basis that Anthony had been denied the right to a fair trial by jury. Judge Hunt denied the request and stated her sentence, a $100 fine. Anthony responded, "I shall never pay a dollar of your unjust penalty."

Anthony never retired from her lifelong effort to promote women's rights. The International Woman Suffrage Alliance was formed in 1904, and Anthony, at the age of 84, was recognized as their leader. At their convention in 1906, she instructed the delegates: "The fight must not stop. You must see that it doesn't stop." At a dinner in her honor in Washington, D.C., on her 86th birthday, she concluded her comments by stating, "Failure is impossible." Susan B. Anthony died on March 13, 1906.

In 1920, the Nineteenth Amendment to the Constitution was ratified. It included the statement that "the right of citizens of the United States to vote shall not be denied or abridged by the United States or by any State on account of sex." It was called the "Susan B. Anthony Amendment." Anthony was right; failure was impossible.

ELIZABETH CADY STANTON (1815-1902) Women's Rights Policy Maker

"Stanton's talents were aptly suited to the role of agitator. Well educated and widely read, she had keen intelligence, a trained mind, and an ability to argue persuasively in writing and speaking. Her personality was magnetic. In conversation and correspondence she was willful and opinionated; in person, she was funny, feisty, engaging. Her most remarkable trait was her self-confidence. It gave her the courage to take controversial stands without hesitation."

> Elizabeth Griffith, *In Her Own Right:*
> *The Life of Elizabeth Cady Stanton*

The conditions that confronted women in the United States in the mid-nineteenth century are difficult to envision today. Women weren't allowed to vote. A college education was denied them. Women couldn't own property, and any wages they earned were turned over to their husbands. The guardianship of children was automatically given to the father in cases of separation and divorce. By law, a woman's inheritance went to her husband. She wasn't entitled to the rights given to the least responsible men, whether they were born in the United States or were immigrants.

Elizabeth Cady Stanton was a leader in the Women's Rights Movement for over 50 years. In order to appreciate her role and her contribution to the movement, it is important to understand her relationship with two other leaders of the movement, Lucretia Mott and Susan B. Anthony. Cady Stanton met Lucretia Mott at the World Anti-Slavery Convention in London in 1840. Mott, a Quaker minister and a reformer active in both the abolitionist and temperance movements, was 22 years older than Cady Stanton and became her mentor.

Cady Stanton and Mott "resolved to hold a convention as soon as they returned home and to form a society to advocate the rights of women." However, the first Women's Rights Convention in the United States wasn't convened until eight years later in Seneca Falls, New York, on July 19 and 20, 1848. The *Declaration of Sentiments*, written by Cady Stanton, was based on the *Declaration of Independence*. The *Declaration of Sentiments*, as adopted at the convention, asserted that "all men and women are created equal."

Elizabeth Cady Stanton and Susan B. Anthony met three years later, in March 1851, after an antislavery meeting in Seneca Falls. Anthony never married and was less of an extrovert than Cady Stanton. Cady Stanton's and Anthony's abilities complemented each other extremely well. Cady Stanton was the policy formulator, effective writer, and moving speechmaker; Anthony's strengths were her organizational ability and her willingness to campaign and make campaign arrangements.

Cady Stanton's first encounter with activists was with abolitionists whom she met at the home of her cousin, Gerrit Smith, in Peterboro, New York. Smith was a political reformer and staunch antislavery activist. Elizabeth met and fell in love with Henry Stanton, a well-known abolitionist, on one of her visits to Peterboro. Henry was a dynamic individual and a powerful, effective speaker. They met in October 1839, when Henry spoke at local antislavery meetings; he was an agent of the American Anti-Slavery Society and secretary of the national society. After a brief courtship, Elizabeth and Henry were married in Johnstown, New York, on May 1, 1840.

Cady Stanton and Henry left for New York City after the wedding to travel to London for the World Anti-Slavery Convention, where Cady Stanton met Lucretia Mott. The convention wasn't a success; agreement wasn't reached on any of its goals. However, it did plant the seed for the Women's Rights Movement in the United States by providing the occasion for two of its leaders to meet.

Mott encouraged Cady Stanton to think independently about religion and individual rights: "When I first heard from her lips that I had the same right to think for myself that Luther, Calvin, and John Knox had, and the same right to be guided by my own convictions, I felt a newborn sense of dignity and freedom."

When the Stantons returned home, Henry read law with Judge Cady in Johnstown for the next 15 months. In late 1842, Henry joined a law practice in Boston. In 1843, Cady Stanton moved to Boston and found it a stimulating city. William Lloyd Garrison and many strong-willed abolitionists lived there; it was, generally, a home for liberal thinkers. The Stantons entertained frequently; their guests included Ralph Waldo Emerson, Stephen Foster, Nathaniel Hawthorne, James Russell Lowell, and John Greenleaf Whittier.

The Stantons were happy in Boston, but Henry developed a chronic lung congestion and needed a less humid climate. In 1847, they moved to Seneca Falls, New York, where Henry resumed the practice of law.

In March 1848, the New York Married Women's Property Act was passed by the Legislature; New York was the first State to pass a bill of this type. The bill, which ensured that married women could hold the title to property in their own names, was first introduced to the legislature in 1836 but didn't pass at the time. Cady Stanton had circulated petitions in support of the bill and had lobbied for its passage with members of the Legislature.

Cady Stanton had difficulty adjusting to the small-town atmosphere of Seneca Falls after the dynamic social and political scene in Boston. The demands of her young, growing family weighed upon her. Henry was busy with his career and was out of town frequently on trips to Albany and Washington. She was pleased to hear that Mott planned to visit Waterloo, just west of Seneca Falls, in July 1848.

Cady Stanton was invited to spend July 13 with Mott at the home of Jane and Richard Hunt in Waterloo. Mott's sister, Martha Wright of Auburn, and Mary M'Clintock were also there that day; all five women were eager to proceed with the conference that Mott and Cady Stanton had discussed eight years previously. Cady Stanton remembered that she "poured . . . out the torrent of my long-accumulating discontent with such violence and indignation that I stirred myself, as well as the rest of the party, to do and dare anything."

The women called a convention for July 19 and 20 at the Wesleyan Chapel in Seneca Falls. A notice appeared in the *Seneca County Courier* on July 14 announcing a "convention to discuss the social, civil, and religious condition and rights of women." All of these women, the nucleus of the convention, were married and had children. All but Cady Stanton were staunch antislavery activists. Mott was the only one of the five who had any experience as a delegate, orator, or organizer. However, all of them had attended temperance and antislavery conventions.

Cady Stanton's *Declaration of Sentiments*, essentially a declaration of women's rights, was the principal document reviewed at the convention and the basis for the resolutions that were passed. Over

100 men and women were present each day. The clause requesting women's right to vote wasn't universally accepted. Both Lucretia Mott and Henry Stanton were against its inclusion in the *Declaration of Sentiments*, but Cady Stanton prevailed; it was left in.

The convention was successful, and a number of resolutions were passed including the following:

- Resolved, that all laws which prevent woman from occupying such a station in society as her conscience shall dictate, or which place her in a position inferior to that of man are contrary to the great precept of nature, and therefore of no force or authority. . . .

- Resolved, that woman is man's equal—was intended to be so by the creator, and the highest good of the human race demands that she should be recognized as such. . . .

- Resolved, that it is the duty of the women of this country to secure themselves their sacred right to the elective franchise. . . .

Some newspaper columnists ridiculed the convention; other editors were sympathetic to the women's cause. Frederick Douglass, writing in the *North Star*, saw no reason to deny women the right to vote because "right is of no sex." The convention was the beginning of the Women's Rights Movement in the United States.

In 1854, Cady Stanton spoke to the New York State Legislature about the need for improvements to the married women's property law. She reviewed the *Declaration of Sentiments*, and discussed the lack of the women's rights to vote, to hold office, to earn wages, and to inherit from their families.

Stanton's speech included a plea for women to be able to own property, to be guardians for their own children, and to be eligible for higher education. She made a strong, favorable impression on the Legislature. In 1860, the New York State Legislature passed a law granting women the right to earn and keep their own wages and to be custodians for their own children.

In 1869, Cady Stanton and Anthony founded the National Woman Suffrage Association; Cady Stanton was elected president, and Anthony was elected secretary. Cady Stanton held this position for 21 years. However, Cady Stanton's strong stands on women's rights weren't for everyone. In late 1869, conservative suffragists who disagreed with Cady Stanton formed a rival organization, the American Woman Suffrage Association. This competing organization was comprised mainly of New Englanders led by Lucy Stone.

In 1888, Cady Stanton convinced Senator Aaron Sargent to introduce a women's suffrage amendment as a supplement to the Fifteenth Amendment to the Constitution. It failed that year, but it was introduced in every session of Congress until finally adopted in 1920.

In 1890, the two major women's suffrage organizations joined forces. Cady Stanton was elected president, Anthony was elected vice-president, and Stone became head of the executive committee of the combined National American Woman Suffrage Association. Cady Stanton presided over the new organization for two years and then turned over the reins to Anthony.

Cady Stanton never gave up her quest for the right of women to vote. On October 25, 1902, the day before she died, she wrote a letter to President Theodore Roosevelt requesting his support in obtaining the vote for women. In the words of author Ida Husted Harper, "If the intellect of Elizabeth Cady Stanton had been possessed by a man, he would have had a seat on the Supreme Bench or the Senate of the United States, but our country has no rewards for great women."

Elizabeth Cady Stanton didn't live to see the fruits of her labor. Her efforts weren't completely rewarded until 18 years after her death. In 1920, the Nineteenth Amendment to the Constitution was ratified. It includes the statement that "the right of citizens of the United States to vote shall not be denied or abridged by the United States or by any State on account of sex." All of society, not just women, benefited from Elizabeth Cady Stanton's lifelong struggle for women's rights.

FREDERICK DOUGLASS (1817-1895) Civil Rights Leader and Editor

"It rekindled the few expiring embers of freedom and revived within me a sense of my own manhood. It recalled the departed self-confidence, and inspired me again with a determination to be free. He can only understand the deep satisfaction which I experienced, who has himself repelled by force the bloody arm of slavery. I felt as I never felt before. It was a glorious resurrection, from the tomb of slavery to the heaven of freedom. My long-crushed spirit rose, cowardice departed, bold defiance took its place, and I now resolved that, however long I might remain a slave in form, the day had passed forever when I could be a slave in fact." (Frederick Douglass, upon winning a fight with a "slave breaker")

Douglas T. Miller, *Frederick Douglass and the Fight for Freedom*

Frederick Douglass was born Frederick Bailey in February 1818, in Talbot County on the eastern shore of Maryland. His mother, Harriet Bailey, was a slave and his father, whom he never met, was a white man. His master was Captain Aaron Anthony.

In March 1826, Frederick was sent to live with a member of Anthony's family, Hugh Auld, in Baltimore. Living in Baltimore was a good experience for Frederick; he had many opportunities to learn.

Thomas Auld, Frederick's legal owner, brought him back to rural slavery in 1833. He was not obedient, so Auld hired him out to an overseer who had reputation as a "slave breaker." After he had endured six months of flogging and other mistreatment, he turned on the slave breaker in a two-hour fight that he won. After that, the overseer didn't bother Frederick, but he was even more committed to winning his freedom. Thomas Auld sent him back to Hugh Auld in Baltimore. He became an experienced caulker in a boatyard, where competition for jobs was fierce between poor white immigrants and slaves. He was attacked and badly beaten because he was thought to have taken a job from a white immigrant.

Frederick continued his self-education by joining the East Baltimore Mental Improvement Society, a debating club. An argument with Hugh Auld motivated Frederick to board a northbound train and escape. Despite some tense moments when he saw two local men who could identify him as a slave, he arrived in Philadelphia safely and continued on to New York City.

Frederick stayed with David Ruggles, publisher of the antislavery quarterly, *The Mirror of Slavery*. Ruggles, who was active in the Underground Railroad, suggested that he move farther north. Frederick traveled to New Bedford, Massachusetts, where he hoped to find work as a caulker, and lived with Nathan Johnson and his wife. Johnson suggested that because Frederick was an escaped slave, he should change his name. Johnson had just finished reading Sir Walter Scott's *Lady of the Lake*; he suggested the surname of "Douglass," the name of the Scottish lord and hero. Frederick Bailey became Frederick Douglass.

When Douglass looked for work as a caulker, he found that prejudice existed in the North as well as the South. White caulkers did not want to work with African Americans. He was forced to take odd jobs as a common laborer. One day he found a copy of William Lloyd Garrison's antislavery newspaper, *The Liberator*, and it changed his life. Garrison was a strong-willed abolitionist. In addition to being an editor, Garrison had helped to establish the New England Anti-Slavery Society. Douglass subscribed to Garrison's paper and was moved by it.

Douglass attended the annual meeting of the New England Anti-Slavery Society in New Bedford on August 9, 1841, and a meeting the next day on the Island of Nantucket. At the second meeting, Douglass was asked to speak. Although he was nervous, he spoke movingly about his life as a slave and was well-received.

Douglass was asked to become a full-time lecturer for the organization. He reluctantly accepted a three month assignment and stayed for four years. He improved his oratorical skills and became one of the Society's most popular lecturers.

It was a dangerous time to be an abolitionist. On September 15, 1843, Douglass was severely beaten in Pendleton, Indiana. He escaped with a broken wrist and bruises. Abolitionist newspaper editor Elijah Lovejoy was killed in Alton, Illinois, while defending his press from an incensed mob. William Lloyd Garrison was dragged through the streets of Boston with a rope around his waist and almost lost his life.

During the winter and early spring of 1844-45, Douglass left the lecture circuit to write an autobiography, *The Narrative of the Life of Frederick Douglass, an American Slave*. In August 1845, he went on a successful lecture tour of England, Ireland, and Scotland.

One month after Douglass's return to America, two English women raised money and negotiated for his freedom. They contacted American agents to buy his freedom from the Aulds for $711.66. The deed of manumission was filed at the Baltimore Chattel Records Office on December 13, 1846, and Douglass was a free man.

Douglass returned to England for a lecture tour in 1847. Upon his return to America, he published an antislavery newspaper. His British friends raised money to help him get started. He was surprised when Garrison advised against it. Garrison did not want competition for his own newspaper.

Douglass started his newspaper despite Garrison's counsel against it. He knew that he would have to choose a base far from Garrison's in New England. Douglass chose Rochester, New York, a booming city of 30,000 on the Erie Canal, where he had been well-received on the lecture circuit in 1842 and 1847. Douglass moved his family there on November 1, 1847.

In December 1847, the first edition of his newspaper, *North Star*, was published. He named it *North Star* because the North Star was the guide that the slaves used when escaping from the South to freedom.

Douglass supported the Women's Rights Movement. On July 14, 1848, his *North Star* carried the announcement: "A convention to discuss the Social, Civil, and Religious Condition and Rights of Women will be held in the Wesleyan Chapel at Seneca Falls, New York, the 19th and 20th of July instant." The masthead that Douglass used for the *North Star* was: "RIGHT IS OF NO SEX — TRUTH IS OF NO COLOR."

In 1851, the *North Star* merged with the *Liberty Party Paper;* the resulting paper was called *Frederick Douglass's Paper.* In 1858, Douglass began publishing *Douglass's Monthly* for British readers. The weekly ran until 1860; he stopped printing the monthly in 1863, thus ending a 16 year publishing career.

Douglass served as a Rochester stationmaster on the Underground Railroad. He hid hundreds of escaping slaves at the *North Star* printing office and at his home and made arrangements for them to travel to Canada.

In January 1871, President Grant appointed Douglass to a commission to Santo Domingo (Dominican Republic). Douglass moved to Washington, D.C., because he thought that more federal appointments would be offered. In 1877, President Rutherford Hayes appointed him United States Marshal for the District of Columbia. He served in that position until 1881, when President James Garfield appointed him Recorder of Deeds for the District of Columbia. He held that office until 1886.

In September 1889, President Benjamin Harrison appointed Douglass Minister-Resident and Consul-General to the Republic of Haiti, where he served until July 1891. Douglass, one of the strongest antislavery voices of his time, died of a heart attack in Washington, D.C., on February 20, 1895.

CHAPTER 3

LUMINARIES / NOTABLES

"I have learned that success is to be measured not so much by the
position one has reached in life as by the obstacles which he has
overcome while trying to succeed."

Booker T. Washington

SCOTT HAMILTON (1958-   ) Figure Skating Champion

"I've always felt a special connection with my audience. It's that bond I share with them that makes performing the thing I love the most."

Scott Hamilton

Scott Hamilton won four consecutive U.S. Figure skating Championships (1981-1984), four consecutive World Championships (1981-1984), and a gold medal at the 1984 Olympics at Sarajevo. His signature skating move was a backflip, which earned him no points but which his fans had come to expect in his routines.

Hamilton was born on August 28, 1958, in Bowling Green, Ohio. He was adopted at the age of six weeks by Dorothy McIntosh Hamilton, an elementary school teacher, and Ernest Hamilton, a professor of biology at Bowling Green State University. Scott has an older sister Susan, his parents' biological daughter, and a younger brother Steven, who was also adopted.

When Hamilton was two years old, he contracted an illness that caused him to stop growing. The disease was difficult to diagnose and several incorrect diagnoses were made, including cystic fibrosis. He was given six months to live. He was taken to Boston Children's Hospital, where the correct diagnosis of Swachman-Diamond syndrome was made. A special diet and exercise regimen allowed the syndrome to correct itself. In 1962, Scott was very sickly with bronchitis and respiratory problems. He was having difficulty digesting his food and seemed to have stopped growing. He was referred to a doctor in Ann Arbor.

The illness continued for two years. The problem appeared to be malabsorption syndrome, the inability to absorb nutrients from the intestines into the bloodstream. Finally, additional tests in Toledo indicated that Hamilton was suffering from celiac disease, the inability for the body to digest gluten in grains such as wheat, rye, and barley. Further tests at Ann Arbor indicated that he had lactose intolerance, an allergy to milk and milk products.

Hamilton's interest in skating began at this time. He also had physical limitations in sports but he developed a real interest skating. In 1967, a regulation-sized skating rink was installed at

70

Bowling Green State University, along with a small practice rink. Hamilton began his skating slowly and, eventually, enrolled in Saturday group lessons with skating instructor Rita Lowery. The group lessons weren't enough so he began to take private lessons. Hamilton's parents noticed that he was always happy after his skating activities. He participated in a skating show after being on skates only a few months. He looked up to the older skaters and began to set goals for himself.

Finally, Hamilton began to gain weight and to increase in height. The family thought that his interest in skating had something to do with it. By 1986, he was taking four lessons a week from Lowery — two in freestyle and two in school figures. Compulsory figures continued to give him difficulty.

In 1969, Hamilton skated in his first competition: the Tri-State Free Skating Competition. It was his first victory. When Rita Lowery left Bowling Green, Hamilton took lessons from Giuliano Grassi, an experienced pro, for about year and then switched to Herb Plata, an ice show star, when Grassi had to meet other obligations. Later, Hamilton trained with Pierre, a former Olympic champion.

The cost of figure-skating training became an issue. The family had given up much to pay for Scott's training. His mother developed cancer and could no longer work to earn an income. In 1976, his parents told him that they could only afford to pay for one more year of training, and then he would have to drop out.

Fortunately, Helena and Frank McLoraine of Toledo heard of Scott's dilemma and agreed to pay for his continued training. Later, Scott would work with the McLoraines in providing philanthropic support for the sport. Hamilton attended Bowling Green State University in his home town. He was going through a learning curve in skating competitions. In his first world championship in Ottawa, he skated to an eleventh-place finish.

Hamilton finished third in the U.S. Figure Skating Championships in 1980, which earned him a place on the U.S. Olympic team. He was given the honor of carrying the American flag in the opening ceremony of the 1980 Winter Olympics. He finished in fifth place. He came in first in the 1981 U.S. Championships with an outstanding performance. From then on, he never lost a competition.

Hamilton won a gold at the 1981 World Figure Skating Championships. He also won gold medals at the 1982, 1983, and 1984 U.S. and World Championships, as well as the gold medal at the 1984 Winter Olympics. He turned professional in April 1984.

Hamilton toured with the Ice Capades for two years and then formed "Scott Hamilton's American Tour," later renamed "Stars on Ice." He co-produced and performed in Stars on Ice for fifteen years before retiring in 2001. In 1990, he was inducted into the U.S. Olympic Hall of Fame. Beginning in 1985, he was a skating commentator for CBS television. He has also been a commentator for NBC television.

Hamilton was diagnosed with testicular cancer in 1997. He returned to skating after his treatment. On November 14, 2002, he married Tracie Robinson, a nutritionist. They have two sons, Aidan McIntosh Hamilton and Maxx Thomas Hamilton.

In November 2004, Hamilton was diagnosed with a benign brain tumor, which was treated at the Cleveland Clinic. On March 8, 2010, "Scott Hamilton: Return to the Ice" was shown on the Bio Channel. The two-hour special told of Hamilton's return to the ice after battling cancer.

In June 2010, Hamilton had brain surgery to prevent the recurrence of the brain tumor, which could have caused blindness if untreated. In November 2010, he returned for surgery for an aneurysm caused by the brain being "nicked" when the brain tumor had been removed. He was certainly resilient.

HELEN KELLER (1880-1968) Humanitarian and Author

"My life has been happy because I have wonderful friends and plenty of interesting work to do. I seldom think about my limitations, and they never make me sad. Perhaps there is just a touch of yearning at times, but it is vague, like a breeze among flowers. The wind passes, and the flowers are content . . . I slip back at times. I fall, I stand still. I run against the edge of hidden obstacles. I lose my temper and find it again, and keep it better. I trudge on. I gain a little. I feel encouraged. I get more eager and climb higher and begin to see widening horizons."

Helen Keller, *The Story of My Life*

Helen Keller was a model of what the human spirit can do when challenged. She was above average in intelligence and in inquisitiveness. Her ability to overcome her triple disabilities of being blind, deaf, and mute is an inspiration to all of us. She could not have accomplished what she did without a very positive outlook and considerable optimism.

Keller led a life of achievement, writing articles and books and supporting causes for the disabled, particularly the blind. She received considerable recognition for her accomplishments. Her academic honors included honorary degrees from Harvard University and the University of Berlin as well as a Doctor of Laws degree from the University of Glasgow and a Doctor of Humane Letters degree from Temple University. She was invited to the White House by every President from Grover Cleveland to John F. Kennedy, and, in 1964, she was awarded the Presidential Medal of Freedom by President Lyndon Johnson.

Keller was a normal infant until the age of 19 months, when, due to an illness, she lost her sight, hearing, and ability to speak. Her resilience in overcoming her disabilities was exemplary. The accomplishments of her teacher, Anne Sullivan, were notable as well.

Keller's devastating illness occurred in February 1882. It was described by doctors as "acute congestion of the stomach and brain" and "brain fever," but it was probably scarlet fever. Helen's doctor did not expect her to live. Hope for Keller to overcome her disabilities came when her mother read Charles Dickens's

73

American Notes, in which he described the progress made by a young girl who was blind and deaf and had been educated at the Perkins Institution in Boston.

Arthur Keller took his daughter to Baltimore for a comprehensive eye examination by the highly regarded oculist, Dr. Chisholm. He gave no encouragement for improvement but suggested that Keller consult with Dr. Alexander Graham Bell in Washington. Dr. Bell, the Scottish-American inventor of the telephone, had a lifelong commitment to helping the deaf. He had been a teacher of speech for the deaf in Boston. Dr. Bell suggested that the Kellers contact the Perkins Institution.

The Institution recommended Anne Sullivan as a teacher for Helen. When Sullivan arrived at the Kellers' home in Tuscumbia, Alabama, to take up her new responsibilities, she was pleased to find a healthy young girl who indicated early that she was clever. However, Sullivan found that Keller was also an unruly, undisciplined child whose behavior was out of control.

Sullivan realized that she would have to establish her authority quickly if she hoped to succeed with her charge. Within several days, Keller demonstrated her unruliness by knocking out two of her teacher's front teeth. Keller would pinch Sullivan when she was disappointed and then lie on the floor and kick and scream.

Sullivan suggested that faster progress could be made if she and Keller were off by themselves. The Kellers realized the importance of establishing discipline and suggested that Sullivan and their daughter move to the garden house, which was a quarter mile from the homestead. After two weeks in the garden house, Keller realized that Sullivan was trying to help her. The young student became not only obedient but loving. Sullivan was overjoyed. Keller began to show a definite interest in learning.

On April 5, 1887, just over a month after Sullivan arrived in Tuscumbia, a significant emotional event occurred for Keller. Sullivan described it in a letter to a friend at Perkins, as cited by Keller in *The Story of My Life:*

> I must write you a line this morning because something very important has happened. Helen has taken the second great step in her education. She has learned that everything has a name, and that

the manual alphabet is the key to everything she wants to know . . . This morning, while she was washing, she wanted to know the word for "water" . . . I spelled "w-a-t-e-r" and thought no more about it until after breakfast . . . We went out to the pump house, and I made Helen hold her hand under the spout while I pumped. I spelled "w-a-t-e-r" in Helen's free hand.

The word coming so close upon the sensation of cold water rushing over her hand seemed to startle her. She dropped the mug and stood transfixed. A new light came into her face. She spelled "w-a-t-e-r" several times. Then she dropped on the ground and asked for its name.

Keller was awakened to the possibilities now open to her; she learned at a frantic pace. During several hours in one day in April 1887, she added 30 words to her vocabulary. Her next goals were to learn to construct sentences and how to read. In May 1887, Keller read her first story. Although Louis Braille had invented a system of printing books for the blind in which characters are represented by raised dots in 1829, no standardized technique for printing books for the blind was used at that time.

Sullivan suggested that Keller move to Boston to take advantage of the materials available at the Perkins Institution to teach the blind. Also, Helen would have the opportunity to meet other children who shared her handicaps. In May 1888, Keller began to learn Braille at Perkins. Keller set herself a goal of learning to speak. Sullivan did not think that this was a good way for Keller to spend her energy; however, Keller insisted.

In March 1890, Keller enrolled at the Horace Mann School for the Deaf in Boston. She described the method used by her teacher: "She passed my hand lightly over her face, and let me feel the position of her tongue and lips when she made a sound. I was eager to initiate every motion and in an hour had learned six elements of speech: M, P, A, S, T, and I. I shall never forget the surprise and delight I felt when I uttered my first sentence: 'It is warm.'"

People had to speak slowly for Keller to understand them. Her teacher also taught her how to lip read by placing her fingers not only on the lips of the person speaking but also on his or her throat.

Keller wanted to study at Radcliffe. Years later, President Woodrow Wilson asked her why she chose Radcliffe. She replied that she thought they didn't want her at Radcliffe, and, because she was stubborn, she decided to go there. Keller carried a full course load. Sullivan went to all of her classes and spelled the contents of the lectures into Keller's hand. Keller was elected vice president of her freshman class.

While at Radcliffe, Keller enrolled in a composition course taught by a highly regarded Harvard professor. Her writing attracted the attention of the editors of the *Ladies' Home Journal*, who asked her to write her autobiography, which was published in 1902. *The Story of My Life* was a success as it had been when published in the *Ladies' Home Journal*. Keller's second book, *Optimism,* based on a 7,000-word essay that she wrote on the goodness of life while an undergraduate at Radcliffe, was published in 1903.

In 1906, Keller was appointed to the Massachusetts Commission for the Blind. She pioneered in bringing the problems of blind newborns to the attention of the public.

In 1909, Keller's third book, *The World I Live In,* was published. In 1927, her book, *My Religion*, was published, followed two years later by *Midstream: My Later Life*. Keller gave lectures sponsored by the American Foundation for the Blind and established the Helen Keller Endowment Fund.

In 1940, Keller wrote *Let Us Have Faith*, in which she discusses "the ultimate ability of man to conquer despair and tyranny." In 1955, her biography of Anne Sullivan Macy, *Teacher*, was published.

Keller died on June 1, 1968, of arteriosclerotic heart disease. She was an optimist for her entire lifetime. She said, "I believe that all through these dark and silent years, God has been using my life for a purpose I do not know. But one day I shall understand, and then I will be satisfied."

PAUL WITTGENSTEIN (1887-1961) One-armed Concert Pianist

"It [learning to play the piano with one hand] was like attempting to scale a mountain. If you can't climb up from one side, you try another."

Paul Wittgenstein

Paul Wittgenstein was a highly regarded concert pianist prior to World War I. While serving in the Austrian army, he was severely wounded in the right arm, which had to be amputated. For most musicians, loss of an arm would have been a career-ending event. Wittgenstein, however, surveyed the music that could be played with one hand and practiced seven hours a day to learn how to play it. In an article in *The Music Review*, E. Fred Flindell commented on this accomplishment:

> Wittgenstein amazed the post-war generation. In the years following the war, a period of bizarre turmoil and stunting cynicism, Wittgenstein not only attained world-wide fame, his example fostered a unique image in the minds of scholars, concertgoers, and musicians alike. Neither his family, his wealth, his heroic war record, nor his musical talent could alone account for or carve out such an achievement. His was simply a boundless idealism, one embodying devotion, endurance, and temerity in the service of music.

Paul Wittgenstein, who was born on November 5, 1887, in Vienna, Austria, was the seventh of eight children of Karl and Leopoldine Kalmus Wittgenstein. Karl owned several steel factories and became known as the "Iron King" of Austria. Leopoldine Wittgenstein, the daughter of a wealthy merchant, played arrangements for four hands on the organ and piano with young Paul as his skill on the keyboard developed. Paul's younger brother, Ludwig, became a renowned philosopher.

The Wittgenstein family was wealthy. They frequently entertained Brahms, Mahler, and Clara Schumann. Paul was fortunate to have the opportunity to play piano duets with Richard Strauss. Bruno Walter and Pablo Casals also performed in the Wittgenstein home. Karl Wittgenstein provided financial support to Arnold Schöenberg.

Young Wittgenstein took piano lessons from the highly regarded teacher, Malvine Brée. Wittgenstein had an incredible memory for music and was a facile sight-reader. His exposure to masters of music in his home elevated his interest in music. He was not concerned about his own limitations in comparison with them. Next he took lessons from Theodor Leschetizky and the blind Austrian composer, Josef Labor. They helped him search for his own musical identity.

Wittgenstein's friend, Trevor Harvey, said about him at this time, "By all accounts in his early days he built up an astonishing left-hand technique, but when I knew him the nervous intensity that he developed led him often to play insensitively and loudly, and not always with great accuracy." He referred to himself as the "Saitenknicker," the mighty key smasher.

In December 1913, Wittgenstein made his debut as a concert pianist at the Grosser Musikverein Saal in Vienna. Three months later, he gave a solo performance with the Vienna Symphony Verein. In August 1914, he was called to active duty as a second lieutenant in the Austrian Army. He was severely wounded while leading a reconnaissance patrol near Zamosc, Poland.

In his book about Wittgenstein, *The Crown Prince*, John Barchilon described what happened when Wittgenstein's patrol was hit by an artillery shell:

> The ground opened up and hurled them in the air, spinning and twisting. Paul saw earth, fire, and sky. Arms, legs, and black dirt swirled around him, and then he began the endless journey back to earth. He fell and fell and fell, landing on something soft. Where were his legs? His arms, hands, where were they? Where was his foot? He heard nothing. Just silence. Black, black nothing. Was this death?

Wittgenstein was taken to an army hospital at Krasnostov, where his right arm was amputated. He was taken prisoner by the Russian Army at the hospital and moved to hospitals in Minsk and in Orel and Omsk, Siberia, where he had access to a piano. In November 1915, through efforts of the International Red Cross, he was sent from Siberia to Sweden, where he participated in a prisoner exchange sponsored by the Pope.

In March 1916, Wittgenstein was promoted to first lieutenant and retired on a medical disability pension. Leopoldine Wittgenstein received a letter from his commanding officer:

> I wish to express my sincere sympathy with you in connection with the severe wounding of your son. You may be proud of him, because owing to the information obtained by his patrol, the efforts of the Russians to attack us at Famorz were frustrated. He has rendered outstanding services, and I sincerely hope he will get official recognition.

In May 1916, Wittgenstein was awarded the Military Cross Class III and the War Decoration Class III. Five months later, he was awarded the Military Cross Class II by the Grand Duke of Mecklenburg. From the summer of 1917 until August 1918, by his own request, he served as a first lieutenant on the Italian front as a general's aide.

From the time of his return to Vienna until he volunteered for the Italian front, Wittgenstein practiced compositions for the left hand. He performed in five recitals, in which he played Labor's *Concertpiece for Piano and Orchestra, Sonata in E-flat for Piano and Violin,* and *Piano Quartet in C Minor.* In September 1918, he returned to Vienna and the concert stage.

Leschetizky had died in 1915. Wittgenstein did not look for another teacher; he practiced seven hours a day, establishing his own regimen. Initially, he tired easily and had to rest frequently. From 1918 to 1921, Wittgenstein searched libraries, museums, and second-hand retail music shops for compositions for the left hand. He liked Brahms's arrangement of Bach's *Chaconne,* as well as Godowsky's *Suite for the Left Hand Alone,* the *Fugue upon Bach,* and the *Intermezzo and Etude Macabre.* He also admired *Studies for the Left Hand* by Reger, *Etudes for the Left Hand* by Saint-Saëns, and Scriabin's *Prelude and Nocturne for the Left Hand,* which the composer wrote after developing tendonitis in his right hand.

One of the earliest one-armed pianists was the Hungarian Count Geza Zichy, who began playing the piano at the age of five; he decided to be a concert pianist after losing his right arm in a hunting accident in 1864, when he was fifteen. His concert in Berlin in May 1915 was the first known public performance of a one-armed pianist. Count Zichy's friend, Franz Liszt, transcribed a song for him, and Emil Sauer wrote *Etude* for him. Wittgenstein did not like the works that Count Zichy composed for himself.

Wittgenstein wrote his own arrangements of piano compositions and operas using the transcription devices of Liszt and of Godowsky. He also commissioned composers to create new works for the left hand. Wittgenstein observed: "Since it is no particular attainment of mine, I think I may honestly say that I am (perhaps) the pianist for whom the greatest number of special compositions have been written." In 1931, he accepted a teaching position at the New Vienna Conservatory, where he was known for his energy and his optimism.

Wittgenstein didn't hesitate to make extensive changes to other composers' works that he had commissioned, similar to his modifications to Brahms's transcription of Bach's *Chaconne*. He made changes to the compositions of Hindemith and Korngold, as well as to Britten's *Diversions on a Theme*, Prokofiev's *Concerto No. 4*, and *Parergon to the Domestic Symphony* by Richard Strauss. They were twentieth-century composers, and Wittgenstein's style was that of the nineteenth century.

Wittgenstein asked Ravel if he would compose a piano concerto for the left hand. Ravel willingly undertook the project. Initially, Ravel and Wittgenstein did not agree on the finished work. Wittgenstein objected to Ravel's inclusion of jazz rhythms in his composition; however, the differences were resolved. Ravel's *Concerto in D for Left Hand* became one of the most frequently played works for one hand.

Wittgenstein continued to perform on the concert stage. One of his students in the 1930s recalled the first time she had heard him play: "I was about twelve years old when I heard Paul Wittgenstein

perform for the first time. I was sitting with my father in our sub-
scription seats in the rear of the Wiener Musikverein Saal. After the
concert, my father asked me if I had noticed anything unusual about
the pianist. I had not. He told me that the pianist had only played
with his left hand. I could not believe it."

In November 1934, Wittgenstein performed the Ravel
Concerto for the Left Hand and Orchestra with the Boston
Symphony. The music critic of the *New York Herald-Tribune*
reported:

> Doubtless the greatest tribute one could pay to
> Paul Wittgenstein, the famous one-armed pianist,
> is a simple statement of the fact that after the first
> few moments wondering how the devil he accom-
> plished it, one almost forgot that one was listening
> to a player whose right sleeve hung empty at his
> side. One found oneself engrossed by the sensi-
> tiveness of the artist's phrasing, the extent to which
> his incredible technique was subordinated to the
> delivery of the musical thought.

Wittgenstein taught at the New Vienna Conservatory until he
immigrated to the United States in December 1938. From 1938
until 1943, he taught at the Ralph Wolfe Conservatory in New
Rochelle, an affiliate of the Mannes Music School; from 1940 until
1945 he was a professor of piano at Manhattanville College of the
Sacred Heart. He became a U.S. citizen in 1946. In 1957,
Wittgenstein published *School for the Left Hand*. In 1958, he
received an honorary Doctor of Music degree from the Philadelphia
Musical Academy.

In a June 1967 interview with Leonard Castle, Wittgenstein
described some of the piano techniques that he used in concerts. He
did not use the middle or harp pedal on the piano. He used two fingers on one key for increased volume, and difficult leaps over the
keys could be avoided by half pedaling that simulated the two-
handed technique. His skill was enhanced by the speed with which
he used his left hand and his precise control.

On March 3, 1961, Paul Wittgenstein died in Manhasset, New
York. In *The Music Review*, E. Fred Flindell wrote what might be
considered an epitaph:

It is, however, astonishing how many works [over forty] the artist took an active part in commissioning, determining, and performing. Few knew that Wittgenstein spent years helping others as president of the Society Against Poverty, or of his countless anonymous and gracious deeds of assistance. Perhaps his nineteenth-century ideas and bearing were at times anachronistic, even quixotic. Still, his endeavor and influence, his courage and skill will remain legendary for generations to come.

ELIZABETH BLACKWELL (1821-1910) First U.S. Woman Doctor

"We may forget the early struggles of the doctors Elizabeth and Emily Blackwell, but what we should never forget is that the dignity, the culture, and the high moral standards which formed their character, finally prevailed in overcoming the existing prejudice, both within and outside the profession. By their standards, the status of women in medicine was determined."

Dr. Elizabeth Cushier

Elizabeth Blackwell's desire to become a medical doctor did not develop slowly. It occurred as a significant emotional event in her early 20s while visiting a friend who was dying of cancer. Blackwell considered the study of medicine. Although she had been content with her social and family life, it was not a fulfilling life for her. She did not feel challenged.

Blackwell entered her personal reflections on pursuing the study of medicine in her diary. "The idea of winning a doctor's degree gradually assumed the aspect of a great moral struggle, and the moral fight possessed an immense attraction for me. This work has taken deep root in my soul and become an all-absorbing duty. I must accomplish my end. I consider it the noblest and most useful path that I can tread."

Blackwell sent out applications to medical schools while teaching to earn money for tuition. She wanted to attend medical school in Philadelphia, which she considered the medical center of the United States because of its four highly regarded medical schools.

Blackwell sent her first inquiry to Dr. Joseph Warrington in Philadelphia. His response was discouraging; he viewed men as doctors and women as nurses and recommended that she pursue a nursing career. However, he added: "If the project be of divine origin and appointment, it will sooner or later surely be accomplished."

She applied to 29 medical schools for admission and received 28 rejections. In late October 1847, Blackwell received an acceptance from the medical school of Geneva College, Geneva, New York. The president of Geneva College was an open-minded individual who had recruited an extremely capable dean for the medical school, Dr. Charles Lee.

The circumstances surrounding Blackwell's acceptance were unusual. Dr. Warrington wrote a letter to Dr. Lee on her behalf. The Geneva faculty was unanimously against the admission of a woman to their medical school. However, they did not want to be responsible for rejecting the highly regarded Philadelphia doctor's request. The faculty turned the decision over to the medical students; they were confident that the students would vote against her admission.

Dr. Lee read Dr. Warrington's letter to the class and informed them that the faculty would let the students determine the issue. He told them that one negative vote would prevent Blackwell's admission. The students were enthusiastic about her admittance, and the single dissenting student was browbeaten into submission. Blackwell received a document composed by the students and signed by the chairman of the class, as noted by Peggy Chambers in *A Doctor Alone, A Biography of Elizabeth Blackwell:*

> Resolved—That one of the radical principles of a Republican Government is the universal education of both sexes; that to every branch of scientific education the door should be open equally to all; that the application of Elizabeth Blackwell to become a member of our class meets our entire approbation; and in extending our unanimous invitation we pledge ourselves that no conduct of ours shall cause her to regret her attendance at this institution.

Blackwell was overjoyed to receive the acceptance. She was not sure what to expect from her fellow medical students; however, she had grown up with brothers and was not an overly sensitive young woman. The Geneva community was not ready for a female medical student, and, initially, she had difficulty finding a place to live. She moved into a drafty attic room in a boarding house.

Eventually, Blackwell became aware that she was being subjected to a form of ostracism. The other boarders were unfriendly at mealtime, the women she passed on the street held their skirts to one side and did not speak, and one doctor's wife snubbed her openly. Although her feelings were hurt by this treatment, she reacted by staying in her room and studying.

Blackwell's professor of anatomy was Dr. James Webster, who was friendly and sincerely glad to have her in his class. He predicted: "You'll go through the course and get your diploma—with great éclat too. We'll give you the opportunities. You'll make a stir, I can tell you."

Nevertheless, within a short time, Dr. Webster prevented Blackwell from attending a dissection. He wrote a note to her explaining that he was about to lecture on the reproductive organs and that he could not cover the material satisfactorily in the presence of a lady. He offered her the opportunity for dissection and study of this portion of the course in private. She knew that Dr. Webster had a reputation for being coarse in covering this material. He sprinkled his lecture with humorous anecdotes. The students liked this approach to the subject matter and responded by becoming somewhat rowdy. Blackwell replied to Dr. Webster, reminding him that she was a student with a serious purpose, and that she was aware of his awkward position, particularly "when viewed from the low standpoint of impure and unchaste sentiments." She asked why a student of science would have his mind diverted from such an absorbing subject by the presence of a student in feminine attire. She offered to remove her bonnet and sit in the back row of benches, but if the class wished she would not attend the class.

Dr. Webster acquiesced, and Blackwell attended the dissection, which she said was "just about as much as I could bear." She noted in her diary: "My delicacy was certainly shocked, and yet the exhibition was in some sense ludicrous. I had to pinch my hand until the blood nearly came, and call on Christ to help me from smiling, for that would have ruined everything; but I sat in grave indifference, though the effort made my heart palpitate most painfully."

Blackwell considered how to spend the summer adding to her medical knowledge. One of the few places open to her was Blockley Almshouse in Philadelphia, which cared for 2,000 lower-class unfortunates. Again, Blackwell had to pay for being a pioneer. The resident doctors snubbed her and left a ward when she entered it. They neglected to enter the diagnosis and the notation of the medication used in treatment on the patients' charts. She had to make many of her own diagnoses. Her major accomplishment that summer was the preparation of a thesis on typhus for which she received compliments from senior staff physicians.

Blackwell worked hard during her second year of medical school. Although she had always received good grades, she approached her final exams with trepidation. When the results were compiled, Elizabeth had the best academic record in the class. However, the administration of Geneva College vacillated on establishing the precedent of awarding the first medical degree to a woman in the United States.

Dr. Webster defended her, saying, "She paid her tuition didn't she? She passed every course, each and every one with honors! And let me tell you, gentlemen, if you hold back, I'll take up a campaign in every medical journal." Blackwell received her medical degree on January 23, 1849. Her brother, Henry, traveled to Geneva to share the experience with her. He documented his recollections of the ceremony, as observed by Ishbel Ross in *Child of Destiny:*

> He [Dr. Lee, who gave the valedictory address] pronounced her the leader of the class; stated that she had passed through a thorough course in every department, slighting none; that she had profited to the utmost by all the advantages of the institution, and by her ladylike and dignified deportment had proved that the strongest intellect and nerve, and the most untiring perseverance were compatible with the softest attributes of feminine delicacy and grace, to all which the students manifested, by decided attempts at applause, their entire concurrence.

As Blackwell left the ceremony, the women of Geneva displayed their smiles and friendly faces to her. She was pleased to see this change in attitude; however, she recorded her true feelings in her diary: "For the next few hours, before I left by train, my room was thronged by visitors. I was glad of the sudden conversion thus shown, but my past experience had given me a useful and permanent lesson at the outset of life as to the very shallow nature of popularity."

Blackwell returned to Philadelphia with the hope of being accepted by the medical community there. She attended lectures at the University of Pennsylvania, but it was obvious that she was not going to be given the opportunity to gain the practical medical experience she needed. She obtained that experience at St. Bartholomew's Hospital in London and at La Maternite in Paris. Again, she encountered bias. She was not given access to all departments at St. Bartholomew's, and at La Maternite, she was considered an aide, not a doctor.

Upon Blackwell's return to New York, she was unable to find a position at the city dispensaries and hospitals. She opened her own dispensary. She lectured on women's health subjects and published two books.

On May 12, 1857, Blackwell opened the New York Infirmary for Women and Children. Charles A. Dana, Cyrus W. Field, and Horace Greeley were trustees of the infirmary. In 1868, Blackwell opened her medical college. For 31 years, the college filled a need in providing medical education for women. In 1899, it was incorporated into the Cornell Medical Center. The infirmary founded by Elizabeth Blackwell is now part of New York Infirmary — Beekman Downtown Hospital.

In 1899, Hobart and William Smith Colleges, successors to Geneva College, named its first residence hall for women Blackwell House. Elizabeth Blackwell was a pioneer who encountered many obstacles. She was sufficiently resilient to overcome them and to make significant contributions to the medical profession.

FLORENCE NIGHTINGALE (1820-1910) Nursing and Medical Pioneer

"It was not by gentle sweetness and womanly self-abnegation that she had brought order out of chaos in the Scutari Hospitals, that, from her own resources, she had clothed the British Army, that she spread her dominion over the serried and reluctant powers of the official world; it was by strict method, by stern discipline, by rigid attention to detail, by ceaseless labor, by the fixed determination of an indomitable will."

Lytton Strachey, *Eminent Victorians*

Florence Nightingale is known principally for her work at military hospitals during the Crimean War. However, her contributions were much greater than that. She was the driving force in the reform of British Army medical services during and after the Crimean War in designing hospitals with the patient in mind, in the establishment of a school of nursing with higher standards than previous ones, and in the administration of medical services for the army in India.

This effort involved guiding those in positions of power in the British government, choosing chairmen for key committees, and generally steering medical and hospital reform, both military and civilian, for over 40 years. Nightingale provided direction for the careers of many Members of Parliament and advice to every Viceroy of India before he left England to assume his new duties.

Virtually all of Nightingale's girlhood friends were contented to become wives, mothers, and hostesses whose principal interests in life were social activities. She was bored with the social whirl and felt obliged to do something meaningful with her life. She viewed this as a call and entered this note in her diary: "On February 7, 1837, God spoke to me and called me to His service."

However, Nightingale did not know what form this service was going to take; she knew that it was going to have something to do with ministering to the sufferings of humanity. It did not become clear to her for seven years that her call was caring for the sick.

In the fall of 1842, while visiting the Baroness and Baron von Bunsen, the Prussian Ambassador to Great Britain, Nightingale asked them what a person could do to relieve the suffering of those who cannot help themselves. The Baron told her about the work at

Kaiserswerth, Germany, where Protestant deaconesses were trained in the institution's hospital to nurse the poor who were sick. Nightingale had not considered nursing as a way of serving those in need, and she did not follow up on this suggestion at the time.

By the spring of 1844, however, Nightingale was certain that her life's work was with the sick in hospitals. Thirteen years later she wrote, "Since I was 24 . . . there never was any vagueness in my plans or ideas as to what God's work was for me."

In June 1844, Dr. Ward Howe, the American philanthropist, visited the Nightingales at Embley. Nightingale asked Dr. Howe: "Do you think it would be unsuitable and unbecoming for a young Englishwoman to devote herself to works of charity in hospitals and elsewhere as Catholic sisters do?" Dr. Howe replied: "My dear Miss Florence, it would be unusual, and in England whatever is unusual is thought to be unsuitable; but I say to you 'go forward.' If you have a vocation for that way of life, act up to your inspiration and you will find there is never anything unbecoming or unladylike in doing your duty for the good of others. Choose, go on with it, wherever it may lead you and God be with you."

Nightingale considered how to present to her parents her plan to spend three months in nursing training at nearby Salisbury Infirmary, where the head physician was Dr. Fowler, a family friend. She broached the subject with her parents in December 1845, during a visit by Dr. Fowler and his wife.

The Nightingales were strongly opposed and could not understand why Florence wanted to "disgrace herself." She wrote later: "It was as if I had wanted to be a kitchen-maid."

Nightingale was distressed because she knew what she had to do, but she was prevented from doing it. Lytton Strachey, in *Eminent Victorians,* observed: "A weaker spirit would have been overwhelmed by the load of such distresses—would have yielded or snapped. But this extraordinary young woman held firm and fought her way to victory. With an amazing persistency, during the eight years that followed her rebuff over Salisbury Hospital, she struggled and worked and planned."

While continuing to perform her social obligations, Nightingale studied hospital reports and public health material. She built up a detailed knowledge of sanitary conditions that ultimately allowed her to become the foremost expert in England and on the Continent in her subject.

Finally, Nightingale was given the opportunity to receive nursing training at Kaiserswerth. Her spartan life started at five o'clock in the morning and the work was hard; but, in her words, "I find the deepest interest in everything here and am so well in body and mind. This is life. Now I know what it is to live and to love life, and I really should be sorry to leave life . . . I wish for no other earth, no other world than this."

Nightingale met Dr. Elizabeth Blackwell, the first woman medical doctor in modern times, in the spring of 1851 in London, where Blackwell had come for further medical training. Nightingale talked with Blackwell about the strength of her own commitment to hospital nursing.

In April 1853, Nightingale heard of an opportunity that suited her parents' requirements. The Institution for the Care of Sick Gentlewomen in Distressed Circumstances had encountered problems and was to be reorganized and moved to another location. Nightingale took charge and was responsible not only for the management of the institution but also its finances.

Nightingale had one year of nursing experience in March 1854, when England and France declared war on Russia. In June, the British Army landed at Varna on the Black Sea. When they embarked from Varna for the Crimea there was a shortage of transport ships, so they had to leave hospital tents and regimental medicine chests behind. On September 30, the British and the French defeated the Russians in the Battle of the Alma with heavy casualties on both sides.

British casualties did not receive proper care, since there were no litters or hospital wagons to transport them to a site to receive medical attention. When the wounded were carried by their comrades to receive the care of a doctor, no bandages or splints were available, nor were there any anesthetics or painkillers.

William Russell's dispatches to the *London Times* brought the conditions of the casualties to the attention of the British public. Two weeks after the Battle of the Alma, he wrote, "It is with feelings of surprise and anger that the public will learn that no sufficient preparations have been made for the care of the wounded. Not only are there not sufficient surgeons . . . not only are there no dressers and nurses . . . there is not even linen to make bandages."

Russell visited the French Army to see how their wounded were being treated. He found that their medical facilities and nursing care were excellent, and that 50 Sisters of Charity had accompanied their army. In another article for his newspaper, he asked, "Why have we no Sisters of Charity? There are numbers of able-bodied and tender-hearted English women who would joyfully and with alacrity go out to devote themselves to nursing the sick and wounded, if they could be associated for that purpose and placed under proper protection."

The Secretary for War during the Crimean War was Sidney Herbert, a good friend of Nightingale and her family. He wrote to ask if she would go to the Crimea to organize and superintend the nurses to care for the wounded.

Nightingale immediately began interviewing candidates and ultimately selected 14 nurses who, along with 10 Catholic Sisters and 14 Anglican Sisters, accompanied her to Scutari. She was appointed Superintendent of the Female Nursing Establishment of the English General Hospitals in Turkey. This title caused her problems, since it was construed to restrict her authority to Turkey and to exclude her from the Crimea in Russia.

Nightingale arrived at the military hospital in Scutari on November 4, 1854, 10 days after the Battle of Balaclava, where the Light Brigade was decimated by pitting cavalry against artillery, and 10 days before the Battle of Inkerman. She encountered a medical support system in total collapse, due to insufficient planning, poor execution of the few plans that did exist, and generally inadequate administration hampered by bureaucratic constrictions.

The Commissariat was responsible for the procurement, financing, transporting, and warehousing of hospital supplies. The Purveyor was responsible for food for the sick but did not procure it; the Commissariat did, and the organizations did not work well together.

Barrack Hospital, with four miles of beds, was not big enough. Nightingale had to plan, equip, and finance accommodations for 800 additional patients when the casualties from the Battles of Balaclava and Inkerman began to arrive. Open sewers, which ran under Barrack Hospital, were filled with lice, rats, and other vermin. Ventilation was poor and the stench was horrible. Working in these conditions is an indication of the strength of Nightingale's empathy for her patients. She became a purveyor of hospital supplies and a supplier of clothing to the patients.

Finances available to Nightingale were money sent to her from private sources in England and funds collected by the *London Times* for aid to the sick and the wounded. An eyewitness wrote, "I cannot conceive, as I now look back on the first three weeks after the arrival of the wounded from Inkerman, how it would have been possible to have avoided a state of things too disastrous to contemplate had not Miss Nightingale been there, with the aid of the means placed at her disposal."

Although Nightingale complied with regulations, her active style offended Dr. John Hall, Chief of the Medical Staff of the British Expeditionary Army. He found ways to obstruct her efforts. In particular, he was initially able to prevent her from supporting the two large hospitals in the Crimea by a strict interpretation of her title, Superintendent of the Female Nursing Establishment in *Turkey*. He claimed that her responsibility did not extend to the Crimea. She had to overcome Dr. Hall's obstructions.

Coworkers were in awe of Nightingale. Dr. Sutherland said, "She is the mainspring of the work. Nobody who has not worked with her daily could know her, could have an idea of her strength and clearness of mind, her extraordinary powers joined with her benevolence of spirit. She is one of the most gifted creatures God ever made."

Nightingale worked incredibly long hours and gave personal attention to the patients, even those with infectious diseases. The administrative load was overwhelming, and she had no secretary to share the paperwork burden. By spring 1855, she was physically exhausted. Nightingale was becoming a legend in England. She received a letter from Queen Victoria:

> You are, I know, well aware of the high sense I entertain of the Christian devotion which you have displayed during this great and bloody war, and I need hardly repeat to you how warm my admiration is for your services, which are fully equal to those of my dear and brave soldiers, whose sufferings you have had the privilege of alleviating in so merciful a manner.

In August 1856, Nightingale returned home from Scutari. Within a few weeks of her return, she visited the Queen and the Prince Consort at Balmoral Castle and made an excellent impression. The Prince wrote in his diary: "She put before us all the defects of our present military hospital system and the reforms that are needed." The Queen observed, "Such a head! I wish we had her at the War Office."

Nightingale became an influential person, and she knew how to use that influence. She negotiated Sidney Herbert's appointment as chairman of a royal commission whose function was to report on the health of the army.

During six months of extremely hard work, Nightingale assembled and wrote in her own hand "Notes Affecting the Health, Efficiency, and Hospital Administration of the British Army." This comprehensive 800-page document contained far-sighted recommendations for reform in the areas of hospital architecture, military medical requirements, sanitation, and medical statistics.

In December 1859, Nightingale published a nursing guide, *Notes on Nursing*. In 1860, she opened the Nightingale Training School for Nurses at St. Thomas Hospital and became known as the founder of modern nursing. She did this concurrently with her ongoing efforts for medical and sanitary reform, which continued for over 40 years. Administration was her strength; she established a cost accounting system for the Army Medical Services between 1860 and 1865 that was still in use over 80 years later.

In November 1907, King Edward VII bestowed the Order of Merit on Nightingale, the first such award given to a woman. She died on August 13, 1910, after serving others for virtually her entire adult life.

During the time when Nightingale was pleading unsuccessfully with her parents to allow her to undertake nursing training, her mother confided her concerns to her friends. As noted by Lytton Strachey in *Eminent Victorians,* "At times, indeed, among her intimates, Mrs. Nightingale almost wept. 'We are ducks,' she said with tears in her eyes, 'who have hatched a wild swan.' But the poor lady was wrong; it was not a swan that they had hatched; it was an eagle."

CHAPTER 4

RESEARCHERS / CEOs / INVENTORS

"One CEO underscored its importance this way: 'More than education, more than experience, more than training, a person's level of resilience will determine who succeeds and who fails. That's true in the cancer ward, it's true in the Olympics, and it's true in the boardroom.'"

D. L. Coutu, "How Resilience Works,"
Harvard Business Review, May, 2002

STEPHEN HAWKING (1942-   ) Cosmologist and Researcher

"It is the most persistent and greatest adventure in human history, this search to understand the universe, how it works and where it came from. It is difficult to imagine that a handful of residents of a small planet circling an insignificant star in a small galaxy have as their aim a complete understanding of the entire universe, a small speck of creation truly believing it is capable of understanding the whole."

Murray Gell-Mann

As an undergraduate, Stephen Hawking was an undistinguished student. He was not highly motivated; he studied an average of one hour a day. In 1963, at the age of twenty-one, Hawking was told that he had amyotrophic lateral sclerosis (ALS), which is known as motor neuron disease in Britain and Lou Gehrig's Disease in the United States. ALS attacks the nerves of the spinal cord and the portion of the brain that controls voluntary motor functions of the muscles. The nerve cells degenerate, causing muscles to atrophy throughout the body, resulting in paralysis. Memory and the ability to think are not affected.

ALS, which worsens in stages, forces the patient to deal with a series of progressively limiting plateaus. Hawking has made incredible contributions to science by ignoring his ailment, to the extent of his ability. He has probably done more than any scientist to expand our understanding of the origin and nature of the universe, and his theoretical work on "black holes" was innovative. He is especially well known for his book, *A Brief History of Time*, a best seller.

Stephen Hawking was born in Oxford, England, on January 8, 1942, the three-hundredth anniversary of the death of the Italian scientist Galileo. Both of Hawking's parents, Frank and Isobel Hawking, had attended Oxford University. Stephen Hawking wanted to major in either physics or mathematics in college, but his father insisted that his son take chemistry so that he could follow him in a medical career.

Hawking won a scholarship to University College, Oxford University. When he completed his undergraduate studies at

Oxford, he took the final examinations upon which admission to graduate school were based. Hawking achieved the first-class honors degree that he needed to be admitted to graduate school at Cambridge University to study cosmology with Dr. Fred Hoyle, the foremost British astronomer of his time. In October 1962, when Hawking began his graduate studies at Cambridge, he could choose between two areas of research, elementary particles—the study of small particles, or cosmology—the study of large objects. Cosmology is the study of the origin, evolution, and destiny of the universe.

In Hawking's words, "I thought that elementary particles were less attractive, because, although they were finding lots of new particles, there was no proper theory of elementary particles. All they could do was arrange the particles in families, like in botany. In cosmology, on the other hand, there was a well-defined theory—Einstein's general theory of relativity."

Instead of studying with Fred Hoyle, Hawking was assigned to Dennis Sciama, an unknown to him. He was discouraged by this until he realized that Hoyle, who traveled abroad frequently, would not have been as good a mentor as Sciama, a respected scientist who conscientiously guided him in his research.

Hawking also had a personal problem with which to contend. He began to have difficulty tying his shoelaces, he bumped into walls and furniture, and, on a few occasions, he fell. Also, he experienced slurred speech without having a drink to blame it on. When he arrived home for Christmas vacation in 1962, his parents, who hadn't seen him for several months, knew immediately that something was wrong. His father thought that he might have contracted a disease in the Middle East during a trip with him over the summer. His parents referred him to a specialist.

At several parties over the holidays, Hawking met and talked with Jane Wilde, the friend of a friend, who attended the local high school. Jane planned to read modern languages at Westfield College in London in the fall. She was attracted to this intellectual and somewhat eccentric character. Their relationship blossomed from their first meeting.

In January, Hawking underwent a battery of tests; the diagnosis was ALS. He faced decreasing mobility, gradual paralysis, and ultimately death as respiratory muscles lost their functionality or he contracted pneumonia. Many ALS patients do not live two years beyond the diagnosis. He went into a deep depression, locked himself in his room, and listened to music. If Hawking had decided to study experimental physics instead of theoretical physics, his career would have been over.

Hawking questioned continuing with his research, because he might not be around long enough to get his Ph.D. Literally, he felt that he had nothing to live for. He was not a deeply religious person; nevertheless, he had an experience that helped to put things into perspective: "While I was in hospital, I had seen a boy I vaguely knew die of leukemia in the bed opposite me. It had not been a pretty sight. Clearly there were people who were worse off than me. At least my condition didn't make me feel sick. Whenever I feel inclined to feel sorry for myself, I remember that boy."

Jane visited Stephen early in his stay in the hospital and was surprised to find that he had lost the will to live. Their relationship strengthened; she was a major factor in Hawking's turning his life around. His interest in his research was revived.

During his first two years at Cambridge, Hawking's physical condition worsened. He had to use a cane, and, occasionally, he fell. He rejected offers of help in getting around. His speech grew increasingly difficult to understand. He and Jane became engaged. She said, "I wanted to find some purpose to my existence, and I suppose I found it in the idea of looking after him. But we were in love." For Hawking, their engagement gave new direction to his life and gave him something to live for.

Hawking met applied mathematician Roger Penrose at a scientific meeting at Kings College in London. Penrose explained his concept of a singularity—a mass with zero size and infinite density—occurring at the center of a black hole, a region in space where gravity is so strong that not even light can escape. He showed that the collapse of a star could lead to the formation of a singularity. One night on the train back to Cambridge from London, Hawking turned to Dennis Sciama and speculated what would happen if Penrose's singularity theory were applied to the entire universe.

Penrose had showed that the collapse of a star could cause the formation of a singularity. Hawking conjectured that an important event had begun with the singularity. The event was the reverse of Penrose's collapse, an outward explosion named by Fred Hoyle the "big bang," the origin of the universe. The "big bang" refers to the tremendous explosion that began the expansion of the universe fifteen billion years ago.

When Hawking applied Penrose's ideas to the entire universe, he really began to devote himself to his work: "I started working hard for the first time in my life. To my surprise, I found I liked it. Maybe it is not really fair to call it work. Someone once said, 'Scientists get paid for doing what they enjoy.'" This effort became the final chapter of Hawking's dissertation, "Properties of the Expanding Universe," the work for which he was awarded a Ph.D by Cambridge University. Hawking looked for a post with a salary so he and Jane could get married. He applied for a theoretical physics fellowship at Caius College, Cambridge University. He was awarded the fellowship, and he and Jane were married in July 1965.

Hawking's condition continued to decline. He now needed crutches to walk, and his ability to speak worsened. He had a difficult time getting around their house, but he refused offers of help. His strong-willed nature presented a challenge for Jane. She said, "Some would call his attitude determination, some obstinacy. I've called it both at one time or another. I suppose that's what keeps him going." When asked whether he ever became depressed over his condition, Hawking replied, "Not normally. I have managed to do what I wanted to do despite it, and that gives a feeling of achievement." He maintained a positive outlook, and he was generally cheerful. He didn't waste time worrying about his health.

In the late 1960s, Jane and their friends convinced Hawking that he should be in a wheelchair. He didn't let this change bother him; in fact, he admitted that it enabled him to get around better. His approach to life didn't change. Jane said, "Stephen doesn't make any concessions to his illness, and I don't make any concessions to him."

Hawking recalls when his first black hole breakthrough occurred. In November 1970, he was thinking about black holes while getting ready for bed. As he remembers it: "My disability makes this a rather slow process, so I had plenty of time. Suddenly, I realized that many of the techniques that Penrose and I had developed to prove singularities could be applied to black holes."

Over a six-year period, Hawking co-authored *The Large Scale*

Structure of Space Time with George Ellis. In March 1974, Hawking became a Fellow of the Royal Society at the age of thirty-two. He continued to collect prizes, six major awards in two years: the Eddington Medal from the Royal Astronomical Society, the Pius XI Medal awarded by the Pontifical Academy of Science in the Vatican, the Hopkins Prize, the Dannie Heineman Prize, the Maxwell Prize, and the Hughes Medal of the Royal Society, which cited "his remarkable results in his work on black holes."

In 1978, Hawking was awarded the Albert Einstein Award by the Lewis and Rose Strauss Memorial Fund. During the following year, Hawking co-authored *General Relativity: An Einstein Centenary Survey* with Werner Israel. Hawking was appointed Lucasian Professor at Cambridge University in 1979, 310 years after Isaac Newton was given the same honor. At about this time, an interviewer asked Hawking again about his disability. He responded: "I think I'm happier now than I was before I started. Before the illness set in, I was very bored with life. It really was a rather pointless existence."

Cambridge University Press hoped that Hawking's latest book, *The Very Early Universe,* would sell better than his previous one, *Superspace and Supergravity*, which even scientists had difficulty understanding. The University Press suggested to Hawking that he write a popular book about cosmology. The Press had success previously publishing popular science books by Arthur Eddington and Fred Hoyle. Hawking was a tough negotiator, and the University Press didn't think that they could afford the generous advance that he demanded. The initial sample of a section of the book that Hawking provided was much too technical. In particular, it contained too many equations. The Press told him that every equation would reduce sales significantly.

Prior to signing with Cambridge University Press, Hawking heard that Bantam Books was interested in his popular book about cosmology. Bantam offered an advance for the United States and Canada. He accepted their offer. Bantam's editors also suggested that the technical content of the manuscript should be reduced.

By Christmas 1984, the first draft of the manuscript was finished. Bantam began to promote the book: "Hawking is on the cutting edge of what we know about the cosmos. This whole business of the unified field theory, the conjunction of relativity with quantum mechanics, is comparable to the search for the Holy Grail."

In 1985, Hawking spent the summer in Geneva, Switzerland, at CERN, the European Center for Nuclear Research, where he continued his research and made corrections to the manuscript of his book. One night in early August, Hawking suffered a blockage in his windpipe and later contracted pneumonia. He was placed on a life-support machine but was not in critical condition. Because he was unable to breathe through his mouth or nose, doctors recommended a tracheostomy. A cut would be made in his windpipe and a breathing device would be implanted. However, Hawking would never be able to speak again.

A California computer technologist, Walt Woltosz, gave Hawking a program called Equalizer that provided a menu of 3,000 words from which to construct sentences. The sentences were sent to a voice-synthesizer that spoke for him with an American accent. Hawking's life was transformed by this technology.

In early spring of 1988, Hawking's popular book about cosmology, *A Brief History of Time: From the Big Bang to Black Holes,* was released. Within a few weeks, this book about equating relativity theory with quantum mechanics was at the top of the bestseller list, where it stayed for many months. Stephen Hawking fan clubs were formed. Sales of the book exceeded everyone's estimates, particularly Bantam's.

More than any previous accomplishment, *A Brief History of Time* made Stephen Hawking a household name. A documentary, "Master of the Universe" won a Royal Television Society award, and ABC presented a profile of Hawking on its *20 / 20* program. Earlier, Commander of the British Empire (CBE) honors had been conferred upon Hawking, and, in 1989, he was made a Companion of Honor by Queen Elizabeth.

Hawking's list of achievements is impressive, particularly when his handicap is considered. However, he has suggested that his accomplishments might not have been as great if he hadn't been diagnosed with ALS at the age of twenty-one. Hawking, a strong-willed individual who was highly motivated, always maintained his sense of humor; his upbeat outlook on life contributed significantly to his success. He observed, "One has to be grown up enough to realize that life is not fair. You have to do the best you can in the situation you are in."

LEE IACOCCA (1924-) Rescuer of Chrysler Corporation

"It is a mistake to suppose that men succeed through success; they much oftener succeed through failures. Precept, study, advice, and example could never have taught them so well as failure has done."

Samuel Smiles

Lido "Lee" Iacocca was born on October 15, 1924, in Allentown, Pennsylvania, to Nicola and Antoinette Iacocca. The Iacoccas were a close-knit family, and young Lee was encouraged to excel in school. Iacocca's interest in cars began in his teens. His first car was a 1938 Ford. In 1942, Iacocca enrolled at Lehigh University, where he completed the engineering program in three years.

When Iacocca graduated, he was one of fifty college graduates who received an offer to work for the Ford Motor Company in Dearborn, Michigan. Because he also received a fellowship to study for a master's degree at Princeton University, he delayed starting his job at Ford until August 1946.

Halfway through Ford's eighteen-month training program, Iacocca realized he didn't want to be in engineering; he wanted to be in sales. He was told that he could switch if he could find his own sales job within the company. Iacocca found a position in fleet sales in Chester, Pennsylvania. By 1949, he was a zone manager in Wilkes-Barre, working with eighteen dealers. He advanced rapidly and, at the age of thirty-six, was promoted to general manager of the Ford Division, the company's largest division.

Iacocca's greatest success with the Ford Division was the introduction of the Mustang in 1964. In January 1965, he was promoted to group vice president of the Ford and Lincoln-Mercury Divisions; in December 1970, Iacocca became president of the Ford Motor Company.

By 1975, the working relationship between Iacocca and Henry "my name is on the building" Ford II began to deteriorate. In July 1978, Henry Ford II fired Iacocca. When he asked the reason, Ford said, "It's personal, and I can't tell you any more. It's just one of those things." Iacocca pressed further and was told, "Well, sometimes you just don't like somebody."

Iacocca rented an office in a warehouse; he had reached the low point of his life. In *Iacocca: An Autobiography,* he explained:

> There are times in everyone's life when something constructive is born out of adversity. There are times when things seem so bad that you've got to grab your fate by the shoulders and shake it. I'm convinced it was [reading the newspaper] that morning at the warehouse that pushed me to take on the presidency of Chrysler only a couple of weeks later. The private pain I could have endured. But the deliberate public humiliation [in the press] was too much for me. I was full of anger, and I had a simple choice: I could turn that anger against myself, with disastrous results. Or I could take some of that energy and try to do something positive.
>
> Fortunately, Chrysler recovered from its brush with death. Today I'm a hero. But strangely enough, it's all because of that moment in the warehouse. With determination, with luck, and with the help of lots of good people, I was able to rise up from the ashes.

Iacocca received offers from many companies, including International Paper, Lockheed, and Tandy Corporation. He also received an offer to be the dean of the New York University business school. However, he had been a car man for thirty-two years, and he didn't want to make a career change at the age of fifty-four. He was courted by Chrysler Corporation, initially by directors on the board and then by John Riccardo, the chief executive officer.

Riccardo knew that Chrysler had problems that he couldn't fix; however, he was willing to give up his job to someone who could. Iacocca realized that he wouldn't be happy for long as the number two man at Chrysler; he had to be CEO. Riccardo promised Iacocca that he would become the Chairman of the Board and CEO of Chrysler within a year.

Iacocca knew that Chrysler had aging plants, low employee morale, high inventory, and reliability problems with their cars, but he was unaware how severe their problems were. He said, "If I had the slightest idea of what lay ahead for me when I joined Chrysler, I wouldn't have gone over there for all the money in the world." Nevertheless, he observed: "I had to do it. I had to prove to myself that I've still got it." He was astounded to find that the design and manufacturing departments didn't talk with each other; neither did manufacturing and marketing.

Iacocca observed the lack of discipline at Chrysler in his first week on the job. An example of the looseness in discipline was use of the office of Gene Cafiero, president of Chrysler, as a thoroughfare. Managers carrying coffee cups from the coffee urn walked through Cafiero's office to get to other offices. Cafiero was unable to conduct a confidential conversation unless he left his office to do it. Iacocca also noticed that Chrysler employees made many more personal calls during working hours than Ford people did.

Iacocca's biggest surprise at Chrysler was the virtual absence of financial controls. The previous CEO, Lynn Townsend, and the present CEO, Riccardo, had come to Chrysler from the Detroit office of Touche Ross, the public accounting firm. However, instead of implementing financial controls, both Riccardo and his predecessor spent inordinate amounts of time visiting Chrysler's bankers, renegotiating loans to alleviate cash flow problems.

Iacocca knew that Chrysler had lost almost $160 million in the third quarter of 1978, the quarter before he joined the company. One year after retired Ford executive Paul Bergmoser started at Chrysler, he showed Iacocca an internal financial report noting that the company had lost a billion dollars in the previous year. However, no analysis of how the money was lost was provided in the report. Engineering had always been considered Chrysler's strength. But when earnings sagged, Townsend had cut funding to engineering and product development. Instead of supporting future development in the United States, he expanded overseas by purchasing Rootes Motors of England and Simca of France. Neither was a good investment.

Shortly after joining Chrysler, Iacocca requested a list of all the plants with their rate of return on investment. The information was not available. He was astounded: "I couldn't find out anything."

When Iacocca attended his first board meeting at Chrysler, he was surprised to find how poorly informed the directors were. He had always thought that Ford directors weren't as well informed about company activities as they should have been. However, Ford's directors knew orders of magnitude more about company operations than Chrysler's directors did.

Chrysler had many managers in positions in which they had no experience. Apparently, managers were considered universal at Chrysler, and they could be moved to areas other than those in which they had experience. The large number of managers out of place was reflected in the company's performance. Many managers were uncomfortable with their assignments.

In order to survive, Chrysler had to solve many problems, including those listed by Iacocca in his book, *Iacocca: An Autobiography*:

- A sound system of financial planning and financial control didn't exist.
- All thirty-five vice presidents ran their area of responsibility as a fiefdom with little communication among the functional areas.
- The actual quality and perceived quality of Chrysler products were low because of the shortcomings of the Plymouth Volare and the Dodge Aspen.
- Cars weren't built to customer and dealer orders. The Manufacturing Division decided how many cars to build and what options they would have, and the Sales Division had to sell those particular cars.
- Managers were reassigned frequently, and many managers were responsible for functions for which they had no experience and little aptitude.
- Chrysler leased cars to companies such as Hertz and Avis instead of selling them. The rental companies leased the new cars for six months and then returned them to Chrysler as used cars.
- The company's manufacturing facilities were old.

Iacocca assembled a capable, experienced team of automotive executives. He brought in managers he had known at Ford, such as

Gerald Greenwald, and other former Ford managers, including Steve Miller from Ford Venezuela. Iacocca named Hal Sperlich, who had moved to Chrysler from Ford two years previously, vice president of product planning and later head of North American Operations. Also, Iacocca persuaded retired Ford executives, such as marketer Gar Laux and quality control guru Hans Matthias, to come out of retirement and help him at Chrysler. Layoffs at Chrysler became the order of the day. Iacocca asserted himself. In less than three years, he replaced thirty-three of the thirty-five vice-presidents that he had inherited.

Upon joining Chrysler, Iacocca observed: "I was confident of my own abilities. I knew the car business, and I knew I was good at it. In my heart I honestly believed that the place would be humming within a couple of years."

Unfortunately, his timing in joining Chrysler couldn't have been worse. In January 1979, less than three months after he joined the company, the Shah was exiled from Iran. The price of gasoline doubled within three weeks.

Chrysler shifted production from the large, gas-guzzling cars to small economy cars, such as the Plymouth Horizon and Dodge Omni. As this shift was occurring, the country went into a recession. Car sales dropped by half.

Chrysler was in a precarious position. Bankruptcy wasn't a good alternative because, among other reasons, few customers would buy a car from a bankrupt company; the buyer couldn't be sure that the company would remain in business to provide parts, service, and warranty repairs.

Many Chrysler assets had been sold, including the division that made tanks for the U.S. Army, and much of the company's real estate had been sold. Also, Chrysler had pursued every lead for a prospective purchaser of the company as well as many merger opportunities, including one with Volkswagen. The only remaining alternative was to seek a loan from the U.S. Government.

Opposition to a bailout, a government loan to a manufacturer, was prevalent, particularly among businessmen. Their motto was "make it on your own or go under." The National Association of Manufacturers came out against federal loan guarantees. However, precedents existed for federal loan guarantees: $250 million to Lockheed in 1971, $111 million to Jones & Laughlin Steel in 1974, and $150 million to the Wheeling-Pittsburgh Steel Corporation. One of the largest loan guarantees was to the Washington, D.C., Metro, which had received $1 billion.

The Treasury Department estimated that it would cost the government $2.7 billion for unemployment insurance and welfare payments in the first year if Chrysler went under. Iacocca asked the federal government to make a choice; pay out $2.7 billion now or guarantee loans for half that amount with a reasonable chance of being paid back. Congress made Iacocca sweat to obtain the loan.

Eventually, Chrysler was in debt to over 400 banks and insurance companies for $4.75 billion. The banks were located all over the world, including Frankfurt, London, Ottawa, Paris, Tehran, and Tokyo. The smallest U.S. bank involved was the Twin City Bank of Little Rock with a loan of $78,000, and one of the largest was Manufacturers Hanover, to which Chrysler owed $200 million.

As a sweetener to prospective lenders, Chrysler issued 26.4 million stock warrants that were valid until 1990. The stock warrants could be exercised when the price of Chrysler's stock reached $13.00, which represented a sizable dilution of Chrysler's equity.

The risk taken by the federal government was less than most people realized. The government took all of Chrysler's $6 billion worth of assets as collateral, including cars, plants, real estate, and tooling. The liquidation value of Chrysler's assets had been appraised at $2.5 billion. The government had the first lien. If Chrysler didn't survive, the federal government would recover $1.2 billion in loans before other creditors' claims were satisfied.

Iacocca negotiated concessions with the United Automobile Workers Union. Initially, union workers gave up $1.15 an hour from their paychecks. Within the first year and a half, that concession grew to $2.00 an hour less pay. Chrysler union members gave up an average of $10,000 in pay while the concessions were in effect.

Chrysler's survival was dependent on the success of the K-cars, the Plymouth Reliant and the Dodge Aries. The company couldn't afford to build more cars like the Plymouth Volare and Dodge Aspen, whose engines stalled and whose hoods flew open unexpectedly. Repair of the Volare's rusty fenders had cost the company $109 million. Fortunately, Reliant and Aries were cars that consumers wanted.

In 1983, Chrysler made an operating profit of $925 million. On July 13, 1983, Iacocca announced his decision to pay off the loan, in its entirety, seven years before it was due. In his autobiography, *Iacocca,* he commented:

> For a variety of reasons, Chrysler turned out to be a hell of a lot worse than I bargained for. But once I was in, once I decided it was what I wanted to do, I never thought seriously of leaving. Of course, that's not always the best policy. People sometimes die with that attitude. They get swamped and overtaken by events, and they're still holding on as the waters rise up above them.

> When I signed on for my new job, I couldn't imagine anything in the automobile business could be that bad. I was wrong. In retrospect, I have to admit that there were several times at Chrysler when I came close to drowning.

Iacocca didn't drown at Chrysler; he was resilient and brought a major automobile manufacturer back from the brink.

R. H. MACY (1822-1877) Founder of Macy's Department Store

"Genius is only the power of making continuous efforts. The line between failure and success is so fine that we scarcely know when we pass it; so fine that we are often on the line but don't know it. How many a man has thrown up his hands at a time when a little more effort, a little more patience, would have achieved success. In business sometimes, prospects may seem darkest when they are really on the turn. A little more persistence, a little more effort, and what seemed hopeless failure may turn into glorious success. There is no failure except in no longer trying. There is no defeat except from within, no really insurmountable barrier save our own inherent weakness of purpose."

Elbert Hubbard

Rowland Hussey Macy was born on August 30, 1822, on Nantucket Island to John Macy and Eliza Myrick Macy, who were Quakers. John Macy, the captain of a sailing ship, was a descendent of Thomas Macy, the first white man to settle on the island. Many of the personal characteristics displayed by Macy in later years were nurtured in Nantucket, including drive, frugality, originality, and perseverance.

Macy's first job was crew member on the three-masted, 368-ton whaler, *Emily Morgan,* out of New Bedford. The ship stopped at Pernambuco, Brazil, sailed around Cape Horn, and put in at Samoa, the Gilbert Islands, Ascension Island, and New Zealand.

On September 26, 1841, the *Emily Morgan* returned to New Bedford loaded with 3,000 barrels of sperm oil, over 100 barrels of whale oil, 1,000 pounds of whale bone, and a cask of ambergris, which was used in making perfume. Nineteen-year-old Macy returned home with his earnings for four years, one 175th share (about $500), which he used later to begin his first retail venture.

Macy moved to Boston and worked in several jobs, including an apprenticeship in a printing shop, before deciding to go into business for himself. In 1844, he opened his first retail store, a small thread and needle store at 78 1/2 Hanover Street in Boston. It failed in its first year. His second attempt in the retail business was a dry goods store at 357 Washington Street, Boston, in 1846. Macy sold mainly European-made items purchased at public auction. This venture wasn't successful either, and he had to close this store in late 1847.

In 1848, Macy worked with his brother-in-law, Samuel S. Houghton, at a store located at 175 Tremont Street in Boston. Macy learned many of his principles of retailing from this early experience. He learned the advantages and disadvantages of doing business on credit and the value of intensive advertising. He learned from his failures.

Macy's next opportunity was in California during the gold rush. In 1849, Macy traveled to California with his brother Charles. In July 1850, Macy and his brother formed a partnership with two other men in Marysville, California, about forty miles north of Sacramento. Macy and Company sold clothing, other dry goods, and provisions.

Macy and Company competed with at least thirty other general stores in the area. Most of their customers were miners; when the gold ran out in the Marysville area, the miners moved on to the next find, and Macy and Company's business was reduced dramatically. In September 1850, they sold out, and Macy returned to Massachusetts with earnings of three to four thousand dollars. He had gained from this experience, since he had become familiar in dealing with customers from all over the world. He also learned about doing business on a large scale in an environment of inflated prices.

In April 1851, Macy began his fifth endeavor in the retail business, a dry goods store on Merrimack Street in the small town of Haverhill, Massachusetts. By this time, Macy was experienced in the retail business. Some of that experience was in what not to do.

Many of the ideas and operating methods that would serve him well in his New York store in later years were first implemented at the Haverhill store. He advocated the concept of selling at a fixed price (which wasn't common in the mid-nineteenth century), buying for cash, selling for cash, and advertising at about three times the rate of his competition.

Macy was his own advertising copywriter, and he was good at it. Not only was his advertising cleverly done, it was innovative, as in the use of considerable white space around his words to draw attention to them. Macy did most of the buying for his store personally. He bought from manufacturers and importers, not from wholesalers and jobbers. He eliminated one layer of middlemen.

However, Haverhill had too many dry goods stores to serve that small market. Macy went out of business just before Christmas, 1851. If imitation is the sincerest form of flattery, he should have been flattered. His competitors copied many of his techniques.

In November 1852, he reopened at a new location in Haverhill, in the New Granite Store at 68-74 Merrimack Street. He sold his goods for the lowest prices in town. However, by 1855, the combined population of Haverhill and nearby Bradford was just over 9,000, and the market he had chosen wasn't large enough to sustain a store. He sold out in July 1855.

In Macy's sixth failure in the retail business, he declared bankruptcy. He promised creditors fifty cents on the dollar, but he was able to pay only twenty-five cents. Macy salvaged two to three thousand dollars on which to live, but this black mark stayed on his credit record for ten years. He had to contend with it three years later when he founded his New York store.

Next, Macy became a stockbroker and exchange broker in Boston. In 1857, he moved to Superior City on Lake Superior in Wisconsin to work as a real estate broker and money broker. Heavy ship traffic was anticipated for the new Soo Locks, and substantial growth was predicted for Superior City. The financial panic of 1857 dashed that optimism. Macy returned to the East in 1858.

At this time, Macy was thirty-six years old and had been a whaler, retailer, gold miner, stockbroker, and real estate broker. He didn't have much to show for his efforts. A potential employer could look at his frequent job changes and not rate his prospects very high. However, that employer would've overlooked the overwhelming resilience of the man. Macy also had good business sense; he knew value when he saw it, and he had considerable persuasive ability.

Macy used his persuasiveness in financing his next venture in the retail business, a small dry goods store at Sixth Avenue near 14th Street at Herald Square in Manhattan. The store, which was twenty feet wide and sixty feet deep, was financed by long-term credit from his suppliers. Considering his lack of cash and his previous track record, his success in obtaining credit was a tribute to his ability to sell himself.

Finally, Macy served a market in which he could be successful. New York had a total population of 950,000 in 1858, including Brooklyn's 200,000 across the East River. New York was the largest city in the United States and was growing rapidly. Approximately two-thirds of U.S. imports came in through the Port of New York, and about one-third of exports left from there. New York was dominant in a number of areas, including banking, finance, clothing manufacturing, and wholesale dry goods.

Macy employed his established methods of operation and was successful beyond his dreams. He used the techniques that he had developed over the years, including selling for cash only, offering only one selling price, selling at low prices based on high volume, and using bold advertising. His offer of returning customers' money within a week if they were not satisfied with their purchase also contributed to his success.

Macy credited much of the success of his New York store to Margaret Getchell LaForge, Macy's first woman executive. A distant relative of Macy's, Margaret Getchell started to work at the store as a cashier in late 1860. She advanced rapidly to a bookkeeping position and then to superintendent of the store. She was fair, tactful, and attentive to detail in supervising the day-to-day operations. She was known for her executive ability and was a strong influence on Macy in establishing policies for the operation of the store.

In 1869, Getchell married Abiel T. LaForge, Macy's lace buyer and a trusted employee. LaForge became a partner of R. H. Macy & Company in 1872; Robert Macy Valentine, Macy's nephew, became a partner in 1875.

On March 29, 1877, Rowland Hussey Macy died while on a buying trip to Paris. Abiel LaForge and Valentine managed the store, but within a brief time LaForge died of tuberculosis. Shortly afterward, both Mrs. LaForge and Valentine died. Charles B. Webster, a former floorwalker who had been made a partner after the death of Macy and LaForge, became store manager.

In 1887, Webster approached Isidor and Nathan Straus, sellers of imported china and glassware in rented space at Macy's since 1874, with an invitation to become partners. In 1898, Webster sold his interest in the store to the Straus family. More than five generations of the Straus family have been involved with the store.

Without resilience, Macy would have been an unknown. By rebounding from failures, his efforts resulted in the largest store in the world under one roof, with 2,200,000 square feet spread over an entire city block. The department store is known for producing the Macy's Thanksgiving Day Parade and as the location for the original version of the movie *Miracle on 34th Street*. To many people, Macy's is an institution.

ISAAC SINGER (1811-1875) Sewing Machine Inventor and Promoter

"People are always blaming their circumstances for what they are. I don't believe in circumstances. The people who get on in this world are the people who get up and look for the circumstances they want, and, if they don't find them, make them."

George Bernard Shaw, *Mrs. Warren's Profession,* Act II

Isaac Singer left home at the age of 12, in his words, "without money, without friends, without education, and possessed of nothing but a strong constitution and a prolific brain" [and without humility]. Singer was good-looking, over six feet tall, blond, and outgoing. He possessed considerable assertiveness and charisma, and he had a knack for winning people over to his viewpoint. Women were charmed by him; he instilled trust in people. He was an amateur actor in his spare time.

Singer worked for a press and developed a machine for carving wooden type for printers. However, Singer's timing was off; wooden type was being replaced by lead type. At this time, Singer was 38 years old, and, by any criteria, couldn't be considered a success. However, his personal qualities of motivation and boundless optimism wouldn't let him settle into a secure but quiet existence. He was a driven man.

George Zieber, a Philadelphia book publisher and jobber, financed the manufacture of a type-carving machine based on Singer's design that was completed in June 1850 and transported to Boston by Singer and Zieber in search of sales. They rented a room on the first floor of Orson Phelps's shop in Boston next door to the main factory area, where Phelps constructed sewing machines designed by J. H. Lerow and S. C. Blodgett.

The Lerow and Blodgett machine used a shuttle that moved in a circular motion instead of back and forth as on other designs. The machine didn't work well and required frequent maintenance. Phelps asked Singer whether he and Zieber could redesign the machine at their own expense and make it more reliable. Singer assured Phelps that he could do the redesign, and that Zieber had money available to finance the development work.

Phelps convinced Singer that more money could be made from sewing machines than from type-carving machines, which had a very limited market. Singer developed a credo that helped to establish his fortune: "I don't give a damn for the invention, the dimes are what I am after." That statement distinguished Singer, the entrepreneur, from Singer, the inventor. Clearly, Singer was primarily an entrepreneur.

Singer redesigned the Lerow and Blodgett machine. Phelps, Singer, and Zieber signed an agreement in which Phelps and Zieber each put up the money to build a model of the machine to obtain a patent, and Singer contributed his ability as an inventor.

Singer worked 12 hour days and skipped many meals to complete the machine in 11 straight days. He took the machine to New York to begin the patent application process. The application was one of the early steps in revolutionizing the clothing industry, the shoe industry, and many other businesses that involved sewing.

When Singer and Zieber began to market their machine, they encountered considerable resistance from those who had tried earlier sewing machines and been dissatisfied with them. People were also concerned that sewing machines would displace thousands of tailors and seamstresses. Also, the price of the machines was more than shops in the clothing industry could afford to pay. Initially, sewing machines couldn't be sold to housewives for use in the home because of their high price.

Singer was in his element in promoting sales of his sewing machine. The actor in him came out as he demonstrated his sewing machine at carnivals and circuses, in rented halls, and wherever people would listen to his pitch. He wrote articles promoting the machines, advertised heavily, and sent out agents to tout the advantages of the sewing machine. Singer was an actor, an inventor, and an entrepreneur, but he demonstrated strongly in this phase of his life that he was, above all, a promoter.

In late 1850, Singer rented space in a clothing store to demonstrate his sewing machine. Elias Howe saw the demonstration and realized that Singer had infringed upon his patents. Howe approached Singer at the machine shop and offered to sell the rights to his patent for $2,000. Singer argued with him and threatened to kick him down the stairs. Singer was frustrated because he and Zieber couldn't raise that amount, even if they wanted to. It was the best offer they ever received from Howe; in fact, they ultimately paid Howe considerably more for the use of his patent.

Zieber had a liquidity problem. The business was saved when orders were received. Singer planned to use part of the money to buy out Phelps. He picked quarrels with Phelps and treated him in a condescending manner.

Singer promised Phelps $1,000 down and $3,000 additional in three installments, along with a verbal agreement to keep his shop busy for five years, the duration of the partnership. Phelps, who wasn't strong enough to contest Singer's aggressive pitch, signed the contract on December 24, 1850. Singer immediately told Phelps that he would have to go on the road selling machines, which Phelps didn't want to do. Singer then sold Phelps's one-third interest to a businessman and treated him as he had treated Phelps.

Singer realized that neither he nor Zieber had the necessary financial or legal background to deal with the venture as it grew. Singer visited Edward Clark, a partner in the law firm of Jordan, Clark, and Company, who had drawn up the contracts for the partnership. Singer offered Clark a one-third share of the business for his services. Clark was the one partner whom Singer couldn't bully. He seemed to have a hold on Singer. Clark told Zieber that, "Singer will not break the agreement I shall make with him." Clark was a vital addition to the enterprise and the source of many innovations that generated profits for the business.

In December 1851, Zieber became ill, and his doctor confined him to bed. He became concerned that if anything happened to him, the friends from whom he had borrowed wouldn't be paid. Singer offered him $6,000 for his share of the business (annual profits at that time were $25,000). Clark drew up the agreement; Zieber signed it in bed the next morning.

Zieber recovered within a short time and realized his mistake. He had given up all claim to Singer's patents and had been replaced as a 50 percent patent holder by Clark. Singer and Zieber had operated as friends (most of the time) as well as partners. Clark and Singer didn't have the same relationship; they were antagonists from their first meeting.

In 1851, Howe visited the Singer and Clark venture to request $25,000 for a license to use his patent and was thrown out again. Clark underestimated the validity of Howe's claim and made a poor business decision, a rarity for him. As before, the Singer partnership ultimately would pay Howe much more than the amount he had requested. During the next three years, almost all of the partnership's profits and most of Clark's energy were spent on legal battles. By 1853, other major sewing machine manufacturers had signed licenses with Howe to use his patent.

In July 1854, Howe won his suit against Singer and threatened to sue him in New Jersey as well as New York. Singer was directed to pay Howe $15,000 and a royalty of 25 dollars per machine. Litigation among the manufacturers of sewing machines didn't settle down until 1856, when one of the sewing machine manufacturers suggested the "combination," a patent pool in which all companies in the combination had the use of the other company's patents for a fee.

In 1855, the United States was in an economic slump—the worst since 1837. Singer sold only 883 machines and was struggling after making payments to Howe. Also that year, Singer designed a smaller, lighter machine for use in the home. The cost of the machine was $125 at a time when the average annual family income was $500. Clearly, housewives needed help in purchasing their first sewing machine. Clark had the idea of leasing the sewing machine to the housewife and applying the lease payments toward the purchase of the machine. Clark's installment plan idea boosted sales to 2,564 machines in 1856; sales tripled in one year.

Clark also suggested selling sewing machines for half price to church ministers to use in establishing sewing societies associated with their churches to show that respectable women sewed. This also introduced the sewing machine to groups and familiarized individual housewives with it.

The production of sewing machines grew rapidly after 1858. By 1870, Singer had produced 127,833 machines using mass production techniques, such as the use of interchangeable parts—a concept devised by Eli Whitney.

European sales were a principal reason for the rapid growth of I. M. Singer and Company; Singer's competitors didn't exploit foreign markets nearly as aggressively as he did. By 1861, Singer had sold more machines in Europe than in the United States. Singer was one of the earliest multinational corporations.

In 1863, Clark and Singer agreed to dissolve their partnership and form a joint stock company. Each received 40 percent of the stock in the company plus an equal share of the bond holdings, and both men agreed to step down from active management of the company. Neither wanted the other in charge; if Clark wanted Singer to give up his control, he would have to give up control also.

Singer developed a heart condition, and the combination of a chill and heart problems caused his death on July 23, 1875. Isaac Singer's life was certainly a Horatio Alger story. He made significant contributions as an inventor. His drive and aggressiveness contributed significantly to his success. However, his ability to promote the sewing machine, using skills developed as an actor, was his most important accomplishment.

JOHN FITCH (1742-1798) Inventor of the Steamboat

"He did persevere. We cannot begin to relate the obstacles he encountered. A considerable volume would scarcely afford the requisite space. Poor, ragged and forlorn, jeered at, pitied as a madman, discouraged by the great, refused by the rich, he and his few friends kept on, until in 1790, they had a steamboat running on the Delaware, which was the first steamboat constructed that answered the purpose of one. It ran with the tide, eight miles an hour, and six miles an hour against it."

National Cyclopedia of American Biography

On a sunny April Sunday in 1785, John Fitch had the idea that led to the development of the steamboat. While walking home from church, hobbled by rheumatism, he watched a neighbor from a nearby town ride by in a horse-drawn carriage. He thought: "What a noble thing it would be if I could have such a carriage without the expense of keeping a horse." His inspiration was to propel a carriage by steam power.

Fitch soon decided against building a steam-propelled wagon because of the poor quality of the roads. However, his experience as a surveyor along the Ohio River motivated him to think about a steam-powered boat. The atmospheric-type steam engine, such as the engines designed by Newcomen, had been in use for years, but Fitch wasn't familiar with them. In 1785, only three steam engines were in use in the United States, two in New England and one in New Jersey that was used to pump water from a mine.

Fitch made a sketch of a steam-powered boat. He would have been surprised to learn that, in England, Watt and Bolt were working on a new double-acting design: power was generated on the upward stroke of the cylinder as well as the downward stroke.

Fitch built a model propelled by flat wooden paddles driven by a loop of chain on a sprocket. He also designed a circular paddle wheel similar to those used later on side-wheelers and stern-wheelers on the Mississippi River. His first technical challenge was to transfer the reciprocal motion of the steam engine to the rotary motion of the propeller. Fitch's greatest challenge, however, was obtaining financing for his project. He hoped that the fledgling U.S. Congress would fund his development. In 1785, Fitch petitioned

Congress for financial support of his development effort. Congress referred his petition to a committee that set it aside and ignored it. Unfortunately, it was not entered into congressional records.

Fitch presented his design to Benjamin Franklin, who usually supported the inventions of others. Fitch also presented his proposal, accompanied by his model, drawings, and a written description of the steamboat, to the American Philosophical Society, of which Franklin was the most prominent member. He received no response from either Franklin or the Society.

Later, Fitch learned that Franklin had his own design for powering a boat. Also, James Rumsey of Virginia developed a design for a boat powered by a wheel driven by river current and assisted by men using a system of poles to generate forward motion. Fitch was relieved to hear that the boat wasn't powered by a steam engine. The boat was impractical because it could only travel with the current and because the weight of the men using the poles limited the amount of cargo it could carry.

Fitch also appealed to the State Assemblies in Delaware, Maryland, New Jersey, New York, Pennsylvania, and Virginia for financial support for his venture. He was unable to obtain financial assistance from the States, but they were willing to grant him the exclusive right to operate a steamboat on their rivers; granting that right didn't cost them anything. In March 1786, the New Jersey Legislature granted him exclusive rights for a period of 14 years. In early 1787, Delaware, New York, and Pennsylvania granted him similar rights to those he had obtained from New Jersey.

Unfortunately, venture capitalists didn't exist in the eighteenth century. Fitch organized a joint-stock company with 15 middle-income backers, who included merchants, shopkeepers, and tavern keepers. He sold 20 shares and kept 20 shares for himself.

Fitch chose Henry Voight, a Philadelphia clockmaker and watchmaker, to build a steam engine for his boat. Fitch considered Voight a mechanical genius and, furthermore, a friend at a time when Fitch had few friends. Their first design was a double-acting engine in which power was generated on both the upward and downward strokes. Unfortunately, the size of the cylinder, one inch in diameter, was too small to generate sufficient power to propel the boat. The first trial on a small skiff with flimsy paddles was unsuccessful. Many spectators on the wharf jeered at their efforts.

Fitch's and Voight's next engine had a three-inch-diameter cylinder without a separate condenser. A pump injected water directly into the cylinder, which cooled the steam and produced condensation. This engine wasn't sufficiently powerful to propel the 45-foot skiff in which it was mounted.

The idea for applying power to the paddles came to Fitch in the middle of the night. His "cranks and paddles" idea was implemented by attaching paddles to arms that were moved by a crank. When the crank went downward, paddles were pulled through the water to the stern of the boat; when the crank moved upward, the paddles were lifted out of the water and returned to the bow. This design was used with a steam engine that had a 12-inch-diameter piston.

Fitch and Voight continued to innovate and to improve their design, including the use of a narrower hull with less water resistance. They redesigned the condenser and placed the furnace directly under the boiler, which eliminated the need for bricks and mortar surrounding the furnace.

Voight lost patience with the project, particularly with the shortage of funds. Voight was replaced by William Thornton. Thornton's first design was a condenser used on an engine with an 18-inch-diameter cylinder. The new condenser worked no better than the old one.

Fitch's stockholders, unhappy with his lack of progress, attempted to push him aside and replace him with Thornton. Fitch not only fought off this maneuver, but he designed a straight-tube condenser that worked better than any of Thornton's designs. Fitch and Thornton conducted a series of successful trials using the engine with the larger cylinder and the new condenser.

The Governor of Pennsylvania, Thomas Mifflin, and members of the Pennsylvania Assembly were impressed with the trial run. Fitch scheduled regular, round-trip passenger runs from Philadelphia along the Delaware River to Burlington, Bristol, Bordentown, and Trenton. Fares were kept low to compete with the stagecoach route along the river. In fact, fares were so low that money was lost on every run.

This steamboat's record was otherwise impressive. She carried passengers a total of just under 3,000 miles from mid-May until the end of September 1790 and traveled over 90 miles in 12 1/2 hours, or over seven miles an hour, upstream. Fitch continued to improve his design. He began construction of a second boat that he named, appropriately, *Perseverance*. In mid-October, *Perseverance* broke loose from her moorings, drifted into the Delaware River, and went aground. By the time she was towed back to the wharf, the season was almost over. Personally, Fitch was in dire circumstances. His clothes were in tatters, and, unable to pay his landlady for his room or his meals, he was totally dependent on her charity.

In the spring of 1791, the Commissioners for the Promotion of Useful Arts (Thomas Jefferson, Henry Knox, and Edmund Randolph) settled the Fitch-Rumsey invention dispute by awarding patents to both of them. Fitch was enraged to hear that the design for which he was awarded the patent wasn't his own successful design, but the Bernoulli-Franklin design that Rumsey sponsored. By this stroke, the commissioners gave any possible commercial value of Fitch's invention to Rumsey. Fitch had no recourse because Congress had made no record of his petition to them; the Patent Office wasn't established until 1802.

Fitch lost the support of his financial backers. He wanted to make improvements to *Perseverance*, but he didn't have the money to make them. He tried, unsuccessfully, to obtain additional funding for steamboat development in England and France. On Fitch's last trial on *Perseverance*, Voight arrived at the dock to taunt the inventor dressed in rags and struggling with a sluggish piston. Voight knew how to fix it; furthermore, he knew how to improve it with little expense, but he wasn't going to help his old friend. Fitch's last memory of his steamboat development was this cruel treatment by Voight.

Despite his many disappointments, Fitch said, "I thank God for the perseverance He has given me, in carrying to such length as I have . . . It would have given me heartfelt pleasure could I have rendered more an immediate service than I have, yet please myself with the idea that . . . my feeble attempts will be found of that use which I now wish them to be."

Fitch was technologically successful in his steamboat development, even if his efforts weren't economically successful. In spite of overwhelming setbacks, he proved that a boat could be propelled by steam power.

CHAPTER 5

STATESMEN / RULERS

"The ability to make adjustments begins with attitude, and the first attitude is accepting that failure is an education, then learning from the experience rather than becoming engulfed in frustration."

Karl Kuehl, *Mental Toughness: A Champion's State of Mind*

NELSON MANDELA (1918-2013) First Native South African President

"During my lifetime, I have dedicated myself to this struggle of the African People. I have fought against white domination, and I have fought against black domination. I have cherished the ideal of a democratic and free society in which all persons live together in harmony and with equal opportunities. It is an ideal which I hope to live for and to achieve. But if needs be, it is an ideal for which I am prepared to die."

Nelson Mandela

Nelson Mandela spent over twenty-seven years in the Union of South Africa's prisons for political activism in striving to eliminate racial segregation and to improve the living and working conditions of blacks in South Africa. In February 1990, he was released from prison and was overwhelmed by the fervor with which he was greeted by the people. In April 1994, for the first time in the history of South Africa, black people voted to elect leaders of their choice. On May 19, 1994, Nelson Mandela was inaugurated as the first black President of the Union of South Africa.

Nelson Rolihlahla Mandela was born on July 18, 1918, at Qunu in the Transkei reserve on the east coast of South Africa. He was the eldest son of Henry and Nonqaphi Mandela, members of the royal family of the Thembu, a Xhosa-speaking people. His Xhosa name, Rolihlahla means "stirring up trouble." Henry Mandela was the chief counselor to the leader of the Thembu people and served on the Transkeian Territories General Council.

Young Nelson worked on the family farm plowing the fields and tending the cattle and sheep. He attended the local school run by white missionaries. When Nelson was twelve, Henry Mandela became ill and sent his son to live with the Chief of the Thembu. Nelson was raised with the Chief's son and attended the Methodist High School.

In 1936, Mandela enrolled in Fort Hare College, a Methodist college in eastern Cape Province. At Fort Hare, he met many future activist leaders, including Oliver Tambo, who later became the leader of the African National Congress. Mandela's political leanings took shape in college. After three years of college, he was suspended for boycotting the Students' Representative Council, of which he was a member, because the college administration had reduced the powers of the council.

Mandela returned to the Transkei. The Chief was disappointed in him; he encouraged him to cooperate with the college administration. Mandela moved to Johannesburg, the center of the gold-mining region in the Transvaal, to avoid the arranged marriage that the Chief had planned for him.

Cosmopolitan Johannesburg was a shock to Mandela, who was used to rural and small-town life. Like all "Bantus," the white name for black South Africans, he lived in a township on the outskirts of the city with no electricity or sewers. Initially, he worked as a guard at a mining compound. In the township of Alexandra, he met Walter Sisulu, owner of a real estate agency, who loaned him money to complete his college degree.

Sisulu also helped Mandela find a job with a Johannesburg law firm to finance his law studies at the University of Witwatersrand. While studying for a law degree, he met a young nurse, Evelyn Mase, whom he married. They lived in Soweto (Southwest Townships) in Orlando Township. Sisulu, a member of the African National Congress (ANC), suggested that Mandela join their organization, which had been formed by journalists, lawyers, teachers, and tribal chiefs to work to end segregation. They wanted to be able to buy property and to be elected to parliament.

In 1943, Mandela joined the Youth League of the ANC. The Youth League planned to push the ANC to fight white domination by participating in protests against the white government and by spurring blacks into militant action. In September 1944, Anton Lembede was elected president of the ANC, and Mandela, Sisulu, and Tambo (Mandela's friend from college), were appointed to the executive committee.

The ANC stated their philosophy: "The Congress must be the brains-trust and power-station of the spirit of African nationalism; the spirit of African self-determination, the spirit so discernible in the thinking of our youth. It must be an organization where young African men and women will meet and exchange ideas in an atmosphere pervaded by a common hatred of oppression."

In 1946, black African mine workers held a strike for better wages in which 70,000 workers participated. Seven mines were shut down; the country's booming economy was slowed. The government reacted violently. Police, aided by army units, cut off all food and water to workers' living quarters, arrested the leaders of the strike, and used batons to beat protesters who would not return to work. After some workers were killed, the strike was broken within a week. The ANC learned lessons from the strike. They realized that in numbers alone they had the power to make social change happen. Mandela said, "We have a powerful ideology capable of capturing the masses. Our duty is now to carry that ideology fully to them."

In 1949 at the ANC annual conference, the Youth League implemented a new policy of action employing strikes, civil disobedience, and noncooperation. They were convinced that they had to become more militant and had to use mass action to fight apartheid, the government's program of racial separation and white supremacy. In 1950, the ANC became allied with the Indian National Congress in South Africa, which was better financed than the ANC. Mandela learned about the passive resistance campaigns waged by Mohandas Gandhi in Africa earlier in the twentieth century. He respected the Indians' hard work and dedication to their cause, but he felt that the African movement should be separate. The Indian National Congress worked closely with the South African Communist Party. Mandela noted, "It is clear that the exotic plant of communism cannot flourish on African soil."

Also in 1950, Mandela completed his law studies and set up a a law practice in Johannesburg with Oliver Tambo. Most of their cases involved victims of apartheid laws. Tambo observed: "South African apartheid laws turn innumerable innocent people into 'criminals.' Every case in court, every visit to the prison to interview clients, reminded us of the humiliation and suffering burning into our people."

On May 1, 1950, the ANC scheduled a one-day national work stoppage. Over half of native South African workers stayed home. The strike was successful; however, nineteen Africans were killed in Johannesburg when police attacked demonstrators. Mandela commented: "That day was a turning point in my life, both in understanding through firsthand experience the ruthlessness of the police, and in being deeply impressed by the support African workers had given to the May Day call."

In 1951, as newly elected national president of the Youth League, Mandela was asked to lead a Defiance Campaign. He toured the country to sign up volunteers. In June 1952 in Port Elizabeth, the Defiance Campaign began their "defiance" by singing African freedom songs, calling out freedom slogans, and using the "Europeans only" entrances to post offices and railroad stations.

In Johannesburg, Sisulu, Mandela, and fifty Defiance Campaign volunteers were arrested for violating the 11:00 p.m. curfew. A volunteer broke his ankle when a guard pushed him down a flight of stairs; he was then refused medical attention. When Mandela protested to the policeman, he was beaten with a nightstick. By the end of December 1952, over 8,000 Defiance Campaign volunteers had been arrested.

Mandela and other ANC leaders were tried in December 1952. Mandela and over fifty of the ANC's most capable leaders were prohibited from participating further in the organization. Mandela was forbidden to travel outside of Johannesburg for two years, and he was not permitted to attend political meetings. By year-end 1952, ANC membership had grown to 100,000.

Mandela was away from home most of the time, putting considerable strain on his marriage. Evelyn was raising their children by herself, and, with his commitment to the ANC, she could foresee no improvement in their relationship. He was never out of the view of undercover police. She moved with the children to Natal. Finally, Mandela and Evelyn were divorced.

On December 5, 1956, 156 people, including Mandela, Sisulu, and Tambo, were arrested and charged with treason as members of "a countrywide conspiracy, inspired by communism, to overthrow the State by violence." The "Treason Trial" lasted for six years, during which time Mandela, who helped to prepare the defense, was alternately in jail and out on bail. During one of the times that he was out of jail, Mandela was introduced to Winnie Nomzamo Madikizela by Oliver Tambo and his fiancée, Adelaide Tsukudu.

Winnie's Xhosa name, Nomzamo, means "she who strives." Winnie, whose parents were both teachers, graduated from Shawbury High School and enrolled in the Jan Hofsmeyr School of Social Work in Johannesburg. Upon graduating with honors from the Hofsmeyr School, she won a scholarship to study for an advanced degree in sociology in the United States. Instead, she accepted a position at the Baragwanath Hospital in Soweto and became the first black medical social worker in South Africa.

Mandela was thirty-eight when he met Winnie. She was nervous because he was a national figure sixteen years older than she. A white resident of Cape Town observed: "I noticed people were turning and staring at the opposite pavement and I saw this magnificent figure of a man, immaculately dressed. Not just blacks, but whites were turning to admire him." While they were dating, Winnie commented: "Life with him was a life without him. He did not even pretend that I would have a special claim on his time."

In June 1958, Mandela and Winnie were married. They moved into a home in the Orlando West township of Soweto. Winnie joined the ANC and enrolled in a course in public speaking. Soon after their marriage, they were awakened in the middle of the night by security police who searched their home but found nothing incriminating.

At a mass demonstration organized by the Women's League of the ANC, Winnie and 1,200 other female protesters were arrested and imprisoned. Winnie, who was pregnant, was struck several times and almost lost her baby. Upon her release from prison, Winnie was told that she had been fired from her position at the hospital. She found a job with the Child Welfare Society.

In 1959, a militant group split off from the ANC because they did not want to cooperate with other racial groups; they advocated "Africa for Africans" and called themselves the Pan Africanist Congress (PAC). In the following year, the PAC planned a campaign against the requirement for all blacks to carry a pass.

On March 21, 1960, in Sharpeville, 10,000 protesters gathered in peaceful support of the ban on passes. The police panicked and fired into the unarmed crowd, killing sixty-seven Africans, including eight women and ten small children. Most were shot in the back as they were running away.

Later, the police fired into a peaceful crowd in the township of Langa, outside of Cape Town, killing fourteen and wounding many others. The government of the Union of South Africa was universally condemned by world opinion. The United Nations Security Council spoke out against the government of the Union of South Africa for the first time. The ANC decided to send one of their leaders outside of the country, beyond the jurisdiction of the police of South Africa. Oliver Tambo was chosen to go.

In March 1961, the chief judge announced a verdict of not guilty in the treason trial. Spectators cheered and shouted "Nkosi Sikelel' iAfrika" (God Bless Africa). Mandela had conducted the defense, cross-examined witnesses, and given testimony himself. He emphasized that the ANC through their Defiance Campaign had conducted nonviolent activities and maintained that, in the long run, civil disobedience would free all Africans. His defense brought him an international reputation and increased his standing within the ANC; he was now considered its strongest leader.

Mandela had responded to the accusation that the freedom of the ANC was a threat to Europeans (whites): "No, it is not a direct threat to the Europeans. We are not non-white; we are against white supremacy and in struggling against white supremacy we have the support of some sections of the European population. We said that the campaign we were about to launch was not directed at any racial group. It was directed against laws we considered unjust."

After spending a brief time with his family, Mandela went on the road. His first stop was the All-in-Africa Conference in Pietermaritzburg, where he was the keynote speaker. He was elected head of the National Action Council. He decided to go underground to plan further protests.

Mandela became known as the "black pimpernel," modeled on the fictional English Scarlet Pimpernel who always eluded his enemies during the French Revolution. He stayed underground for a year and a half, surfacing only for meetings. On one occasion, he had to climb down a rope from an upstairs window in the back of a house while police entered the front.

Winnie would be given a message to meet someone in a car at a certain location. She would change cars frequently: "By the time I reached him I had gone through something like ten cars. The people who arranged this were mostly whites. I don't know to this day who they were. I would just find myself at the end of the journey in some white house; when we got there they were deserted."

One day at work, Winnie was told to drive to a particular corner of the city. She described the incident: "When I got there, a tall man in blue overalls and a chauffeur's white coat and peaked hat opened the door, ordered me to shift from the driver's seat and took over and drove. That was him. He had a lot of disguises and he looked so different that for a moment, when he walked toward the car, I didn't recognize him myself."

By June 1961, the ANC realized that the tactic of nonviolence had failed. They were going to have to "answer violence with violence." A new organization was formed, the Umkhonto we Sizwe (Spear of the Nation, or MK), to conduct violent attacks against the government. The MK was not a terrorist organization; they limited their attacks to sabotage, mainly of power plants, railroad freight cars, and transmission lines where innocent bystanders wouldn't be injured. If caught, MK saboteurs faced the death penalty. The police stepped up their search for Mandela.

In January 1962, Mandela traveled out of South Africa for the first time. Oliver Tambo asked him to speak at the Pan African Freedom Conference in Addis Ababa, Ethiopia. He was moved by the open environment outside of South Africa: "Free from white oppression, from the idiocy of apartheid and racial arrogance, from police molestation, from humiliation and indignity. Wherever I went, I was treated like a human being." For leaving the country without a passport, Mandela was charged with an additional "crime."

Mandela returned to South Africa. As the result of a tip from an informer, on August 5, 1962, he was captured returning to Johannesburg from a meeting in Natal. He was accused of inciting a strike in 1961 and of leaving the country illegally. At his trial in Pretoria, Mandela shouted to the gallery, "Amandla!" (power), and the crowd in the gallery answered "Ngawethu!" (to the people).

Mandela told the court: "I consider myself neither legally nor morally bound to obey laws made by a parliament in which I have no representation. In a political trial such as this one, which involves a clash of the aspirations of the African people and those of whites, the country's courts, as presently constituted, cannot be impartial and fair." He was found guilty on both charges and sentenced to ten years of hard labor. He was imprisoned in Pretoria, where he sewed mailbags, and then transferred to the maximum-security prison on Robben Island in the Atlantic Ocean, seven miles off Cape Town.

On July 12, 1963, the police raided the ANC's Rivonia farm and captured Walter Sisulu. They found many ANC documents, including Mandela's diary of his tour of Africa and incriminating evidence that documented his role in the MK violence. On trial, he stated to the court: "I do not deny that I planned sabotage. I did not plan it in a spirit of recklessness, nor because I have any love of violence. I planned it as a result of a calm and sober assessment of the political situation that had arisen after many years of tyranny, exploitation, and oppression of my people by the whites."

On June 11, 1964, Mandela was sentenced to life imprisonment. A staff writer for the *New York Times* wrote, "To most of the world, the Rivonia defendants are heroes and freedom fighters, the George Washingtons and Ben Franklins of South Africa." The *London Times* added, "The verdict of history will be that the ultimate guilty party is the government in power."

On Robben Island, Mandela had a small cell without electricity or sanitary facilities. It was furnished with a mat, a bedroll, two light blankets, and a bucket. He was issued cotton shorts, a khaki shirt, and a light jacket. The guards told him that he was going to die there. He rejected the offer of a special diet and did not use his international reputation to obtain special privileges. All prisoners at Robben Island considered him their leader and spokesperson. He worked in a limestone quarry, chained to another prisoner.

Every six months, prisoners were permitted one half-hour visit and were allowed to mail one letter of 500 words and to receive one letter. On Winnie's first visit, she was instructed that they could not speak in the Xhosa language, and that political subjects could not be discussed. She could not bring any presents, and their daughters could not visit their father until they were fourteen. They communicated with microphones and headsets through a glass partition that gave a distorted view of the other party.

Winnie was forced to leave her job at the Child Welfare Society. To support her family, she worked at menial jobs—in a dry cleaners, a furniture store, and a laundry—but lost the jobs when the security police threatened the owners with reprisals. Spies and informers were everywhere she went, and the police maintained an ongoing program of harassment.

The children suffered. Winnie was frequently in jail, and friends and neighbors had to care for the young girls. On one occasion, she spent seventeen months in jail; the first five months were spent in solitary confinement in filthy living conditions. She believed that this treatment made her a stronger person. Finally, she sent their daughters to Swaziland to attend school. She lived on the charity of her friends and her supporters.

On June 16, 1976, during a mass protest in Soweto, the cruelty of the government was again displayed. A Soweto leader observed:

> I saw a stream of schoolchildren marching past my house. They had just reached the Orlando West school when the police tried to stop them marching any further. The children kept on walking so the police released dogs. Then the police panicked and fired into the mass of children. I will never forget the bravery of those children. They were carrying [trashcan] lids to protect themselves and deflect the bullets. The police had dogs and tear gas and batons, but they chose instead to use bullets against those unarmed kids. The saddest sight anyone can see is a dying child crippled by bullets.

The people of Soweto responded with an uprising. Over 1,000 protesters died, and over 4,000 were wounded. Across South Africa, over 13,000 were arrested, 5,000 of whom were under eighteen. The government of the Union of South Africa was condemned in world news. The government did not respond to international opinion. In September 1977, Steve Biko, the leader of the Black Consciousness Movement, died in jail from beatings and torture.

In May 1977, Winnie Mandela was banished to Brandfort in the Orange Free State, where she lived for ten years, in an attempt to minimize her role as a national leader. She was moved into a three-room concrete-block house without running water, electricity, or a sewer system. It had a dirt floor; access was by openings in the front and side walls that could not be closed. Communication was difficult. Local people spoke only the African languages, Sotho and Tswana; Winnie spoke English and Xhosa. To communicate with the outside world, Winnie began to use the international press.

Winnie received an honorary doctor of laws degree from Haverford College, and two Scandinavian newspapers awarded her the Freedom Prize. In January 1985, U.S. Senator Edward Kennedy visited Winnie at Brandfort while on a trip to South Africa.

While Winnie was receiving international attention, Nelson Mandela continued to lead even while in prison. The United Democratic Front stated their opinion: "You [Nelson Mandela] are a true leader of the people. We will not rest until you are free. Your release and the release of all political prisoners is imperative. Your sacrifice for your people is affirmed. We commit ourselves anew to a free South Africa in which the people shall govern." Bishop Desmond Tutu said, "The government has to come to terms with the fact that the black community now says, 'Our leader is Nelson Mandela and any other persons are just filling in.'"

The government offered to release Mandela if he would reject violence unconditionally. He responded, "Only free men can negotiate. Prisoners cannot enter into contracts. I cannot and will not give any undertaking at a time when I and you, the people, are not free. Your freedom and mine cannot be separated. I will return."

Samuel Dash, chief counsel for the U.S. Senate Watergate Committee, observed on a visit that the guards treated Mandela "as though he were their superior, unlocking gates and opening doors on his command as he led me on a tour of his building." When Dash commented on the whites' fear of the black majority, Mandela pointed out that "unlike white people anywhere else in Africa, whites in South Africa belong here—this is their home. We want them to live here with us and to share power with us."

Dash noted: "I felt that I was in the presence not of a guerrilla fighter or radical ideologue, but of a Head of State." Mandela reiterated the principles of the ANC to Dash:

• A unified South Africa without artificial "homelands"
• Black representation in the central parliament
• One man, one vote

On February 11, 1990, Nelson Mandela was released from prison. His first speech to the people was given in Cape Town at the Grand Parade, a large square in front of the old City Hall.

Mandela greeted the reception committee and the huge crowd. "Friends, comrades, and fellow South Africans. I greet you all in the name of peace, democracy, and freedom for all! I stand here before you not as a prophet but as a humble servant of you, the people. Your tireless and heroic sacrifices have made it possible for me to be here today. I therefore place the remaining years of my life in your hands."

In late February, Mandela traveled to Lusaka to attend a meeting of the National Executive Committee of the ANC. He enjoyed being reunited with comrades that he hadn't seen in many years. He also spoke with heads of State of other African countries, including Angola, Botswana, Mozambique, Uganda, Zambia, and Zimbabwe. After the conference, Mandela traveled around Africa and visited the Egyptian president, Hosni Mubarak, in Cairo. While in Egypt, Mandela stated at a press conference that the ANC was "prepared to consider a cessation of hostilities." This was a message for the government of South Africa.

Upon Mandela's return to South Africa, the ANC leadership, including Mandela and Walter Sisulu, met with government officials in a first round of talks to discuss their differences. In early June, Mandela went on a six-week trip to Europe and North America. He met with world leaders in France, Switzerland, Italy, Ireland, and England as well as the United States and Canada. After visiting Memphis and Boston, he traveled to Washington and addressed a joint session of Congress.

Upon his return to South Africa, Mandela realized that violence was continuing to obstruct the peace process. He traveled around the country in an attempt to soothe some of the ill feelings. On December 20, 1991, the first serious negotiations, called the Convention for a Democratic South Africa (CODESA), started between the ANC, other South African parties, and the government.

On June 3, 1993, negotiations resulted in setting a date for the first non-racial, one-person-one-vote national election in South Africa on April 27, 1994. For the first time in the history of South Africa, black voters could elect the leaders of their choice. In 1993, Mandela and President de Klerk shared the Nobel Peace Prize. Mandela accepted the prize on behalf of the people of South Africa. He acknowledged that Mr. de Klerk had made a serious, vital contribution to the peace process.

Mandela and de Klerk had one television debate before the presidential election. In his remarks, Mandela looked at de Klerk and said, "Sir, you are one of those I rely upon. We are going to face the problems of this country together." Mandela extended his hand to de Klerk and added, "I am proud to hold your hand for us to go forward." The gesture surprised de Klerk, but he agreed to work together.

Mandela won the election with 62.6 percent of the vote. He realized that now he would have to heal the country's wounds, to promote reconciliation, and to instill confidence in the leadership of the government. At his inauguration, Mandela declared:

> We have, at last, achieved our political emancipa-
> tion. We pledge ourselves to liberate all our people
> from the continuing bondage of poverty, depriva-
> tion, suffering, gender, and other discrimination.
> Never, never, and never again shall it be that this
> beautiful land will again experience the oppression
> of one by another. The sun shall never set on so
> glorious an achievement. Let freedom reign. God
> bless Africa.

After his swearing-in ceremony, the ranking generals of the South African Defense Force and the security police saluted the new president and affirmed their loyalty as jet fighters, multi-engine aircraft, and helicopters of the South African Air Force flew overhead. Ceremonies were concluded with blacks singing "Die Stem van Suid-Afrika," the anthem of the republic, and whites singing "Nkosi Sikelel' iAfrica."

In *Long Walk to Freedom*, Nelson Mandela wrote:

> I have walked that long road to Freedom. I have
> tried not to falter; I have made missteps along the
> way. But I have discovered the secret that after
> climbing a great hill, one only finds that there are
> many more hills to climb. I have taken a moment
> to rest, to steal a view of the glorious vista that sur-
> rounds me, to look back on the distance I have
> come. But I can rest only for a moment, for with
> freedom comes responsibilities, and I dare not
> linger, for my long walk is not yet ended.

FRANKLIN DELANO ROOSEVELT (1882-1945)
Overcame Polio to Lead the U.S.

"No matter whether Governor Smith wins or loses, Franklin D. Roosevelt stands out as the real hero of the Democratic Convention of 1924. Adversity has lifted him above the bickering, the religious bigotry, conflicting personal ambitions and petty sectional prejudices. It has made him the one leader commanding the respect and admiration from all sections of the land . . . Roosevelt might be a pathetic, tragic figure but for the fine courage that flashes in his smile. It holds observers enchained."

New York Evening World

In July 1921, Franklin Delano Roosevelt was an ambitious young man attempting to defend his position as Assistant Secretary of the Navy during World War I. He worked long days to respond to fifteen volumes of testimony of a Senate subcommittee investigating the administration of naval affairs during the war. He successfully defended his role and the Navy Department's performance during the war.

Roosevelt had been looking forward to spending the month of August vacationing with his family on the island of Campobello in the Bay of Fundy, as he did every year. When he got off the boat at Campobello, he was surrounded by his five children. Eleanor Roosevelt and Mrs. Louis Howe, the wife of his political advisor and good friend, also greeted him.

Roosevelt spent the next few days deep-sea fishing in the Bay of Fundy. On the last day of fishing, he fell overboard into the ice-cold water of the bay. He was chilled to the bone. He was used to swimming in the cold water of the bay, but he had never experienced the paralyzing cold of the water that day. Perhaps he was affected by the contrast of the water with the hot, humid weather in addition to the heat of the engine near where he had been fishing on the deck.

During the next day, Roosevelt was tired, and his golf game was off. After assembling gear for a camping trip with the children planned for the following day, he took them for a sail in the family sailboat. As they sailed, they saw a fire on one of the islands. They landed, and Roosevelt cut evergreen branches for everyone to use in beating the flames from a grove of spruce trees that was on fire. When the fire was under control, the exhausted firefighters sailed for home.

Roosevelt suggested that the sweaty, bedraggled group go for a swim in Glen Severn, a small lake on the other side of the island. After jogging back to the cottage after the swim, he couldn't resist another swim in the Bay of Fundy; he didn't even consider his chill of the previous day. The swim was exhilarating, but his tiredness persisted. He had several chills and decided to go to bed, to bundle up, and to have supper in his bedroom. The chill stayed with him and the following morning, when he got out of bed, he noticed that his left leg ached and was sluggish. He had a temperature of 102. Eleanor called the family doctor, Dr. Bennett, who examined Roosevelt and diagnosed an ordinary cold, but a severe one. He prescribed bed rest.

The next morning, Roosevelt experienced tenderness in the front of his thighs; even the weight of the covers caused him pain. When he got out of bed, his right knee buckled. His temperature remained at 102. His muscles became more sensitive, and he could barely move his legs. The following day, his legs were completely paralyzed, and his back ached. Louis Howe arrived at Campobello that afternoon and acted immediately. He took the launch to Bar Harbor, Maine, to bring back Dr. W. W. Keen, a well-known diagnostician who was vacationing there.

Dr. Keen found that Roosevelt was completely paralyzed below the waist, and his arms were heavy. His diagnosis was a blood clot in the lower spinal cord. He thought that Roosevelt would recover, but that it would take many months. He prescribed rigorous massaging of Roosevelt's thighs and lower legs, beginning immediately. Until a masseuse could get to Campobello from New York, Eleanor and Howe massaged his legs, causing him considerable pain. His condition worsened; he was helpless. Dr. Keen changed his diagnosis from a clot on the lower spinal cord to a lesion on the lower spinal cord.

Eleanor wrote to Roosevelt's uncle, Frederic Delano, describing the illness. Uncle Frederic was not satisfied with the diagnosis and immediately contacted Dr. Robert W. Lovett, a prominent Boston specialist. Dr. Lovett was out of town, so uncle Frederic described the symptoms to Dr. Lovett's colleague, Dr. Samuel A.

Levine, who immediately diagnosed the ailment as poliomyelitis. He suggested discontinuing the massages; they were doing more harm than good. Roosevelt's temperature continued to fluctuate; however, his temperament was better than everyone expected it would be.

Dr. Lovett came to Campobello to examine Roosevelt. He agreed with Dr. Levine's diagnosis and his suggestion to stop the massages. Dr. Lovett recommended warm saline baths and suggested that Roosevelt spend time in the hospital to help speed his recovery.

Roosevelt was admitted to Presbyterian Hospital in New York under the care of his old Groton classmate, Dr. George Draper, who struck a balance between encouragement and realism. Dr. Draper made a statement about his patient's condition to the newspapers. Louis Howe, always alert to public relations, added the following statement to that of Dr. Draper: "He will not be crippled. No one need have any fear of permanent injury from this attack."

Dr. Draper recommended that straps be installed in the ceiling over Roosevelt's bed, so he could pull himself up to a sitting position and turn in bed. Later, straps were also installed over his bed at Hyde Park. Dr. Draper forwarded a progress report on his classmate to Dr. Lovett in Boston:

> I am much concerned at the slow recovery both as regards the disappearance of pain, which is generally present, and as to the recovery of even slight power to twitch the muscles. There is marked falling away of the muscle masses on either side of the spine in the lower lumbar region . . . The lower extremities present a most depressing picture. There is a little motion in the long extensors of the toes of each foot.
>
> I feel so strongly . . . that the psychological factor in his management is paramount. He has such courage, such ambition, and yet at the same time an extraordinarily sensitive emotional mechanism that it will take all the skill which we can muster to lead him to the recognition of what he really faces without crushing him.

Roosevelt kept his spirits up and greeted all visitors heartily. He didn't complain or seek pity for his bad luck. He joked and laughed with his visitors; if they weren't in a happy frame of mind when they arrived, they were when they left his room. He referred to his paralyzed lower extremities as "my somewhat rebellious legs." After six weeks in the hospital, he was allowed to go home even though he was still weak, and the fever kept returning. Dr. Draper was concerned with the slow progress. He entered the evaluation "not improving" on Roosevelt's chart.

Upon his release from the hospital, Roosevelt moved into one of the twin houses on East Sixty-fifth Street owned by his mother, Sara Roosevelt. He was confident that he would recover and would walk again. However, early in the following year, his right knee buckled followed by his left knee; his tendons were tightening. Dr. Draper had both legs encased in plaster casts, causing considerable pain. Every day, part of the cast was chipped away at the back of the cast to allow a wedge to be driven in to stretch the muscles. After two weeks, the muscles in the legs were loosened and straightened.

Roosevelt displayed enormous endurance. After his legs were straightened, he was fitted for braces. Because he was tall, he had a high center of gravity, which made it more difficult to maintain balance. The braces were heavy and had to be sent back for adjustment several times. Using crutches caused sores in his armpits unless he distributed his weight evenly to his shoulders, wrists, and hands. He gradually extended the distance that he walked on crutches.

In May 1922, Roosevelt moved to Hyde Park on the Hudson River for the summer. He had a set of parallel bars constructed on the south lawn of his home, Springwood. They were ten feet long on a circular base with waist-high lower bars and shoulder-high upper bars. He used the parallel bars daily until he slipped one day and tore some ligaments. Also, he swam in neighbor Vincent Astor's heated pool until he could have one built at his home. He enjoyed swimming and was a strong believer in water therapy. He said that water had gotten him into this predicament, and that he was counting on water to get him out of it.

Roosevelt taught himself to crawl to increase his ability to move around the house. He placed his weight on his wrists and hands and dragged his legs behind him. He was fitted for a lighter pair of braces and a corset to help hold him erect. He wrote an article about the relations between the United States and Japan that was published in *Asia* and talked about writing a history of the U.S. Navy, but he didn't seriously pursue it. In September, he moved back to New York City.

Dr. Draper had advised Roosevelt to become active in business or politics instead of concentrating exclusively on physical fitness. Roosevelt went to his office at 120 Broadway, which was easily accessible for him, for a few hours each day. His old law office, Marvin, Emmett, and Roosevelt, that he had formed with two friends after his vice presidential campaign in 1920, was only accessible by a flight of stone stairs.

At Hyde Park, Roosevelt had practiced getting out of a car—a laborious process involving many steps. He had to:

- Ensure that his braces were locked
- Grip the back of the "jump-seat," and pull himself forward
- Move his inflexible legs out of the car
- Push his legs in front of him
- Grip the "jump-seat," place his weight on the armrest and hoist himself up and out of the car
- Shift his weight to the driver, who handed his crutches to him
- Place the crutches under his arms, move forward, and smile all the time

One day Roosevelt fell going to work at his office, and his driver wasn't strong enough to pick him up by himself. Roosevelt had to ask a young onlooker for a hand. Another onlooker, a lawyer with an office in the building adjacent to Roosevelt's office, was impressed with the spirit his neighbor had shown in recovering from the fall. Basil O'Connor later became a partner and a lifelong friend.

Roosevelt enjoyed going to the office, but he missed the sunshine and the swimming therapy. He decided to rent a houseboat and to spend at least part of the winter in Florida. Sunshine and swimming would help him to improve, and he enjoyed fishing. His upper body muscles gained strength to compensate for the weakness in his lower limbs. After he returned to Hyde Park, he tried horseback riding. Initially, his daughter Anna led him around the estate on a docile pony.

Roosevelt experimented with a new means of locomotion using a crutch under his right arm and the strong arm of an assistant to grip with his left hand. With his braces locked into position, he could swing on his arms and shoulders and force his body forward by brute strength. Initially, his chauffeur, James Depew, and then his son, James, supported him. They had to learn to synchronize their steps with his and, above all, to smile and not look strained.

Roosevelt rejoined the political scene by accepting the position of pre-convention campaign manager for Governor Al Smith for President. He was asked to make the nominating speech for Al Smith at the Democratic National Convention at Madison Square Garden in New York. As Roosevelt approached the podium, he realized that no one had checked to see if it was sturdy enough to hold him. He asked a national committeeman to test the podium, and it was strong enough. Since he had to hold onto the podium and couldn't lift his arms, he smiled and lifted his head. He was greeted by loud applause and many cheers.

Roosevelt became more confident the longer that he spoke. He described Al Smith: "He has a power to strike at error and wrongdoing that makes his adversaries quail before him. He has a personality that carries to every hearer not only the sincerity but the righteousness of what he says. He is the 'Happy Warrior' of the political battlefield." Delegates responded noisily in one of the most tumultuous demonstrations ever seen in Madison Square Garden. Smith didn't win the nomination; John W. Davis did.

Roosevelt returned to Hyde Park to continue his physical therapy. One of his visitors was New York banker George Foster Peabody, who told him of a mineral spring at Warm Springs, Georgia, that had virtually cured a young boy of infantile paralysis. Roosevelt decided to check out Warm Springs on his next trip to Florida. It had been an "in" resort before the Civil War but had encountered hard times. Its main building, Meriwether Inn, had fallen into disrepair, and the grounds had become overgrown. The 50 by 150 foot pool was the principal attraction of the place.

Geologists explained that the source of the water was rain that fell on Pine Mountain, five miles away, and "runs down 3,800 feet to a deep pocket of rock, where it is warmed by the inner earth, and then returned to the surface at a temperature of 88 degrees Fahrenheit at a rate of 800 gallons a minute." The mineral content of the water provided its buoyancy. Roosevelt dipped his feet into the water and immediately had a tingling sensation in his toes. He called the water "marvelous," and said that he had "more life [in his toes] than he'd felt in them since August 1921."

Roosevelt wrote to his mother: "When I get back, I am going to have a long talk with Mr. George Foster Peabody, who is really the controlling interest in the property. I feel that a great 'cure' for infantile paralysis and kindred diseases could well be established here." He envisioned a prosperous resort for all victims of paralysis. When Roosevelt returned to New York, he became a partner of Basil O'Connor in the practice of law. He persuaded his new partner to evaluate the property in Warm Springs and later to become one of its organizers. Roosevelt went to Florida for the winter. He returned to Warm Springs to find that publicity had attracted additional sufferers of paralysis to the spa. Roosevelt worked with the newcomers, always radiating hope and enthusiasm. He stressed that they had to have confidence that they were going to improve.

Roosevelt began to lay out plans for a beautiful resort. He decided to forego his houseboat trips and fishing expeditions in Florida and visit Warm Springs every winter.

About this time, Roosevelt traveled to Marion, Massachusetts, to receive treatment from Dr. William McDonald. McDonald advocated less time in braces to strengthen the muscles and exercise on a "walking board." The walking board was a rectangular wooden platform surrounded by wooden railings. The patient, without leg braces, pulled himself or herself around the platform with a hand-over-hand motion. One day, Roosevelt exercised too long, and one of his knees locked.

Roosevelt described the exercises to Dr. Draper: "Where Lovett gave a single direct pulling exercise for the quadriceps in the direction of gravity, McDonald exercises the quadriceps with and against gravity, direct motion singly, in pairs, alternately, reciprocally and also with a rotary motion, singly, in pairs, alternately and reciprocally." Late in his stay in Marion, he was able to walk a block wearing only one brace and using a cane. He was willing to try any treatment in the chance of improving, and it paid off. "I'll walk without crutches, I'll walk into a room without scaring every-one half to death. I'll stand easily in front of people so that they'll forget that I'm a cripple."

Roosevelt continued his efforts as consultant and "architect" in improving Warm Springs. A table was installed twelve inches below the surface of the water to help patients with their exercises and ramps were installed at all buildings to improve access for the handicapped. He ensured that an active social life was provided, including bridge, poker parties, and picnics. He decided to buy the property and to run it as a nonprofit organization. Eventually, the spa received recognition as a "hydrotherapeutic center" from the American Orthopedic Association.

In September 1926, Al Smith asked Roosevelt to be temporary chairman of the New York State Democratic Convention and to make the keynote speech. Louis Howe advised him not to be drawn into any run for public office. Even though Roosevelt radiated health because of his exercise and his life outdoors, Howe knew that his candidate was at least two years away from public office.

Governor Smith asked him again in 1928 to give the keynote speech at the Democratic National Convention. Will Durant, who covered the convention in Houston for the *New York World-Telegram* wrote:

> Here on the stage is Franklin Roosevelt, beyond comparison the finest man that has appeared at either convention . . . A figure tall and proud even in suffering; a face of classic profile; pale with years of struggle against paralysis; a frame nervous yet self-controlled with that tense, taut unity of spirit which lifts the complex soul above those whose calmness is only a solidity; most obviously a gentleman and a scholar. A man softened and cleansed and illumined with pain . . . Hear the nominating speech; it is not a battery of rockets, bombs, and tear-drawing gas—it is not shouted, it is quietly read; there is hardly a gesture, hardly a raising of the voice. This is a civilized man; he could look Balfour and Poincaré in the face. For the moment, we are lifted up.

Al Smith was nominated on the first ballot.

Al Smith asked Roosevelt to run for Governor. He declined. Howe was relieved that his man wasn't going to run in 1928. Smith continued to pursue Roosevelt and arranged for Herbert Lehman, the Democratic candidate for Lieutenant Governor, to offer to stand in for Roosevelt when he went to Warm Springs.

Finally, Smith called Roosevelt to ask him if he were nominated by the delegates at the convention, he would refuse the nomination. Roosevelt hesitated, and Smith knew that he had the answer that he wanted. Roosevelt realized that public office would probably limit improvement of his physical condition.

The press was critical of Governor Smith for talking Roosevelt into running for Governor, so that he could improve his own chances for the presidency. Journalists concentrated on Roosevelt's handicap. Smith responded, "A Governor does not have to be an acrobat. We do not elect him for his ability to do a double back-flip or a handspring." Roosevelt promised to go more places and make more speeches than any office seeker in New York State.

In one sense, Roosevelt's illness improved him as a candidate. Jean Gould commented upon this in *A Good Fight*:

> Here the habit of listening that he formed during the last six years stood him in good stead. People whom he once would have considered bores, back in the days when he was a State Senator, when he could (and often did) turn and walk away from them, he now found himself listening to, not only because he couldn't help himself, but because he was interested in their project, in finding out what what Mr. Average Man thought, felt, and did.

When Roosevelt went to vote at the Hyde Park town hall, newspaper journalists and photographers were gathered at the entrance. He looked at the photographers, smiled, and asked them to take no photographs of his getting out of the car; they complied. From then on in his public career, he was photographed only from the waist up or after posing for a standing shot.

Governor Smith lost the presidential election overwhelmingly to Herbert Hoover. Roosevelt became Governor of New York State by just 25,000 votes. This margin was improved to 725,000 votes when he ran for reelection in 1930. When he became a serious candidate for President of the United States, a national magazine suggested that a report of his daily routine and the state of his health be made by a panel of doctors. He agreed immediately.

Three doctors: a diagnostician, an orthopedist, and a neurologist examined him and reported:

> We have today examined Franklin D. Roosevelt. We find that his organs and functions are sound in all respects. There is no anemia. The chest is exceptionally well developed, and the spinal column is perfectly normal; all of its segments are in alignment, and free from disease. He has neither pain nor ache at any time.
>
> Ten years ago, Governor Roosevelt suffered an attack of acute infantile paralysis, the entire effect of which was expended on the muscles of his lower extremities. There has been progressive recovery of power in the legs since that date; this restoration continues and will continue . . . We believe that his powers of endurance are such to allow him to meet all the demands of private or public life.

In January 1932, Roosevelt announced his candidacy for the office of President of the United States. In November, he won the election with almost 23,000,000 votes, fifty-seven percent of the popular vote. The "brain trust" that he had assembled in Albany followed him to Washington, including Adolf A. Berle, Jr., James Farley, Frances Perkins, Samuel Rosenman, and Rexford Tugwell. Many programs that they had tried at the state level were polished and expanded for the federal level. Because of his reduced mobility, people came to him instead of his going to them. Eleanor Roosevelt became his traveling eyes, even to the extent of descending into a mine to inspect the working conditions of miners.

When historians are polled, Franklin Delano Roosevelt is always listed as one of the five "great" presidents. Early surveys ranked him third behind Lincoln and Washington. A later survey ranked him second after Lincoln and before Washington. Eleanor Roosevelt was once asked if she thought that her husband would have become President if he hadn't had poliomyelitis. She replied that, in her opinion, he would have become President, but a different (lesser) President.

WINSTON CHURCHILL (1874-1965) British World War II Prime Minister

"Never give in, never give in, never, never, never, never—in nothing, great or small, large or petty—never give in except to convictions of honor and good sense."

Prime Minister Winston Churchill, in a speech at the Harrow School, October 29, 1941

Winston Churchill displayed the quality of perseverance throughout his lifetime with one notable exception, the academic arena. He wasn't a good student because he didn't apply himself. His parents decided that he wasn't suited for the academic rigors of Cambridge or Oxford. Since he had always displayed an interest in the military, they suggested the Royal Military College at Sandhurst, the West Point of Great Britain.

Churchill failed to gain admission to Sandhurst on his first two attempts, but was successful on his third try after taking a cram course taught by a professional tutor. He received no parental praise on his ultimate admission to Sandhurst. His father, Randolph Churchill, wrote: "I am rather surprised at your tone of exultation over your inclusion in the Sandhurst list. There are two ways of winning an examination, one credible, one the reverse. You have unfortunately chosen the latter method and appear too much pleased with your success. Thus the grand result that you came up among the second and third rate class who are only good for commissions in a cavalry regiment." The top of the class went to the best infantry regiments.

In 1899, Churchill became a celebrity during the Boer War. Retaining his commission in the British army, he went to South Africa as a correspondent for the *Morning Post*. Captured by the Boers when they derailed the train on which he was a passenger, he was escorted to prison in Pretoria. He made plans to escape from prison with two other officers. At the last minute, the two other officers backed down, but Churchill escaped alone to Portuguese East Africa and freedom. He was an instant hero when he arrived back in British-held territory in Durban.

Churchill had lost his first bid for Parliament in the constituency of Oldham prior to leaving for South Africa; however, the publicity surrounding his escape from the Boers helped him to win a seat on his second attempt. He became a vocal and visible Member of Parliament and, in 1908, became president of the Board of Trade.

Churchill advanced through increasingly responsible positions in government. In 1910, he was appointed Home Secretary, a major cabinet post, and, in 1911, when the expansion of the German military became obvious, he was appointed First Lord of the Admiralty. His first major setback was the failure of the Dardanelles campaign, a serious British defeat in World War I, of which he had been the principal architect. He received most of the blame, and he resigned from the Admiralty in 1915 at the age of 41.

Five months later, Churchill was dismissed from the cabinet, although he continued to be a Member of Parliament. He revealed his feelings to a friend: "I'm finished. I am banished from the scene of action." His father had a similar experience at the age of 37 and was never able to overcome it. Not so with Winston who, in his early years in Parliament, was called "Pushful, the younger."

Churchill served creditably with the Sixth Royal Scots Fusiliers in France, until, in 1917, he was asked to become the Minister of Munitions. In 1921, he became the Secretary of State for the Colonies. Earlier, he had left the Conservative Party for the Liberal Party. His party lost favor in 1923, and he left office at the time. He lost his next two campaigns for Parliament.

Churchill approached the Conservative Party about rejoining it and ran as a Conservative candidate. He lost again. Finally, a safe seat was found for him as the candidate from Epping, and he was back in Parliament. Not only was he back in Parliament, but he was appointed Chancellor of the Exchequer, the second most powerful position in the British government. His father had held the office at the peak of his career. In 1929, however, when the Conservatives were turned out of office, began a 10 year period during which Churchill held no office. At the age of 55, it appeared that his political career was over.

With the increasing threat of war in 1939, Churchill was invited back into the government at his old post of First Lord of the Admiralty. The message, "Winston is back," was sent to all Royal Navy ships and stations. In May 1940, Prime Minister Chamberlain resigned, and Churchill was asked to become Prime Minister. He said that he had nothing to offer the British people but "blood, toil, tears, and sweat."

Summarizing the aim of the British government, Churchill said, "You ask, what is our aim? I can answer in one word: victory—victory at all costs, victory in spite of all terror, victory however long and hard the road may be; for without victory, there is no survival." He played a significant role in the British policy in World War II. "You ask, what is our policy? I will say: It is to wage war by sea, by land, and air, with all our might and all the strength God can give us: to wage war against a monstrous tyranny, never surpassed in the dark, lamentable catalogue of human crime. That is our policy."

Churchill was 65 years old and assuming leadership of a country at war at a time when many of his peers were retiring. However, he felt as if "I were walking with destiny, and that all of my past life has been but a preparation for this hour and this trial."

Churchill was widely recognized as the one to lead Britain during World War II. He said, "Let us therefore brace ourselves to our duties, and so bear ourselves that, if the British Empire and Commonwealth last for a thousand years, men will say, 'That was their finest hour.'" He downplayed his role as leader, according to Mollie Keller in *Winston Churchill:*

> I have never accepted what people have kindly said—namely, that I inspired the nation. Their will was resolute and remorseless, and it proved unconquerable. If it fell to me to express it, and I found the right words you must remember that I have always earned my living by my pen and by my tongue. It was the nation and the race dwelling all around the globe that had the lion's heart. I had the luck to be called upon to give the roar.

ABRAHAM LINCOLN (1809-1865) A Man for His Time

"To thousands who never saw him, but who know him through his letters and speeches, and through the record of his private and public life, he is an inspiration. The story of his overcoming the difficulties of his early life has put courage into many a young heart; his resolute stand by what he thought to be right has helped countless souls to be true to their duty; and the kindness and goodwill which flowed from his great heart—even to his foes—made the cherishing of malice and bitterness seem unworthy and shameful."

Wilbur F. Gordy, *Abraham Lincoln*

Abraham Lincoln had many strong qualities. Leadership and vision went together; resilience was another. He persisted in his ambition to attain public office while encountering three defeats along the way. In 1832, he was defeated in his first bid for public office when he ran for the Illinois State Legislature. However, he won in his second attempt for that office in 1834 and was reelected several times. In 1846, he was elected to the U.S. House of Representatives. He was defeated in his first bid for the U.S. Senate in 1855 and again in 1858 when he ran against Stephen Douglas.

In 1856, Lincoln began to develop a national reputation when he was considered as a candidate for Vice President at the Republican Convention; however, he didn't have enough votes to be placed on the ticket. In his campaign for the Senate against Stephen Douglas, Lincoln achieved celebrity status in a series of debates. During the Lincoln-Douglas debates, he gave his famous house-divided speech, as cited by Olivia Coolidge in *The Apprenticeship of Abraham Lincoln:*

> A house divided against itself cannot stand. I believe this government cannot endure permanently half slave and half free. I do not expect the union to be dissolved—I do not expect the house to fall—but I do expect it will cease to be divided. It will become all one thing or all the other. Either the opponents of slavery will resist the spread of it, and place it where the public mind can rest in the

belief that it is on the course of ultimate extinction; or its advocates will push it forward until it shall become alike lawful in all States, old as well as new, North as well as South.

In February 1860, Lincoln gained additional national exposure from his speech at Cooper Union, New York City. His closing remarks were "Let us have faith that right makes might; and in that faith let us, to the end, dare to do our duty as we understand it." Newspaperman Horace Greeley stated that "I do not hesitate to pronounce it the very best political address to which I have ever listened, and I have heard some of Webster's grandest."

At the Republican Convention in Chicago in May 1860, Lincoln won the party's nomination for President on the third ballot, beating front-runner William H. Seward of New York. The real tests of Lincoln's leadership began immediately after he was elected. His cabinet included three of his rivals for the Presidency, and virtually every member of his cabinet considered himself superior to Lincoln and more capable of doing the President's job. Members of Lincoln's cabinet were:

William Seward—Secretary of State
Caleb Smith—Secretary of the Interior
Salmon Chase—Secretary of the Treasury
Gideon Welles—Secretary of the Navy
Simon Cameron—Secretary of War
Frank Blair—Postmaster General
Edward Bates—Attorney General

Secretary of State Seward actually suggested that Lincoln give him the powers of de facto President. President Lincoln responded that he had been elected President, that he would carry out the responsibilities of the office, and that no one could do it for him.

On April 12, 1861, just over a month after his inauguration, Lincoln was confronted with the beginning of the Civil War when the Confederates fired on Ft. Sumter in Charleston harbor. Many of the country's most capable generals were from the South. With its plantation economy and culture of chivalry, soldiering was considered a noble occupation. Lincoln had counted on the services of

Robert E. Lee as Commander in Chief of the Union army. However, after much soul-searching, Lee declared his loyalty to his native State, the Commonwealth of Virginia. Finding a general who was capable of leading the Union Army to victory in the field became a crucial test for the new President.

General Winfield Scott was the senior Union general, but he was in his mid-60s and wasn't considered a field commander. Lincoln's first appointment as Commander of the Army of the Potomac was General McDowell. McDowell was unequal to the task and his forces were dramatically defeated by Confederate General Beauregard at the First Battle of Bull Run.

The Army of the Potomac required further training, and General McClellan replaced General McDowell to provide it. General McClellan did an outstanding job with the training assignment, and he was a good administrator; however, he wasn't an aggressive general. In fact, he became extremely cautious on the eve of battle. McClellan was slow in attacking Richmond, and, within five miles of the city, he let the Confederates attack first. The Army of the Potomac was driven back in defeat.

The Army of the Potomac returned to Washington. By withholding support to General Pope, who commanded the Union Army facing Lee's forces, McClellan contributed to the Union defeat at the Second Battle of Bull Run. Lincoln replaced General McClellan with General Burnside, who was defeated with significant Union losses at Fredericksburg.

Burnside accepted the blame and was replaced by one of his severest critics, General "Fighting Joe" Hooker, who, in turn, was defeated with considerable loss of lives at Chancellorsville. Subsequently, General Hooker quarreled with General Halleck, Lincoln's military advisor, and resigned. He was replaced by General Meade, who pursued Lee's army north to Gettysburg to win one of the decisive battles of the war.

As Lee was retreating southward from Gettysburg, Lincoln was notified of General Grant's victory at Vicksburg and his capture of 32,000 men. Finally, the Union had found a general who could beat the Confederate army. After being promoted to Lieutenant General and placed in charge of all Union forces, Grant moved on Richmond. He sent a message to President Lincoln via Secretary of War Stanton, who had replaced Simon Cameron when Cameron was appointed Minister to Russia, "I propose to fight it out on this line if it takes all summer." Lincoln observed that "It is the dogged pertinacity of Grant that wins."

Lincoln displayed his leadership again in achieving the goal of freeing American slaves. He knew that timing was critical in freeing the slaves; however, he was criticized for his delay in taking action. He wrote the Emancipation Proclamation, but waited until McClellan's victory at Antietam to announce it.

In August 1861, General Fremont, Commander of the Western Department of the Union army, had announced that in his department, the slaves of owners who were fighting against the Union were free men. In May 1862, General Hunter had declared the freedom of slaves in Florida, Georgia, and South Carolina. In both cases, Lincoln rescinded the declarations. He received considerable criticism, but he persisted and announced the Emancipation Proclamation when he considered the time to be right.

The United States was fortunate to have had a President with Lincoln's personal qualities, including empathy, optimism, and emotional control, during his critical time in office. Historians consider him one of the five "great" Presidents of the United States. The consensus of historians is that he was the finest President in the history of the country.

In an interview, historian Doris Kearns Goodwin observed that Lincoln's emotional intelligence contributed heavily to his success. She noted that Lincoln was an excellent communicator, both in writing and speaking, and that he relied heavily on teamwork. He had reason to question the loyalty of his cabinet members but he worked well with them and did not bear a grudge.

ROBERT BRUCE *(1274-1329)* King Robert I of Scotland

"Our greatest glory is not in never failing, but in rising up every time we fail."

Ralph Waldo Emerson

In 1305 and early 1306, Scotland was ruled by Edward I of England, a strong, cruel Plantagenet king. Scotland had been a conquered country, or at least partly under English control, since 1296. The Scottish patriot, William Wallace, tried to throw off the English yoke with a rousing victory at Stirling Bridge in September 1297, but his forces lost the battle of Falkirk to the English longbow the following July and were reduced to guerrilla actions. Wallace was a commoner with no aspirations to the crown of Scotland.

In 1306, the two Scottish lords with the greatest claim to the throne were John Comyn of Badenoch, "the Red Comyn," who was the nephew of the previous king, John Balliol, and Robert Bruce, whose grandfather had been King of Scotland. John Comyn had been in communication with Edward I of England. When Robert Bruce heard of these discussions, he suggested that Comyn meet with him in the Church of the Minorite Friars in Dumfries.

The heirs to the throne argued heatedly near the high altar, and Robert Bruce fatally stabbed the Red Comyn. Bruce's companions claimed that it was self-defense. Bruce was concerned about losing the support of the Church by this act but was pardoned by the patriotic Bishop of Glasgow, Bishop Wishart. On Palm Sunday, 1306, Bruce was crowned Robert I, King of Scotland, at Scone.

Scotland was a divided country, and many Scottish lords sided with the English. Bruce's early encounters with the English and their Scottish allies were a series of defeats. In June 1306, he was routed at the battle of Methven, his first battle as King of Scotland. During the battle, Bruce was taken prisoner briefly but was rescued by his brother-in-law, Christopher Seton. Bishop Wishart was captured by the English and imprisoned. Six of the knights who had supported Bruce at his coronation were also captured, and sixteen nobles, including Christopher Seton, were hanged at Newcastle without a trial.

Bruce's rule was at an ebb, and many of his supporters were discouraged. He attempted to enlist men for his small army at Athol.

In August 1306, Bruce and his party camped on land belonging to John of Lorne, a distant Comyn relative. John of Lorne had heard that Bruce was in the area and had asked his tenants to watch for him and his men. Bruce's party was surprised by John of Lorne's men, and the King of Scotland was defeated again. Many of Bruce's party dispersed to avoid capture.

With a small following, Bruce "took to the heather," sleeping in caves and eating only a mixture of raw oatmeal and water, called drammock. After crossing Loch Lomond to Castle Donaverty, Bruce and his men traveled among the Islands of Kintyre and the Hebrides, participating in several forays and skirmishes along the way. They wintered on the Island of Rathlin off the coast of Ireland. The Irish natives didn't provide aid to the refugee Scots but, because they were also hostile to the English, didn't betray them to King Edward's forces.

According to a story passed down from generation to generation, the incident of the spider occurred at Rathlin. Bruce thought that his problems might be due to his killing the Red Comyn in the church at Dumfries, and he considered performing an act of contrition for this great sin. He thought about abandoning his quest to free Scotland from English rule to crusade in the Holy Land against the Saracens. However, he didn't want to shirk his duty as King of Scotland to free his country of the English invaders. He was torn between performing his duty to Scotland and atoning for his past sins. According to Sir Walter Scott in "History of Scotland" from *Tales of a Grandfather*:

> While he was divided twixt these reflections, and doubtful of what he would do, Bruce was looking upward toward the roof of the cabin in which he lay; and his eye was attracted by a spider which, hanging at the end of a long thread of its own spinning, was endeavoring, in the fashion of that creature, to swing itself from one beam in the roof to another, for the purpose of fixing the line on which it meant to stretch its web.

The insect made the attempt again and again without success, and at length Bruce counted that it had tried to carry its point six times, and been as often unable to do so. It came to his head that he had himself fought just six battles against the English and their allies and that the poor persevering spider was exactly in the same situation as himself, having made as many trials, and had been as often disappointed in what he had aimed at.

"Now," thought Bruce, "as I have no means of knowing what is best to be done, I shall be guided by the luck which guides this spider. If the spider shall make another effort to fix its thread and shall be successful, I will venture a seventh time to try my fortune in Scotland; but if the spider shall fail, I will go to the wars in Palestine, and never return to my home country more."

While Bruce was forming his resolution, the spider made another exertion with all the force it could muster, and fairly succeeded in fastening its thread to the beam which it had so often in vain attempted to reach. Bruce, seeing the success of the spider, resolved to try his own fortune; and as he had never before gained a victory, so he never afterward sustained any considerable or decisive check or defeat.

Bruce defeated the English decisively at Bannockburn in June 1314 and finally, in 1328, achieved his goal, the formal recognition of the independence of Scotland by the English Parliament.

CHAPTER 6

SOLDIERS / SAILORS / AIRMEN

"If we fail we can always get up and try again. To be defeated need not mean we are out of the race. Life gives us new contests and new opportunities in which happiness can prevail."

Nancy Sherman, *Stoic Warriors: The Ancient Philosophy Behind the Military Mind*

CARL BRASHEAR (1931-2006) U.S. Navy Master Diver and Amputee

"The Navy diver is not a fighting man.
He is a salvage expert.
If it's lost underwater, he finds it.
If it's sunk, he brings it up.
If it's in the way, he moves it.
If he's lucky, he dies two hundred feet beneath the waves,
Because that's the closest he will ever come to being a hero.
No one in their right mind would ever want the job.
Or so they say."

The Diver's Creed

Carl Brashear set a goal for himself at a young age and had the motivation to achieve that goal despite having to overcome racial discrimination as well as a major physical injury. Paul Stillwell of the U.S. Naval Institute summarized Brashear's achievements:

> To become the first black master diver in the Navy, Carl Brashear used a rare combination of grit, determination, and persistence, because the obstacles in his path were formidable. His race was a handicap, as were his origin on a sharecropper's farm in rural Kentucky and the modest education he received there. But these were not his greatest challenges. He was held back by an even greater factor: in 1966, his left leg was amputated just below the knee because he was badly injured on a salvage operation.

> After the amputation, the Navy sought to retire Brashear from active duty, but he refused to submit to the decision. Instead, he secretly returned to diving and produced evidence that he could excel, despite his injury. Then, in 1974, he qualified as a Master Diver, a difficult feat under any circumstances and something no black man had accomplished before. By the time of his retirement, he

had achieved the highest rate for Navy enlisted personnel, master chief petty officer. In addition, he had become a celebrity through his response to manifold challenges and thereby had become a real inspiration to others.

Carl Brashear was born on a farm in Tonieville, Kentucky, in January 1931, the sixth of nine children of McDonald and Gonzella Brashear. McDonald Brashear was a hard-working sharecropper with a third-grade education. Young Carl helped his father work the farm and attended a one-room, segregated school through the eighth grade. His mother, who had completed nine years of school, augmented his education with home schooling.

At the age of fourteen, Brashear decided that he wanted to be a military man, possibly a soldier. He was influenced by a brother-in-law in the Army. When he was seventeen, he went to the U.S. Army recruiting office to enlist. However, everyone yelled at him, making him so nervous that he failed the entrance examination. He was supposed to return to retake the exam, but he went to the U.S. Navy recruiting office instead. The Navy chief petty officer treated him well, so he enlisted in the Navy.

In February 1948, Brashear reported to the Great Lakes Naval Training Center for basic training and was assigned to an integrated company. He encountered no racial prejudice in boot camp; however, upon completion of his training, steward was the only assignment available to him. He was assigned as steward to an air squadron in Key West, Florida. The Naval Base in Key West was segregated at the time; opportunities for African-American personnel were limited.

At Key West, Brashear met Chief Boatswain's Mate Guy Johnson, who steered him toward a major turning point in his career. Chief Johnson arranged for Brashear to leave the steward assignment and work for him as a beachmaster, beaching seaplanes from the Gulf of Mexico. Brashear strongly preferred his new assignment over his old one. His duties as a beachmaster required him to get along with people, to respect others, and to work with little supervision. Chief Johnson taught him basic seamanship, gave him guidance on being a good sailor, and introduced him to the qualities of leadership.

While stationed at Key West, Brashear decided that he wanted to be a diver. One day, a buoy needed repair, and a self-propelled seaplane wrecking derrick, a YSD, was brought out to repair it. A diver with a face mask and shallow-water diving apparatus went down to make the necessary repairs.

Brashear watched the diver work and realized that diving was what he wanted to do. Brashear requested diving duty on his first two shipboard assignments, on the escort aircraft carriers *USS Palau* (CVE-122) and *USS Tripoli* (CVE-64). He was assigned to the sail locker, with boatswain's mate's duties such as splicing wire and sewing canvass. He learned about fueling rigs and anchoring and mooring methods.

While Brashear was stationed on the *Tripoli,* a TBM Avenger torpedo bomber rolled off the jettison ramp, and a deep-sea diver went down to attach wires to pull the plane out of the water. Brashear watched the diver go down and come up and observed, "Now, this is the best thing since sliced bread. I've got to be a deep-sea diver." He requested diving school routinely until he was admitted in 1954.

Brashear joined the boxing team on the *Tripoli* and won many bouts. He met Sugar Ray Robinson, who taught him how to throw jabs and to keep his hands up. Sugar Ray showed him how to be a better defensive boxer. Brashear fought in the light-heavyweight championship of the East Coast, but he lost that fight.

Brashear made boatswain's mate third class on the *Tripoli* and gained experience with paravane gear used for minesweeping and with the operations of a tank landing ship (LST). He was responsible for a division of men and learned about leadership and supervision. He had done well, but he realized that further education would increase his opportunities for advancement.

In 1953, Brashear made boatswain's mate second class. While at that rate, he won "sailor-of-the-year" honors and was called "Mr. Navy." He enrolled in United States Armed Forces Institute (USAFI) courses and passed his general educational development (GED) examination, the high-school equivalency test, in 1960. A high school diploma wasn't required for the first phase of diving school, but it was for later phases, such as mixed-gas diving.

Brashear's next assignment was in Bayonne, New Jersey, at diving school, which involved hard work and psychological stress.

When he reported for duty, the training officer thought he was reporting in as a cook or steward. When he found out that Brashear was there as a student, he told him, "Well, I don't know how the rest of the students are going to accept you. As a matter of fact, I don't even think you will make it through the school. We haven't had a colored guy come through here before."

When classes started, Brashear found notes on his bunk: "We're going to drown you today, nigger! We don't want any nigger divers." Brashear was ready to quit, but boatswain's mate first class Rutherford, on the staff of the diving school, talked him out of it. Over a beer at the Dungaree Bar, Rutherford said, "I hear you're going to quit." Brashear admitted that he planned to leave the school. Rutherford told him, "I can't whip you, but I'll fight you every day if you quit. Those notes aren't hurting you. No one is doing a thing to you. Show them you're a better man than they are." Rutherford's pep talk was the only encouragement Brashear received. One person's upbeat advice was enough to keep him on his chosen career path.

The first week of diving school was orientation; physics courses were given in the second week. Diving medicine and diving physics were followed by four weeks of pure diving, which included introduction to hydraulics and underwater tools as well as underwater welding and cutting. The course included two weeks of demolition and several weeks of salvage operations, which involved becoming familiar with beach gear and learning how to make splices.

Brashear worked hard in the sixteen-week-long diving school and didn't fail any exams. The school was stressful; the instructors continually challenged the students. Teamwork was emphasized. When working underwater, divers rely on their teammates working alongside them and rely heavily on support personnel topside. Seventeen out of thirty-two that started with the class graduated.

In March 1955, Brashear was assigned to a salvage ship, USS Opportune (ARS-41), which had eighteen divers out of a crew of over 100. The Opportune was involved in many salvage jobs, including raising a gas barge in Charleston, South Carolina, recovering an antisubmarine plane that had sunk in the Virginia Capes, and pulling a cargo ship off the beach in Argentia, Newfoundland. His experiences on the Opportune increased his understanding of teamwork and the importance of knowing other team members' capabilities in diving. He was promoted to boatswain's mate first class while in Argentia, Newfoundland.

Brashear's next duty station was Quonset Point (Rhode Island) Naval Air Station, where, as leading petty officer, he was in charge of the boat house. One of his assignments was retrieving aircraft that had crashed in Narragansett Bay. A collateral duty was to escort President Eisenhower's boat, the *Barbara Ann*, with a 104-foot crash boat with a crew of thirteen and two 20-millimeter guns mounted on the wings of the bridge, from Delaware to Newport, where Ike played golf. Brashear also escorted the *Barbara Ann* on pleasure cruises.

One of Brashear's next assignments was the *USS Nereus*, homeported in San Diego, California, where he made chief petty officer and was assigned to first-class diver school in Washington, D.C. First-class diver school was demanding, with courses in medicine, decompression, physics, treatments, mathematics, and mixing gases to the proper ratio. Brashear flunked out. Most salvage divers who failed first-class school left as a second-class diver.

Brashear was astounded to hear that he was leaving as a non-diver. After seven years of diving experience, he had reached the low point in his career. He wrangled a set of orders to the fleet training center in Hawaii, which he knew had a second-class diver school. Lieutenant j.g. Billie Delanoy, whom Brashear knew from a previous assignment, was in charge of that school. Delanoy knew that his old shipmate should be a diver and enrolled him in the school, which was not difficult for Brashear. He passed it easily and returned to a level he had mastered previously.

While in Hawaii, Brashear dove to inspect the hull of the *USS Arizona* (BB-39) before she could be converted into a memorial. The amount of list had to be determined before they could proceed with the work to build the memorial. Using plumb lines, they determined that the *Arizona* had two degrees of list. It gave him an eerie feeling diving around a hull containing the 1,100 shipmates that didn't survive the Japanese attack on Pearl Harbor.

While assigned to the fleet training center in Hawaii, Brashear received temporary additional duty (TAD) to report to Joint Task Force Eight as a diver supporting nuclear testing during Operation Dominic in 1962. Thor intermediate-range ballistic missiles

(IRBMs) with 20 or 30 megaton warheads were tested on Johnston Island. Brashear was skipper of a large self-propelled harbor tug (YTB-262) and was also a diver.

After studying math for two years, in 1963 Brashear got a second opportunity to attend first-class diving school in Washington, D.C. He thought that he would go through fourteen weeks of training with the class of thirty salvage divers, learning about diving medicine, diving physics, mixing gases, and emergency procedures. However, the training officer made him go through twenty-six weeks of class as though he had never been a salvage diver. He graduated third out of seventeen who completed the course.

After serving a year on the fleet ocean tug *USS Shakori* (ATF-162), Brashear was assigned to the salvage ship *USS Hoist* (ARS-40), where he could train to become a master diver. The *Hoist* participated in the search for a nuclear bomb that was dropped into the sea off Palomares, Spain, when a B-52 bomber and a refueling plane collided in midair. The bomb was found by the deep-diving research vessel *Alvin* six miles off the coast in 2,600 feet of water after a search of two and a half months. Brashear rigged a spider, a three-legged contraption with grapnel hooks, to the bomb to bring it to the surface.

A mechanized landing craft (LCM-8) was moored alongside the *Hoist* to receive the bomb. Brashear was bringing the bomb up with the capstan to place it in a crate in the landing craft when a line parted, causing the boat to break loose. He saw what had happened and ran to push one of his men out of the way of the line. A pipe tied to the mooring came loose, sailed across the deck, and struck Brashear's left leg just below the knee, virtually severing it. The bomb fell back into 2,600 feet of water.

The *Hoist* had no doctor and no morphine and was six and a half miles from the cruiser *USS Albany*, the location of the nearest doctor. Corpsmen placed two tourniquets on his leg, but, because Brashear's leg was so muscular, the bleeding couldn't be stopped. He was placed on board a helicopter to be transported to the hospital at Torrejon Air Force Base in Spain.

Brashear had lost so much blood that he went into shock. By the time he reached Torrejon, he had hardly any heartbeat or pulse. The doctor thought that Brashear was going to die. He came to after they had given him eighteen pints of blood. He was told that they would try to save his leg, but that it would be three inches shorter than his right leg. However, his leg became infected, and gangrene set in. Brashear was air-lifted to the Portsmouth, Virginia, Naval Hospital where he was told that his rehabilitation would take three years.

Brashear decided that he couldn't wait that long to get on with his life, so he told the doctor to amputate. The doctor responded, "Geez, Chief! Anybody could amputate. It takes a good doctor to fix it." Brashear told them that he planned to go back to diving; they thought that he shouldn't even consider it. In July 1966, another inch and a half of his leg had to be amputated.

Brashear had read about an air force pilot with no legs who flew fighter aircraft. That was Douglas Bader, a Royal Air Force ace in World War II. He also read that a prosthesis could be designed to support any amount of weight.

Brashear was sent to a prosthesis center in Philadelphia to be fitted. He refused to have people wait on him. Brashear told the doctor, "Once I get a leg, I'm going to give you back this crutch, and I'll never use it again." They told him that he couldn't do it. In December, he was fitted with an artificial leg; he never used crutches again.

Brashear returned to the Portsmouth Naval Hospital and visited Chief Warrant Officer Clair Axtell, who was in charge of the nearby diving school. He told Axtell, whom he knew from salvage diving school, "Ax, I've got to dive. I've got to get some pictures. I've got to prove to people that I'm going to be a diver." Axtell reminded Brashear that if anything happened to him, his own career would be over; nevertheless, he obtained a photographer and gave him a chance. Brashear dove in a deep-sea rig, in shallow-water equipment, and with scuba gear while the photographer documented his activities. He returned for a second set of dives and another set of pictures.

Brashear's medical board was convened at the naval hospital, where Rear Admiral Joseph Yon from the Bureau of Medicine and Surgery (BuMed) talked with him about returning to diving. Brashear took the initiative to endorse his own orders, "FFT (for further transfer) to the second-class diving school," and reported to the school. A lieutenant commander from BuMed called Brashear at the diving school and asked how he got into the diving school.

Brashear replied, "Orders, sir," which caused some confusion.

Brashear had ignored the first physical evaluation board; now they told him to report to a second one. He had sent all of his diving photographs along with the findings of the medical board to BuMed. They said, "Well, if he did that down there [in Virginia], he can do it up here, " and invited him to spend a week with a captain and a commander at the deep-sea diving school in Washington, D.C. BuMed sent observers to evaluate his performance.

At the end of the week, Captain Jacks, policy control, called Brashear in and told him: "Most of the people in your position want to get a medical disability, get out of the Navy, and do the least they can and draw as much pay as they can. And then you're asking for full duty. I don't know to handle it. Suppose you would be diving and tear your leg off." Brashear said, "Well, Captain, it wouldn't bleed." Captain Jacks jokingly told him to get out of his office.

Brashear reported back to diving school in Virginia. Brashear dove every day for a year, including weekends. He led calisthenics every morning and ran every day. Occasionally, he would return from a run and find a puddle of blood from his stump in the artificial leg. Instead of going to sick bay, he soaked his stump in a bucket of warm salt water. At the end of the year, Brashear received a very favorable report, and returned to duty with full diving assignments—the first time in naval history for an amputee.

Brashear received orders to the boat house at the Norfolk Naval Air Station, where he was a division officer in charge of the divers. Their principal duties were search and rescue and recovery of downed aircraft. They picked up helicopters and jet aircraft that had crashed and assisted civilian divers at the Norfolk Naval Shipyard.

Brashear considered becoming a warrant officer or a limited duty officer, an officer who came up from the enlisted rates. However, a Master Diver must be a chief petty officer, a senior petty officer, or a master chief petty officer, and Brashear's goal was still to be the first African-American Master Diver in the Navy.

In 1970, Brashear went from the Norfolk Naval Air Station boat house to saturation diving school at the Experimental Diving Unit in Washington, D.C. Saturation diving involves going to extreme depths and staying down for long periods of time. Upon graduation from saturation diving school, he attended master diving school. A Master Diver is proficient in all phases of diving, submarine rescue, and salvage; it is the highest position in diving.

Evaluation is done by Master Divers, ex-Master Divers, and the commanding officer and the executive officer of the Master Diving school. Emphasis is placed on emergency procedures. Considerable pressure is placed on participants, and many attempts are made to rattle them. At times, participants are given an incorrect order; they are expected to know better than to obey it. Self-confidence is a requirement. Master Divers have to know how to treat all types of diving accidents. Four out of six in the class made Master Diver, including Brashear. The commanding officer of the Master Diving school called Brashear into his office and told him, "If there was a mark that we'd give, you made the highest mark of any man that ever came through this school to be evaluated for Master. You did not make a mistake. We vote you Master."

Brashear was assigned to the submarine tender *USS Hunley* (AS-31) in Charleston, South Carolina. He was a division officer on the *Hunley*, which was a tender for nuclear submarines, both fast attack submarines and "boomers" with missiles. Divers, who were required to dive when nuclear reactors were critical, used film badges to check their radiation exposure levels. They had to make security checks, looking for foreign objects attached to the hull.

Brashear's next duty was on the salvage ship *USS Recovery* (ARS-43). He preferred salvage work to duty on a tender because salvage jobs were less repetitive. *Recovery* divers evaluated the feasibility of raising a ship that had sunk off Newport News in 1918 and salvaged a helicopter off the coast of Florida. They also dove in a flooded engine room on the *USS Saratoga* (CVA-60).

Recovery was a happy ship; Brashear contributed to this environment by being fair, leading by example, and following a policy of admitting an error when one was made. Men respected him.

Brashear's next assignment was the Naval Safety Center in Norfolk. He represented the Safety Center in investigating diving accidents, determining the cause, and making recommendations to prevent future accidents. He also conducted safety presentations and wrote "safety grams." While at the Safety Center, he was mentioned in newspapers and magazines and received television coverage. Robert Manning of the Office of the Navy's Chief of Information suggested making a short movie about Brashear; a four-and-a-half minute movie was made for TV.

From that beginning, Manning suggested that Brashear should be a candidate for the "Come Back" program about people who have been injured or stumbled in their career and made a comeback. That year a thirty-minute documentary was made about Brashear as well as Rosemary Clooney, Neil Sadaka, Freddie Fender, and Bill Veeck.

Brashear's final tour of duty in the Navy was reassignment to the *USS Recovery*. The commanding officer of the *Recovery* had requested him. Breashear considered it a feather in his cap to finish his Navy career on the *Recovery*.

Brashear retired in April 1979. His retirement ceremony was planned for the *USS Hoist*, the ship on which he had lost his leg. However, the *Hoist* was too small to accommodate everyone, so his retirement ceremony was moved to the gymnasium at the Little Creek Amphibious Base. It was announced in the newspapers three days in advance, and posters were put up all around the Amphibious Base. The gymnasium was filled; two television stations covered the event.

Brashear had the resilience to reach his goal in the Navy and enjoyed an exciting, rewarding career. As with many successful people, Brashear always displayed the "can do" spirit. His life is an inspiration to us.

DOUGLAS BADER (1910-1982) World War II R.A.F. Ace

"The nerve that never relaxes, the eye that never blanches, the thought that never wanders — these are the masters of victory."

Burke

On Monday morning, December 14, 1931, Royal Air Force pilot Douglas Bader was flying near Kenley, England, when he saw two fellow pilots take off from the airfield. He recalled that the pilots, Phillips and Richardson, were flying to Woodley airfield near Reading to visit Phillips's brother, who was stationed there. Bader joined them on their flight.

While visiting Woodley, one of the pilots questioned Bader about the aerobatics he had performed at the air show at Hendon and asked if he would do some aerobatics for them. Bader declined the request. He vividly recalled a reprimand from his commanding officer, Harry Day, for showing off in the air and taking too many chances. Also, the Gloster Gamecock they flew at Hendon had been replaced with the more modern and faster Bulldog. However, the Bulldog was heavier than the Gamecock and wasn't as maneuverable; furthermore, it had the tendency to drop out of a roll.

When the pilots prepared to return to Kenley, Bader was again asked to perform some aerobatics. This time, he took it as a dare. As he climbed, Bader banked and turned back to the airfield to make a low pass at the clubhouse. He rolled to the right and felt the Bulldog begin to drop. He attempted to come out of the roll when the left wingtip hit the ground. His plane crashed, and the engine was separated from the fuselage.

Bader was pinned in the aircraft by his straps. He heard the loud noise of the crash, but didn't feel much pain; however, he noticed that his legs were in unusual positions. His left leg was buckled under the seat, and he could see a bone sticking out of the right knee of his coveralls and a spreading stain of blood. His first thought was that he wouldn't be able to play rugby on Saturday.

A steward came over from the clubhouse with a glass of brandy and offered it to him. Without thinking, Bader said, "No, thanks very much. I don't drink." The steward leaned over, saw all of the blood in the cockpit, became very pale, and drank the brandy himself. The plane had to be cut away with a hacksaw before Bader could be lifted from the wreckage. He was taken to the Royal Berkshire Hospital, where both legs were amputated.

Bader was fitted for artificial legs by the Dessouter brothers at Roehampton Hospital. Robert Dessouter fitted him for the artificial legs and told him that he would never walk without a cane. Bader told him that he would never walk *with* a cane.

After many tries on the first day with the new legs, Bader hobbled a few steps, unaided, over to the parallel bars. Dessouter had never seen an individual with one artificial leg do that on the first day; it was an incredible achievement for someone with two artificial legs. While Bader practiced using his new legs, Dessouter admitted that he had never seen anyone with his tenacity and resolve.

Bader asked the garage at Kenley where he had stored his MG sports car to switch the positions of the brake and clutch pedals so he could take advantage of his stronger leg and to make it easier for him to drive. When the MG was ready, a mechanic drove it to the hospital at Uxbridge where Bader was recuperating.

When Bader asked the mechanic if he had any trouble driving the car over from Kenley, the mechanic said that trouble wasn't the word for it. He kept depressing the brake pedal to shift gears and putting his foot on the clutch to stop, which was even more disconcerting. Finally, he had to drive with his legs crossed, or he would never have made it.

Bader learned how to drive his MG. He participated in dances and played squash and golf. By the summer of 1932, he was able to fly an airplane again. He applied for flight status in the Royal Air Force.

Bader reported to the Central Medical Establishment at Kingsway for a physical examination. He passed but was given an A2H rating, which meant restricted flying; he wasn't allowed to fly solo. He was assigned to the Central Flying School at Wittering for their evaluation of his abilities.

Bader's training went well at Wittering; he was confident that he would be reinstated as a pilot. He reported back to the Central Medical Establishment at Kingsway to see the Wing Commander, who acknowledged that the Central Flying School had given him a favorable report; however, he said, "Unfortunately, we cannot pass you for flying because there is nothing in the King's Regulations which covers your case."

After Hitler's invasion of Poland, Bader again asked to return to flight status. In early October 1939, he received a telegram requesting him to report to a selection board at Kingsway. Air Vice Marshal Halahan, his old commandant from the Royal Air Force College at Cranwell, was in charge of the board. Halahan was interviewing applicants for ground jobs only.

Bader wanted to fly; he requested General Duties (flying) and a A1B rating—full flying category. Air Vice Marshal Halahan forwarded a note to the Wing Commander responsible for making the decision: "I have known this officer since he was a officer at Cranwell under my command. He's the type we want. If he is fit, apart from his legs, I suggest you give him A1B category and leave it to the Central Flying School to assess his flying capabilities." The Wing Commander agreed, and he was in.

In November 1939, Bader returned to flying duties. Within three months, he was assigned to a squadron that flew Spitfires, which were much more advanced aircraft than the Gamecocks and Bulldogs he had flown in the early 1930s.

Initially, he was assigned as Squadron Leader to No. 12 Air Group at Duxford, Cambridgeshire, whose mission was to protect the industrial Midlands. He missed the first three weeks of the Battle of Britain because, in August 1940, most cross-Channel fighter sorties were flown from No. 11 Air Group fields in Kent, Sussex, and Essex. On August 30, Bader's squadron received orders to support No. 11 Air Group in the Battle of Britain.

By the end of 1940, Bader had been awarded the Distinguished Service Order (DSO), a decoration given for leadership, as well as the Distinguished Flying Cross (DFC), for individual initiative in action. Ultimately, he received the bar for each medal; he was only the third person to receive them. By August 1941, he had shot down over twenty-two enemy aircraft.

On August 9, 1941, Bader was returning from a mission over Bethune, France, when a Messerschmitt collided with his plane's tail. His right artificial leg caught on the cockpit as he jumped from the aircraft. Eventually, his leg harness broke, allowing him to open his parachute. If it had been his real right leg, he would probably have been pulled down with the aircraft. He landed in St. Omer, France, where he was captured by the Germans and taken to a hospital. The Germans found his right artificial leg and repaired it for him. Later, a spare leg was parachuted into St. Omer by the R.A.F.

As soon as he could walk, Bader formed a rope out of knotted bedsheets and escaped from the hospital with the aid of one of the nurses. Unfortunately, another nurse informed on the one who had helped him, and he was recaptured. He was moved to a prison camp where he made another escape attempt; eventually, after trying to escape a third and fourth time, he was transferred to the maximum security prison at Colditz. After three and a half years as prisoner of war, he was liberated. When he returned home, he was promoted to Group Captain.

In September 1945, Bader was asked to plan and lead the first Battle of Britain fly-past over London to celebrate the peace and to commemorate the fifth anniversary of the Battle of Britain. In 1956, the Queen awarded him a Commander of the British Empire (CBE) in recognition of his services. In 1976, he was knighted by the Queen. Douglas Bader rebounded from his injuries to achieve his goals and use his talents to defend his country.

REGINALD J. MITCHELL (1895-1937) Designer of the Supermarine Spitfire

"When things go wrong, as they sometimes will,
    When the road you're trudging seems all uphill,
    . . . When care is pressing you down a bit,
    Rest, if you must—but don't you quit.
    . . . Often the goal is nearer than
    It seems to a faint and faltering man,
    Often the struggler has given up
    When he might have captured the victor's cup."

Edgar A. Guest

Reginald Joseph Mitchell was born on May 20, 1895, in the English village of Talke, Staffordshire. His father was a teacher who later became a school headmaster. At the age of seventeen, Mitchell was apprenticed to Kerr, Stewart, and Company locomotive works at Stoke-on-Trent. He studied mechanics and mathematics as part of his engineering studies in addition to studying drafting in night school. In 1917, he accepted the position of assistant to the chief engineer and designer at the Supermarine Aviation works near Southampton. Mitchell was married in 1918 and settled in Southampton. In 1920, he was promoted to chief engineer and designer at Supermarine. At the time, most of his projects involved the design of large military flying boats such as the Martlesham Amphibian, for which he won a government prize.

"RJ" Mitchell established his reputation as an aircraft designer by creating aircraft to compete in the Schneider international seaplane races from 1922 to 1931. The Schneider Trophy race was the world's major aeronautical event. Lieutenant James Doolittle of the U.S. Army was the winner of the race in Baltimore in 1925; he flew a Curtiss biplane on twin floats at an average speed of 232.57 miles per hour. Britain won the Schneider race in 1929 and again in 1930. Britain would become the permanent holder of the Schneider cup with a win in 1931.

Due to the worldwide depression in the 1930s, government expenditures were significantly reduced. Prime Minister Ramsay MacDonald decided not to finance an entry in the 1931 Schneider cup race. The British public protested strongly. In January 1931, Lady Houston, the wealthy widow of a shipping magnate, contributed £100,000 to finance an entry in the 1931 race. The Supermarine S.6B, winner of the 1931 Schneider Trophy, was an early prototype of the Spitfire fighter aircraft. Thus a private citizen, Lady Houston, was a contributor to the development effort of one of the high-performance fighter aircraft of World War II.

All of the major design criteria for the evolving Spitfire had been defined by the summer of 1935. Changes to the design incorporated into the final prototype, which was built in the fall of 1935, included a thinner, elliptically-shaped wing, ducted radiator cooling, and eight machine guns instead of the four machine guns originally specified.

Mitchell was appointed chief designer but unfortunately was able to spend only limited time on the project. In 1933, "RJ" was diagnosed as having cancer and underwent an operation. If he had followed his doctor's advice and either taken an extended leave of absence or reduced his efforts, he might have been cured of cancer, or at least have extended his life. However, he continued to drive himself to develop the Spitfire prototype.

Mitchell was motivated by a visit to Germany in 1934, where he observed the production of military hardware by the Nazis. He was familiar with the Dornier, Heinkel, and Junkers airplanes, and he knew about the Bayerische Flugzeugwerke BF 109 fighter (the ME 109), which was designed by Willie Messerschmitt. Mitchell strongly believed that Britain must respond to the German threat and that Britain needed reliable, high-performance fighters that could be produced in quantity. He drove himself to ensure that his greatest design effort, the Spitfire, would be ready in time to defend England against a German attack.

On March 5, 1936, Spitfire prototype K5054 flew for the first time; it was piloted by chief test pilot J. "Mutt" Summers from the Eastleigh Airport in Hampshire. Mitchell watched his airplane perform. He knew that his perseverance had been rewarded, and that he had accomplished what he had set out to do—to develop a revolutionary high-performance fighter for which a critical need existed. Having a high-performance aircraft was crucial for England in the late 1930s, when war was increasingly seen as unavoidable.

The two principal British fighter aircraft in World War II were the Spitfire and the Hawker Hurricane, which was designed by Sidney Camm. The Hurricane was actually a monoplane version of the Hawker Fury biplane that Camm had designed earlier. The Hurricane was more of a traditional aircraft in that it was built of wood and fabric and stiffened by tubular metal framework. Surprisingly, the fabric-covered fuselage survived cannon shells better than the metal-skinned Spitfire.

The Hurricane was a design halfway between the biplanes of the 1930s and the aircraft design of the 1940s, such as the Spitfire. In the Battle of Britain, the Hurricanes actually downed more German aircraft than the Spitfires, because of the way they were deployed. The faster Spitfires were assigned to engage the German fighters escorting their bombers. The Hurricanes, although slower than the Spitfires, provided an excellent gun platform for attacking the German bombers.

The ME 109 was the leading German fighter; it had similar flight characteristics to the Spitfire. The ME 109 had a tighter turning radius than the Spitfire, but the pilots rarely used this advantage because the ME 109's wings weren't strong enough to withstand the stress of tight turns. The visibility provided by the Spitfire's bubble canopy was superior to the ME 109, whose view to the rear was blocked by the fuselage. Also, the Spitfire pilot had the advantage of armor plate behind his seat. Mitchell never fully regained his strength after his operation in 1933. His condition worsened in early 1937, and his wife, Florence, accompanied him on a visit to a specialist in Austria; however, his cancer was too advanced to operate again. He returned to Southampton, where he died at his home in June 1937 at the age of forty-two.

The importance of Mitchell's design efforts should not be underestimated. A high-performance fighter, such as the Spitfire, was critically needed in the Battle of Britain to counter Germany's high-performance ME 109. By winning the Battle of Britain, England prevented Hitler's planned invasion across the English channel, and Hitler turned his attention to Russia.

Mitchell's drive in pushing the development of the Spitfire while in failing health resulted in an important contribution to Britain's war effort. It is virtually certain that Mitchell would have received a knighthood for his design efforts had he lived, as Sir Sidney Camm did for his design of the Hawker Hurricane.

ULYSSES S. GRANT (1822-1885) Victor of the Battle of Vicksburg

"Everyone has superstitions. One of mine has always been when I started to go anywhere, or to do anything, never to turn back or to stop until the thing intended is accomplished."

Ulysses S. Grant

The Battle of Vicksburg was a major turning point in the U.S. Civil War and one of Grant's notable victories. In the spring of 1862, the U.S. Navy won victories at Memphis and New Orleans, leaving Vicksburg as the last major obstacle on the Mississippi River. Vicksburg was a railroad center, but a lesser one than Memphis. To reach the Confederate fort at Vicksburg, commanded by General John Pemberton, Grant had to overcome many natural obstacles.

The town of Vicksburg is located high on a bluff 200 feet above the Mississippi River. Grant's goal was to reach the high ground east of the river, so he could attack Pemberton's army. Bayous, swamps, and thickets blocked his passage in the east and north, and a high, flood-swollen Mississippi blocked him in the west. The Confederate army held several strong points south of Vicksburg.

The Vicksburg campaign began on November 2, 1862, when Grant sent a dispatch to his superior, General Halleck, notifying him of his movement to Grand Junction, south of Vicksburg. Grant preferred moving back to Memphis and repairing the railway southward from Memphis to use in moving his army to Vicksburg. However, the war wasn't going well for the North in 1862, and that movement would be perceived as a retreat. Therefore, in Grant's words, "There was nothing left to be done but to go forward to a decisive victory." Unfortunately, the winter of 1862-63 was marked by heavy rains and continual high water along the lower section of the Mississippi River. Grant's first attack on Pemberton's army was ill-fated. Grant sent General Sherman north along the Yazoo River, which flows into the Mississippi north of Vicksburg. Sherman assembled his 32,000 men at Chickasaw Bluffs, one of the few places where it was possible to maneuver an army along the Yazoo's swamps and thickets.

Grant planned to approach from the east as part of a coordinated attack. However, when Grant was informed that the Confederate

General Van Dorn had destroyed the Union supply base at Holly Springs in his rear, he was forced to retreat. Communications were poor, and Sherman didn't know about this retreat; he attacked as planned and incurred significant casualties. The plan was a poor one since Grant and Sherman were too far apart to coordinate their movements effectively, and many natural barriers restricted their mobility.

The second attempt to reach Pemberton's army was made north of Vicksburg, where a tributary of the Yazoo River was joined to the Mississippi by a waterway called the Yazoo Pass. The State of Mississippi had built a strong levee across the waterway to reduce the risk of flooding the plantations to the south along the Yazoo River. Grant breached the levee to provide a channel from the Mississippi to the Yazoo that would allow gunboats to approach Vicksburg by the back door. However, the Union gunboats encountered the Confederate Fort Pemberton on high ground in their path. This Union attempt also failed. Next, Admiral Porter and his gunboats were ordered to pass through Steele's Bayou to enter the Mississippi River north of Vicksburg. Steele's Bayou emptied into the Yazoo River between Haines Bluff north of Vicksburg and the Yazoo's confluence with the Mississippi. Steele's bayou was narrow and lined with a heavy growth of trees that overhung the bayou and the adjoining Deer Creek and Big Sunflower River.

The Confederates had felled many trees in front of the gunboats and had positioned about 4,000 sharpshooters to stop the boats. The sharpshooters were successful. Admiral Porter almost blew up his boats to prevent them from falling into Confederate hands, but he was finally rescued by General Sherman.

Another scheme involved cutting a canal across a hairpin turn in the Mississippi River west of Vicksburg to allow the gunboats to get below Vicksburg without having to run the gauntlet of the town's batteries; the gunboats would not be able to defend themselves because their guns couldn't be elevated high enough. General Williams and his men came up from New Orleans to dig the canal. They planned to start digging the canal and then let the power of the river's waters enlarge it and make it suitable for navigation. The canal was almost finished when the retaining dam at the head of the canal burst prematurely, creating a sea of mud.

Grant planned to use a part of the old Mississippi River bed called Lake Providence, located well south of Vicksburg. He had little hope for this plan, but he wanted to keep his men busy. Lake Providence flows out through two treacherous bayous, Bayou Baxter and Bayou Macon, which in turn drain to rivers, including the Red River, that empty into the Mississippi River near Port Hudson.

However, Port Hudson was in enemy hands. The concentration of Confederates in the area, in addition to the natural obstacle of decades of fallen trees, caused the abandonment of this alternative. The press was relentless in complaining about the delays that Grant had encountered. Reports were so negative that President Lincoln sent Assistant Secretary of War Charles Dana to travel with Grant's army as an observer. Dana became a strong supporter of Grant.

Rumors of Grant's drinking stayed with him throughout the Civil War. Lincoln's supposed response to stories of Grant's heavy drinking has never been verified. According to the story, however, President Lincoln asked critics of Grant's drinking to find out what brand of whiskey Grant drank, so that he could send a barrel to the other Union generals—because "he fights." Eventually, Admiral Porter's gunboats and steamers were able to run past Vicksburg's guns and meet Grant's army at Bruinsburg to ferry it across the Mississippi River. Grant had intended to cross the river at Grand Gulf, which was heavily defended, but a visitor to Grant's camp advised them to cross at Bruinsburg. Finally, Grant was able to say, "I was on high ground on the same side of the river with the enemy."

Grant advanced on Vicksburg before Confederate General Joseph E. Johnston could join forces with General Pemberton. Pemberton wouldn't surrender, and a long siege ensued. Finally, on July 3, 1863, with food and supplies running critically low, Pemberton surrendered. Grant captured 32,000 men.

Grant's resilience and the experience he had gained in logistics in the Mexican War served him well. After this victory, Grant became a Major General in the regular army and was in position to become Lieutenant General, commanding general of all Union forces. Grant took eight months to win the Battle of Vicksburg. It was not the way he won the battle or how long it took that was noted, but his having the staying power to win a major victory. He was a leader; "he fights."

JOHN PAUL JONES (1747-1782) Victor Over the HMS Serapis

"The conditions of conquest are always easy. We have but to toil
awhile, endure awhile, believe always, and never turn back."

William Gilmore Simms

In September 1779, during the Revolutionary War, American
Commodore John Paul Jones's squadron patrolled the Yorkshire
coast of England. His crew, which included Arabs, Malays,
Maltese, and Portuguese, had signed up to fight. He had American
officers, but his ship had been commissioned in France, and he had
not been permitted to recruit French sailors. Benjamin Franklin, the
U.S. Minister to France, had helped to obtain the ships for
Commodore Jones's squadron. The East Indiaman *Duras* was
renamed *Bonhomme Richard* in honor of Franklin's *Poor Richard's
Almanac*.

Jones raided Newcastle-on-Tyne to intercept the winter's supply
of coal en route to London. He had four ships: his flagship,
Bonhomme Richard, with forty worn-out guns that had been
scrapped by the French Navy, the frigate *Alliance*, the frigate
Pallas, and the cutter *Vengeance*.

While sailing off Flambough Head on September 23, 1779,
Jones saw a fleet of forty-one sails rounding the Head and
approaching his small squadron. The English pilot on the *Richard*,
who had come aboard thinking she was a Royal Navy ship, told
Jones that this Baltic convoy was escorted by the frigate *Serapis*
(44 guns) and the sloop of war *Countess of Scarborough* (20 guns).

The *HMS Serapis*, commanded by Captain Richard Pearson,
Royal Navy, was rated at 44 guns but actually had 50: 20 eighteen-
pounders on the lower gun deck (vs. *Richard's* 6 eighteen-
pounders), 20 nine-pounders on the upper gun deck (vs. *Richard's*
28 twelve-pounders), and 10 six-pounders on the quarterdeck (vs.
Richard's 6 nine-pounders). Captain Pearson knew that Jones's
squadron was in the area; the bailiffs of Scarborough had sent out
a boat to warn him of the danger.

At 6:00 p.m., Jones made the signal, "Form line of battle," but
the other captains in his squadron ignored it. *Alliance* dropped

back, leaving *Richard* to engage *Serapis*; *Pallas* veered off but later returned and engaged the *Countess of Scarborough*, and *Vengeance* sailed away and looked on from a distance. At 6:30 p.m., *Richard* rounded the port quarter of *Serapis*, and the ships sailed west on the port tack alongside each other.

Captain Pearson asked the *Richard* to identify herself. Jones directed Master Stacey to respond that they were the *Princess Royal*. Pearson asked where they were from. Jones, who was flying the British flag, hesitated in responding. Pearson demanded a response; otherwise he would commence firing. Jones replaced his British colors with the American ensign and commanded his starboard batteries to fire. Simultaneously, Pearson ordered his batteries to fire. Two of Jones's old eighteen-pounders burst when they were fired, destroying the battery as well as the deck above the guns and killing many men.

Each captain attempted to place his ship across the other's bow or stern to use a raking pattern of fire. Pearson, having the faster ship, was more successful in maneuvering. After absorbing several broadsides, Jones realized that he would lose a broadside-to-broadside duel. His only hope was to grapple and board. He dropped astern of the *Serapis*, ran up on her starboard side and attempted to board. His men were repulsed. Next, Pearson tried to place his ship across *Richard's* bow to rake her. He failed, but the relative position of the two ships allowed Jones to run *Richard's* bow into the stern of *Serapis*. Captain Pearson asked Jones if his ship had surrendered. Jones responded with his famous reply, "I have not yet begun to fight."

Jones was unable to bring any of his cannon to bear on the *Serapis*. He tried to get clear and position the *Richard* across the bow of *Serapis*; he almost succeeded. However, the tip of the bowsprit of the *Serapis* became entangled in the support rigging of the *Richard's* mizzen mast. The wind caused both ships to swing around, causing the fluke of *Serapis's* starboard anchor to pierce the bulwarks of the starboard quarter of the *Richard*. The resulting side by side linkage of the two ships was exactly what Jones wanted.

Captain Pearson tried valiantly to separate the two ships to take advantage of his ship's superior fire power. He ordered *Richard's* grappling hooks to be thrown back or their lines cut. However, twenty French Marines commanded by de Chamillard were positioned on the poop deck of the *Richard* and picked off any *Serapis* hands who attempted this. Captain Pearson also tried dropping his anchor, hoping that the tide and the wind would force the ships apart. This, too, was unsuccessful. The ships were so close that their gun muzzles were touching. The starboard gun ports on the *Serapis*, which had been closed early in the battle when the port guns were firing, couldn't be opened and had to be shot open. *Richard's* gunners had to push their staves into *Serapis's* gun ports to load and to ram their charges into their own gun barrels.

Sails on both ships were on fire on several occasions. Crews stopped the battle to repair damage. By 8:30 p.m., the *Richard* was in bad shape. Jones couldn't use his eighteen-pounders for fear that they would blow up, and his main battery of twelve-pounders had been blasted by *Serapis's* two decks of eighteen-pounders. The only cannons that Jones could bring to bear were three of the six nine-pounders on the quarterdeck. He helped to move one of these to the port side and fired it himself. Jones had the advantage of the excellent marksmanship of the French Marines and of the gunners posted on his masts.

While the two antagonists remained locked together in battle, the *Pallas* continued to engage the *Countess of Scarborough*. On the other hand, Captain Landais in the *Alliance* proved to be a disloyal member of Jones's squadron. When the *Serapis* and the *Richard* became linked together, Landais sailed by and raked the *Richard*, killing two men and driving others from their battle stations. About two hours later, he fired a broadside into the port quarter of the *Richard* that included shots below the water line. His third broadside into the *Richard* took a greater toll when he fired into the forecastle, where men who had been driven from their battle stations had gathered. This time he caused many casualties and several fatalities, including a chief petty officer.

In later testimony, Landais claimed that his broadsides forced Captain Pearson to strike his colors and surrender. Of course, it was to Captain Pearson's advantage to claim that he was beaten by two frigates, not one. These attacks on the *Richard* by a member of her own squadron were not accidental. The battle scene was illuminated by a nearly full moon, and the *Richard* had her night recognition signals burning. Also, the upper decks of the *Richard* were painted black; the topsides of the *Serapis* were painted yellow. After the battle, Landais told a French colonel that he intended to help the *Serapis* sink the *Richard* and then to board and capture the *Serapis,* thus emerging as the hero of the battle.

Jones continued personally to fire one of the remaining nine-pounders on his quarterdeck since Purser Mease, the officer in charge of the battery of nine-pounders, had received a bad head wound. At one point, a sailor came up to Jones and pleaded with him to lower his colors. Jones responded that he would never strike and went back to firing the nine-pounder. Eventually, Jones's sharpshooters on deck and in the tops picked off so many of the *Serapis's* gunners that the boys bringing up powder cartridges from the magazines could find no one to give them to. They just left the cartridges on the deck.

William Hamilton, a Scottish seaman in Jones's crew, carried a basket of hand grenades up to a yardarm that was directly over an open hatch on the *Serapis*. He dropped a grenade through the hatch, exploding the powder cartridges that the boy "powder monkeys" had left lying on deck. Twenty men were killed, and many were badly burned. Jones loaded his three remaining nine-pounders with double shot to fire at the mainmast of the *Serapis*.

Captain Pearson seriously considered surrendering after the explosion. On the *Richard*, three petty officers decided that the *Richard* would sink if she didn't strike. One of them, Chief Gunner Henry Gardner, ran aft to haul down the ensign to surrender, but found that the flagstaff with the ensign had been shot away. He pleaded with Jones to surrender.

Captain Pearson heard Gardner's pleas and asked Jones if he was asking for quarter. Jones answered, "No sir, I haven't as yet thought of it, but I'm determined to make you strike." Captain Pearson responding by ordering "Boarders away." However, his boarders were repulsed; they returned to the *Serapis* immediately.

At 10:00 p.m., *Richard's* Master at Arms released about one hundred men in the hold from ships that had been captured earlier. They were told to man the pumps if they wanted to survive. One of the prisoners, the Master of the prize ship *Union*, escaped through an open gun port on the *Serapis*. He told Captain Pearson that the *Richard* had five feet of water in her hold and was sinking.

The situation was grim. The *Richard* had sporadic fires in multiple locations and holes below the water line. Jones's officers were weary; his chief petty officers were asking for quarter. He had only three nine-pounders in service and was receiving fire from four eighteen-pounders into his side.

At 10:30 p.m., Jones's double-loaded shot brought down the mainmast of the *Serapis*. Captain Pearson surrendered. He personally had to tear down the ensign, which was nailed to its staff; everyone around him was either dead or wounded. Lieutenant Dale of the *Richard* went aboard the *Serapis* to take possession and to escort Captain Pearson to the *Richard* to introduce him to Commodore Jones. Captain Pearson presented his sword to Jones, who returned it with comments on the gallantry of the *Serapis's* defenders. Jones invited the defeated captain to his cabin for a ceremonial glass of wine.

The battle had lasted about four hours. The *Richard* was in terrible condition. Her transom was almost entirely shot away, and her quarterdeck was about to fall into the gunroom below it. Her upper decks had gaping holes, and the timbers aft of the mainmast on her lower deck were "mangled beyond my power of description," according to Jones.

Commodore John Paul Jones's determination and perseverance in not giving up, when all indications suggested it, were the significant factors in this battle. He certainly displayed his leadership qualities in achieving victory by rebounding from overwhelming odds.

CHAPTER 7

ORGANIZERS / PLANNERS

"There's no defeat, in truth, save from within; unless you're beaten there, you're bound to win."

Henry Austen, *Perseverance Conquers All*

STEVE JOBS (1955-2011) Founder of Apple Computer Corporation

"His tenacity is what makes him great. Several years after leaving Steve's employ, Susan Barnes conducted a study about family run businesses. She found that the key to success was 'pure staying power, persistence, continually believing in something, doggedness to get things done, and continual optimism.' That was a good description of Steve Jobs. Steve was beaten down many times but 'he kept getting off the mat,' she says."

Alan Deutschman, *The Second Coming of Steve Jobs*

Steve Jobs was one of the first to envision that people would buy a computer for their home for business tasks or educational applications for themselves or their children. Furthermore, he foresaw the need to link the home with a "nationwide communications network," the Internet.

Jobs became interested in electronics at the age of 10. Many Hewlett-Packard engineers lived in his neighborhood in Mountain View, California, and he was intrigued with many electronics projects assembled in neighborhood garages. One neighbor instructed Jobs in electronics and enrolled him in the Hewlett-Packard Explorer Club, where he learned about calculators, diodes, holograms, and lasers. Jobs's first project for the Explorer Club was building a frequency counter. He needed parts and obtained them with the assertiveness for which he became known. He looked up Bill Hewlett in the Palo Alto phone book. Hewlett answered the phone and talked with Jobs for 20 minutes. He not only gave Jobs the parts he needed but also gave him a summer job at Hewlett-Packard assembling frequency counters. Later, when Jobs needed another part, he called the Burroughs Corporation in Detroit collect, and asked them to donate it.

Jobs's future partner, Steve Wozniak, was only 19 when he met Jobs, but his knowledge of electronics was advanced for his age. He had won prizes in local electronics fairs against tough competition. Wozniak dropped out of Berkeley during his junior year and accepted a position as an engineer in Hewlett-Packard's calculator division. He became a regular attendee at meetings of the

Homebrew Computer Club, a gathering place for computer hobbyists, engineers, programmers, and suppliers.

Attendance at club meetings increased exponentially after the January 1975 issue of *Popular Electronics* was circulated. It included an article about the Altair 8800 computer kit produced by MITS in Albuquerque, New Mexico. The Altair central processing unit used an Intel 8080 microprocessor. The Altair was a collection of parts with meager documentation and little input / output capability. Orders from hobbyists for this first mail-order computer overwhelmed MITS. BASIC programming language for the Intel 8080 was developed by Bill Gates and Paul Allen, who later founded Microsoft Corporation.

Wozniak designed his own computer. He took his computer to meetings of the Homebrew Computer Club, but they were not interested in it because it was not based on the integrated circuit used in the Altair. He offered to give away circuit diagrams of his computer to club members, but Jobs suggested that they sell them. Better yet, Jobs suggested that they make the circuit-board computers and sell them. On April 1, 1976, Jobs and Wozniak formed a partnership called Apple Computer to make and sell computers. Jobs developed a reputation as a tough negotiator. He was called "the rejector," because he usually turned down early designs and estimates.

Jobs met an electronics retailer at a Homebrew Club meeting who offered to buy 50 circuit-board computers, called Apple I. Apple Computer needed start-up capital to build them. Jobs's loan requests were turned down by banks and by his previous employer at an electronics warehouse store.

Finally, Jobs found a supplier of electronics parts in Palo Alto who would sell them parts on credit with no interest if they paid within 30 days. When Wozniak designed the next generation computer, Jobs contracted out the insertion of components into circuit boards. The company he chose did not want the work, but Jobs succeeded with his assertive "I'm not going to leave here until you agree" approach.

Until this time in his life, Jobs had been an individual in search of a cause. In promoting the personal computer, he had found his cause. He had a knack for convincing talented people to undertake projects for Apple.

One of Jobs's important early decisions was his choice of an advertising / public relations firm. He was referred to the Regis McKenna Agency. McKenna turned him down. Again Jobs asserted himself; he called McKenna three or four times a day until he agreed to take on Apple as a client.

The fledgling enterprise needed capital to expand. Mike Markkula was recommended as the venture capitalist. Markkula offered to devote four years to Apple and provide money to develop and manufacture the Apple II in return for a one-third ownership in the company. On January 3, 1977, Apple Computer Corporation was incorporated.

Apple II, because of Wozniak's original design and Jobs's efforts as "rejector," was a work of art. It was easy to produce and it looked good when the cover was raised. Jobs negotiated bargain-basement prices for Apple's components.

In early 1977, Apple II was demonstrated in an attention-gathering booth at a computer fair in San Francisco. Thirteen thousand attendees were captivated by Apple II, and 300 orders were placed. Markkula worked hard to obtain additional capital to fuel Apple's growth. He was amazingly successful.

Apple's next product was an enhanced Apple II, Apple III. In addition to enhancements, the company provided improvements that customers and dealers had requested. Sales of Apple III were fewer than forecasted. Fortunately, sales of Apple II, which had little competition in 1979, were strong.

Following Apple III's limited success, Jobs needed a new goal. He sought a partner; he considered IBM and Xerox despite the fact that Apple considered IBM the enemy.

Xerox had invested in Apple's second private investment placement. Jobs contacted the Xerox Development Corporation, the company's venture capital unit, and offered to let them invest in Apple if they would give him a tour of their Palo Alto Research Center (PARC). PARC had a talented staff of computer scientists who had made many breakthroughs that Xerox had failed to exploit. Xerox purchased 100,000 shares of Apple at $10.00 and opened their doors to Jobs. The 25-year-old entrepreneur had gotten his way again.

Larry Tesler of PARC demonstrated their Alto personal computer to Jobs and seven Apple developers, who were enthusiastic when they saw the Alto's potential. User interaction with the Alto made innovative use of icons, menus (action lists), partitions of the screen (windows), and a "mouse." Jobs was moved by what he saw. He shouted: "Why aren't you doing anything with this? This is the greatest thing! This is revolutionary!" After the demonstration, Jobs hired Tesler to work for Apple. Later, Alan Kay, one of PARC's principal computer science visionaries, joined Apple and eventually became an Apple Fellow.

In August 1980, Markkula reorganized Apple into three divisions. Jobs had hoped to be given line authority of a division; instead, he was named Chairman of the Board. On December 12, 1980, Apple Computer Corporation went public. Apple's shares sold out within the first hour.

In 1981, Wozniak crashed his Beechcraft Bonanza light plane and underwent a long recuperation period. He did not return to Apple full time. Jobs and Wozniak made significant contributions to the computer industry. They succeeded where large corporations failed; they pioneered the personal computer revolution. In 1985, President Reagan awarded National Technology Medals to Jobs and Wozniak at the White House.

Without line responsibility in the reorganization of Apple, Jobs was again without a project. He needed a subject for his evangelism. The Macintosh personal computer was the next project to provide an outlet for his zeal. Macintosh was in the R & D phase. Developers planned a "luggable" machine that would be easy to use and would sell for about $1,000. Hardware and software designers would work together from the beginning, and software would be offered as part of the purchase price of the machine. Jobs took over the project and brought in developers from the successful Apple II. Jobs headed the Macintosh Division when it was formed.

Markkula was in a difficult position when his four-year arrangement with Apple was almost over. He looked outside Apple for a new president. He wanted John Sculley, President of Pepsi-Cola USA, who had taken market share from Coca-Cola. Initially, Sculley was not interested in joining Apple. Jobs flew to New York City and courted Sculley. After many long conversations about the future of Apple, Jobs asked Sculley if he intended to sell sugar water to children for the rest of his life when he could be doing something important with personal computers.

Sculley accepted the presidency of Apple and spent many hours learning the technology. Within his first year on the job, he realized that cuts would have to be made. Apple II was carrying the company. He streamlined the organizational structure and eliminated 1,200 jobs to keep the company profitable. Jobs retained his position as manager of the Macintosh Division in addition to serving as Chairman of the Board. Sculley redirected the company from producing most of its own software to increased reliance on outside software developers.

The first disagreements between Jobs and Sculley occurred in 1983. By 1984, when Macintosh sales were considerably below Jobs's estimates, the rift was obvious to everyone. Apple lowered the price of Macintosh, but sales continued to be disappointing. At the Board meeting on April 11, 1985, Sculley dismissed Jobs as manager of the Macintosh Division. Jobs then attempted to have Sculley removed as president and CEO. However, he misjudged Sculley's support from the Board of Directors. Finally, their disagreements became so disruptive that the Board suggested that Sculley force Jobs out of the company.

Jobs founded NeXT, a computer company that produced an expensive computer for academic users. Tim Berners-Lee invented the World Wide Web on a NeXT computer. Nevertheless, it had a limited market, so NeXT concentrated on software development. Jobs then founded Pixar, which produced computer-automated cartoons, such as the highly profitable *Toy Story*.

In 1996, Apple bought NeXT to use its software as the foundation for the next-generation MAC operating system. NeXT software became the basis for all future Apple operating systems. Jobs came with the purchase of NeXT. In 1997, Apple's sales and earnings plummeted, and Jobs was appointed interim CEO and led Apple's rebound. He became CEO in 2000.

In 2001, Apple introduced the iPod and became a consumer electronics company and the major company in the media-player market. In 2007, Jobs announced the iPhone, a powerful pocket-sized personal computer, which incorporated a new touch screen and interface and dominated the smart phone market. The iPad, a highly successful tablet computer, was introduced by Apple in 2010.

Jobs was diagnosed in 2004 with a rare form of pancreatic cancer that could be controlled. He underwent surgery and returned to work.

In 2005, Jobs gave the commencement address at Stanford University. He said, "Your time is limited, so don't waste it living someone else's life. Don't be trapped by dogma, which is living with the results of someone else's thinking. Don't let the noise of others' opinions drown out your own inner voice. And most important, have the courage to follow your heart and intuition. They somehow already know what you truly want to become. Everything else is secondary."

In 2009, Jobs received a liver transplant and was able to continue his work until August 24, 2011, when he turned over his CEO responsibilities to Tim Cook, the Chief Operating Officer. Jobs died from complications of pancreatic cancer on October 5, 2011.

In 2011, Apple's market capitalization exceeded that of ExxonMobil, making it the world's most valuable company. Jobs revitalized six industries: personal computers, animated movies, music, telephones, tablet computing, and digital publishing. He also had a significant impact on retailing with the establishment of the Apple retail stores.

Jobs, who considered himself an artist, had a passion for design. He combined art, technology, and ease of use in his products. Jobs did no market research. He did not ask customers what they wanted; rather, he gave them what he thought they should have.

Steve Jobs was the greatest business executive of the late twentieth and early twenty-first centuries. It is thought that historians will rank him with Henry Ford and Thomas Edison.

AL NEUHARTH (1924-2013) Creator of *USA Today*

"[Potential] headlines about the end of the world:
Wall Street Journal: STOCK EXCHANGE HALTS TRADING AS
  WORLD ENDS.
New York Times: END OF WORLD HITS THIRD WORLD
  HARDEST.
Washington Post: WORLD ENDS; MAY AFFECT ELECTIONS,
  SOURCES SAY.
USA Today: WE'RE GONE . . . STATE-BY-STATE DEMISE
  ON 6A. FINAL SCORES ON 8C."

John Quinn, in a speech to the National Press Foundation

Al Neuharth, while chief executive officer of the Gannett Corporation, was willing to innovate and to create new products. He paid great attention to detail and was a strong promoter of his visions. When *USA Today* losses continued at $10 million a month, he convinced employees to work harder, work leaner, and provide a higher quality paper at a lower cost. Neuharth's strongest qualities in creating a new national newspaper were his assertiveness, his leadership, and his ability to implement a vision.

Al Neuharth, the younger of two sons of Daniel and Christina Neuharth, was born in Eureka, South Dakota, in 1924. Daniel Neuharth farmed eighty acres until he injured his leg in a farm accident, developed tuberculosis, and died in 1926. Christina took in laundry and sewing and waited on tables to support the family. Her motto was "do a little bit more tomorrow than you did today, a little better next year than you did this year."

At the age of eleven, Neuharth delivered the *Minneapolis Tribune* and, at thirteen, he worked after school in the composing room of the *Alpena Journal*. In 1942, he graduated from high school and enrolled briefly at Northern State Teachers' College before enlisting in the U.S. Army. He served as a combat infantryman in World War II, won a Bronze Star, and earned sergeant's stripes.

In 1946, Neuharth returned home and enrolled at the University of South Dakota on the G. I. Bill. He was a sports announcer for the college radio station before shifting to the college newspaper, *The*

Volante, and becoming its editor. In 1950, he was elected to Phi Beta Kappa, graduated from the University of South Dakota, and became a reporter for Associated Press.

In 1952, with $50,000 from the sale of shares, Neuharth and a friend started *SoDak Sports*, a statewide sports weekly modeled on the national *Sporting News*. Within a year, circulation had increased to 18,000, but sales of advertising space were sluggish. Their few advertisers began to shift to television commercials.

In 1954, Neuharth and his partner tried unsuccessfully to sell their weekly; they declared bankruptcy, and their creditors received less than thirty-five cents on the dollar. Neuharth looked upon it as a learning experience. Their biggest error was the lack of a business plan. They had not projected sales revenue or advertising revenue or anticipated profit and loss. It was a mistake that Neuharth would not make again.

Neuharth accepted a job as a reporter for the *Miami Herald*. He wrote a series of articles about mail order scams and was at the right place at the right time on some fast-breaking stories. His career took off, and he was given an assignment with the *Herald's* Washington bureau. In 1959, he was promoted to assistant managing editor of the *Herald* and was chosen to open its Brevard County bureau to cover the news from the Cape Canaveral Space Center.

In the following year, Neuharth was appointed assistant to the executive editor of the *Detroit Free Press*. He worked in both the news and business operations. His performance was noticed both inside Knight Newspapers and outside of it. In 1963, he accepted a position with Gannett Newspapers as general manager of their Rochester, New York, newspapers: the *Democrat and Chronicle* and the *Times-Union*. He was viewed as the heir apparent to Paul Miller, chief executive officer of Gannett Newspapers.

Neuharth suggested to Miller that Gannett start a daily newspaper in Brevard County, Florida, that would serve the Cape Canaveral area. Miller had tried unsuccessfully to buy a small Florida daily as a nucleus for expansion; he was receptive to Neuharth's suggestion even though it bucked the national trend of fewer daily newspapers.

Neuharth bought the *Cocoa Tribune* for $1.9 million, but, instead of revamping it, decided to start a new paper with a fresh format. He called it *Today: Florida's Space Age Newspaper*, and supplemented the small staff with "loaners" from other Gannett newspapers.

Neuharth did not repeat the two mistakes he had made in starting *SoDak Sports*. First, he authorized the preparation of a comprehensive business plan; second, he knew that he had sufficient funds to pay for the start-up. Neuharth was a hands-on manager, who was on-site in Cocoa functioning as the managing editor.

Neuharth organized the new paper into three distinct sections: News, Business, and Sports. The comics section was printed in color, a *Today* innovation. *Today* was profitable in twenty-eight months, which was due mainly to the boldness, innovation, and determination of Neuharth.

In 1973, Neuharth became chief executive officer of Gannett Newspapers and added the title of chairman upon the retirement of Paul Miller in 1978. Neuharth had considered the idea of a national newspaper for ten years; finally, he decided to proceed with the idea for both professional and personal reasons. He thought that the newspaper journalism profession could do a better job than it was doing, and, personally, he needed new worlds to conquer.

Improvements in satellite communications helped to make the idea achievable. Neuharth's lack of modesty was apparent in his goal: "We'll reinvent the newspaper." He wanted to create a newspaper so captivating that it would attract millions of readers, including many who currently read no newspaper. He also wanted to innovate the design and content of the new paper to "pull the rest of the industry into the twenty-first century, albeit kicking and screaming."

By late 1979, Gannett had newspapers across the United States, including many in the major city markets. In areas where Gannett did not own a printing plant, they could make contract printing arrangements. Neuharth considered three start-up possibilities:

- a national sports daily, similar to the *Sporting News* and *Sports Illustrated*
- a daily and / or Sunday supplement for the Gannett community newspapers with national news and advertising
- a national general-interest daily newspaper

He sought the opinion of three key Gannett managers: John Quinn, the chief news executive; Jack Heselden, president of the newspaper division; and Douglas McCorkindale, the chief financial and legal officer. At the year-end board of directors' meeting, Neuharth announced that he was going to set aside $1 million in 1980 to "study what's new in newspapers and television and especially whether we can harness the satellite to deliver more news to more people in more ways."

The R & D effort was called Project NN. NN meant "National Newspaper" but Neuharth promoted the idea outside of Gannett that it stood for "New Newspapers." Project NN soon became known outside of the company as "Neuharth's Nonsense." A five-person project team was assembled in Florida. Neuharth chose Vince Spezzano, the veteran publisher of *Today* in Florida, as coordinator of the team.

Neuharth courted the board of directors' support for his project and kept them informed. In October 1980, the Project NN report was presented to the board, and an additional $3.5 million was budgeted for planning and prototypes in 1981. In August 1981, research conducted by Lou Harris and Associates and Simmons Market Research Bureau was presented to the board, and the prototypes were reviewed. In December 1981, the board of directors voted to launch *USA Today* by a unanimous 12-0 vote, even though the finance organization of Gannett counseled against going ahead. The next phase was called GANSAT, Gannett Satellite Information Network. Neuharth personally worked on the news product and circulation planning; he continued to be a hands-on manager. John Quinn, the chief news executive, worked virtually full-time on prototype plans.

The team decided that *USA Today* must be different, both in appearance and in content. The early goals were:four highly organized sections, emphasis on color, easy-to-read stories, frequent use of charts and graphics, news from all fifty States, and a concentration on sports, TV, and weather. Neuharth used "intrapreneurship" on *USA Today* by obtaining "loaners" from the other Gannett papers. These loaners were gone from their parent newspapers for an average of four months and weren't replaced. It provided a broadening experience for young newspaper journalists and introduced them to new techniques and technology.

On September 15, 1982, *USA Today* was launched at a party in Washington, D.C., attended by President and Mrs. Ronald Reagan, Speaker of the House "Tip" O'Neill, and Senate Majority Leader Howard Baker. Red, white, and blue *USA Today* banners waved from the 60-foot-wide by 140 foot long tent erected on the Mall. The 800 guests included cabinet members, representatives, senators, publishers, and executives. The party on the Mall was followed by dinner at *USA Today* headquarters across the Potomac River in Rosslyn, where food from every State was served.

In 1983, circulation passed 1,000,000. The only other newspapers with circulation over a million were the *Wall Street Journal,* the *New York Daily News*, and the *Los Angeles Times*. Signing up advertisers was a problem, however, because the only official circulation numbers were those provided by the Audit Bureau of Circulations (ABC), who wouldn't consider circulation until after the first year of operation. Neuharth commissioned the public accounting firm of Price Waterhouse to conduct a circulation survey, which verified that circulation had surpassed 1,000,000. However, Madison Avenue didn't view the results as official. Finally, in late June 1984, ABC verified that annual sales were 1,280,000.

In August 1984, Neuharth estimated that *USA Today*'s losses would be $124 million in 1984, $81 million in 1985, and $25 million in 1986, but that it would break even in 1987. He also estimated that the cumulative losses since start-up would approach $400 million before taxes by the end of 1987. That evaluation of *USA Today*'s finances was "as close as we ever came to folding the tent." Advertising increased notably after Cathleen Black was brought in from *New York* magazine as president of *USA Today* and placed in charge of advertising.

Losses continued at $10 million a month during 1984, which translated into $339,726 per day, $14,155 per hour, and $236 per minute. Neuharth decided that serious steps would have to be taken to save the paper. On Sunday, November 11, 1984, Neuharth held a meeting of *USA Today*'s management committee at his Florida home. He told the committee that things could not continue in the current mode. He listed two alternatives: to quit or to make a concerted effort to make many changes.

Neuharth asserted himself; he said that, to reduce their losses, they had to substitute management for money, including:

- We must produce and present even more news, with fewer people, in less space, at lower cost.
- We must sell and present even more advertising, at higher rates, with fewer people, at lower cost.
- We must produce and print more newspapers, with even better quality, with fewer people, at lower cost.
- We must circulate and sell even more newspapers, at higher prices, with fewer people, at lower cost.

He directed that payroll costs be reduced by five percent by the end of 1985. He also set a goal for 1985 losses of under $75 million.

USA Today was not viewed as a serious newspaper by many members of the journalism community; it was called McPaper. *USA Today* staffers heard the name McPaper and commented that many papers were stealing their McNuggets. John Quinn admitted that if *USA Today* ever won a Pulitzer Prize, it would probably be for "the best investigative paragraph."

Gannett's other eighty-eight papers carried the financial load for *USA Today*. By mid-1985, the "Nation's Newspaper" began to turn the corner financially. Gannett reported a twenty percent earnings increase compared with the first half of 1984, an indication of the company's financial strength. Cathy Black increased the advertising revenue 106 percent compared with the previous year. The price was increased from thirty-five cents to fifty cents when the volume of the paper went to sixty pages. The losses were still staggering: $102 million in 1985 followed by $70 million in 1986.

In May 1986, Neuharth stepped down as the CEO of Gannett, but retained the title of chairman. He wanted to ensure that the transition with president John Curley was orderly. He planned to stay on as chairman until 1989, when he would be sixty-five.

In July 1986, Simmons Market Research conducted a survey noting that *USA Today* had 4,792,000 readers per day, the most readers of any U.S. daily. The *Wall Street Journal's* paid circulation was still much higher, but each *USA Today* was read by three readers while the *Journal* was read by only two readers on the average. Increases in advertising followed the increases in readership.

On June 15, 1987, Curley sent a telegram to Neuharth, who was on a business trip: "McPaper has made it. *USA Today* broke into the black with a profit of $1,093,756 for the month of May, six months ahead of schedule." "The Nation's Newspaper" became profitable faster than many other new media ventures: *Sports Illustrated* required ten years, *Newsweek* nine years, and *Money* magazine took eight years to move into the black.

Neuharth's vision, assertiveness, and pure strength of will brought a daily national newspaper into existence when many said it couldn't be done. He noted in *Confessions of an S. O. B.:*

> The most satisfying victories are those where the odds against your winning are the greatest. But long odds don't necessarily make the job more difficult. In fact, the more that people tell you that it can't be done, the more likely that you have a winner. That usually means that you know something that they don't know. Or that your idea is so different or so daring that they can't comprehend it. If your sights are clearly set on a goal, the fact that others say it can't be done shouldn't slow you down. It should spur you on.

DOROTHY DAY (1897?-1980) Caregiver to the Poor and the Outcast

"We were richly blessed to have her among us . . . She was an ordinary woman whose faith caused her to do extraordinary things. The Gospel caught fire in this woman and caused an explosion of love. Perhaps the most important thing we can say is that she taught us what it means to be a Christian. She was a follower of Jesus Christ who fell in love with His kingdom and made it come alive in the most wretched circumstances of men and women . . . Dorothy's heart never failed us."

Sojourners Magazine

Dorothy Day was born in New York City to a middle-class family. When she was in her teens, her father was a journalist in Chicago, where the family lived on the South Side. Day left the University of Illinois at Urbana after two years to work in New York City for *The Call,* a Socialist newspaper. She became a part of the radical Greenwich Village scene.

Day was not as interested in ideology as she was in observing the people and the conditions around her. She was an idealist with a strong sense of justice. She maintained these interests for the rest of her life. She wrote pamphlets observing the poverty and human suffering in the post-World War I era. She was an avid reader who enjoyed the New York intellectual scene. She knew some of the prominent writers, including Hart Crane, Max Eastman, John Dos Passos, Eugene O'Neill, and Malcolm Cowley.

Day was first jailed in 1917 in Washington, D.C., where she had gone to march in a suffragist parade. Upon her return to New York, she left *The Call* and went to work for *The Liberator,* a radical magazine. Day moved to Chicago, where she was jailed for the second time, along with her fellow activists of the International Workers of the World, known as "Wobblies." At age 28, Day returned to New York and rented a cottage on the beach in Staten Island. She entered into a common law marriage and had a daughter against the wishes of the child's father. Also, about that time, she began to have doubts about her past life. Baptized an Episcopalian, she began to consider converting to Catholicism. This was the final straw for her common law husband. He left her.

In her autobiography, *The Long Loneliness,* Day noted, "Something happened to me when I was around 25. I think I began to see myself drifting toward nowhere. I had lived a full and active life, and I was glad I had met so many good people, interesting and intelligent people. But I yearned for something more than a life of parties and intense political discussions."

Day's daughter was baptized in July 1927, and Day was baptized shortly afterwards. She observed, "I think I realized on the day I was baptized how long I had been waiting for that moment— all my life." She felt that her life was just beginning. In his biography of Dorothy Day, Robert Coles observed, "She had married into the church, not as a nun does, for she was hardly eligible for that vocation, but as her own kind of lay convert, and she was ready to give herself, voluntarily, body and mind and soul to an institution, no matter the doubts weighing on her."

During the Great Depression, Day was upset by the widespread poverty and the homeless men and women walking the streets. She was concerned that neither the Church nor any of the institutions of the country were willing to help with food, shelter, and clothing. She wrote articles for *Commonweal,* a liberal Catholic magazine. After a trip to Washington, D.C., to observe a "hunger march," she found a man named Peter Maurin waiting for her in New York.

Maurin had grown up in France, where he was a member of a Catholic brotherhood who taught the poor. He wrote "Easy Essays" stating the nature of social problems with suggestions for practical responses to them in the spirit of the teachings in the Bible. Day and Maurin recognized the similarity of their views and their willingness to combine politics and religion as activists. Maurin became Day's mentor.

In 1933, Day and Maurin began to publish *The Catholic Worker* with very limited funds. Within a few years, it had a circulation of over 150,000. Shortly after they began to publish *The Catholic Worker,* Maurin said, "We need houses of hospitality to give the rich an opportunity to serve the poor." As Robert Cole observed in his biography of Day, "Maurin envisioned . . . a place where 'works of mercy' were offered and acknowledged in a person-to person fashion, as opposed to the faceless, bureaucratic procedures of the welfare state."

Day and Maurin began their first hospitality house with little money, not much of which came from the rich. The difference between their houses of hospitality and those of other organizations was that Day and Maurin lived there. Maurin didn't even have a room. He would return from a trip and have no place to sleep. The first house of hospitality was a rented apartment, "a rat-ridden place, heatless and filthy, abandoned even by slum dwellers."

As Cole describes, "They started . . . preparing soup, serving food to the homeless, finding clothes for them, offering them, when possible, a place to sleep, and very important, sitting with them, trying to converse, hoping in some way to offer them friendship and affection." Eventually, they had over 30 houses of hospitality.

Not all of the young adult volunteers were Catholics; in fact, some were atheists and agnostics. Cole also noted: "The hospitality houses are places where one can do concrete work on behalf of others. Many young men and women who feel within themselves surges of idealism don't know what to do about it. A skeptic might say they don't look hard enough, but it isn't always easy for people to find opportunities for charity in the biblical sense of the word, free of the implication of condescension. In hospitality houses, there is an immediacy to the charitable gesture, a directness, unmediated by bureaucracy and self-consciousness, that many young people find appealing."

Day died on November 29, 1980, three weeks after her 83rd birthday. She was active in publishing *The Catholic Worker* and in working in the houses of hospitality until her death.

Dorothy Day is an outstanding example of an individual who started out in life on a path that she realized would not lead to a life of accomplishment. She changed her lifestyle and spent the rest of her life helping the poor and the disadvantaged.

CHAIM WEIZMANN (1874-1952) Zionist and First President of Israel

"Difficult things take a long time; the impossible takes a little longer."

Chaim Weizmann

Chaim Weizmann persevered an entire lifetime working in the interests of Zionism, the movement to establish a national home for Jews in the Holy Land, which succeeded in founding the State of Israel in 1948. Weizmann wasn't the first leader of the worldwide Zionist movement, and he was replaced in the early 1930s for not proceeding fast enough; nevertheless, for most of the forty years leading to the founding of Israel, he was the movement's spokesman. This lifelong effort resulted in his election as the first President of Israel. Weizmann's motivation over a sixty-year period is notable; however, the determination of the Jewish people in reestablishing a Jewish State in the Holy Land after an absence of two thousand years is unprecedented. Jerusalem was conquered by the Babylonians in 586 BC, and many Jews became slaves.

The dispersal of Jews from their homeland is called the Diaspora (derived from the Greek word for dispersion). Also, the Romans issued expulsion orders in AD 70 and AD 135 that dispersed the Jewish people initially to cities around the Mediterranean Sea and eventually throughout the world.

Chaim Weizmann was born on November 27, 1874, in the village of Motol in Byelorussia. Motol was located in the Pale of Settlement, a region containing five million Jews along the western boundary of Russia that was the only place in Russia where Jews could reside legally. Persecution was a way of life in the Pale, and Jews were continually threatened with pogroms. Weizmann's father, Ozer Weizmann, was a lumber merchant who inherited his lumber business from his father-in-law. Ozer's family was middle class, but they lived more comfortably than most others in the Pale. They spoke three languages—Yiddish, Hebrew, and Russian—and had many books in their home in each of these languages.

Weizmann attended high school in Pinsk, where he could receive a better education than in Motol. After school he worked in a chemical plant owned by the Luries, the family with whom he stayed in

Pinsk. He developed an early interest in chemistry, and this practical experience reinforced his inclination to major in the subject. He joined a Zionist group called the Hoverei Zion (Lovers of Zion) and first heard about Jews emigrating to Palestine to establish a homeland. By the age of sixteen, he considered himself a Zionist.

Weizmann enrolled at the Charlottenburg Technical College in Berlin. Subsequently, he earned a doctorate in chemistry magna cum laude at the University of Fribourg in Switzerland.

While studying in Berlin, Weizmann joined the Russo-Jewish Academic Society, which he considered the "cradle of the modern Zionist movement." An active member of the society was Asher Ginsberg, known to fellow Zionists as Ahad Ha'am, which means "one of the people" in Hebrew. Ha'am advocated a patient approach to Zionism, not an aggressive one, realizing that its ultimate success depended upon some form of agreement with the Arabs who had lived in Palestine for centuries. Ha'am became Weizmann's mentor in the Zionist movement.

The Zionist movement underwent significant changes when Weizmann was in Berlin. In 1896, a strong leader emerged in Theodor Herzl, a Hungarian Jew, who published *Der Judenstaat* (The Jewish State). A sophisticated lawyer and journalist, he was the Paris correspondent for the Viennese newspaper, *Neue Freie Presse*.

Herzl wrote his book using examples of anti-Semitism he had seen in Vienna and Paris, particularly the Dreyfus affair in 1894. The French government falsely convicted a Jewish French Army captain, Alfred Dreyfus, with passing military secrets to the Germans. Evidence indicated that Dreyfus was innocent, but it wasn't until 1906 that the government conceded the anti-Semitic basis for their case and acknowledged the findings as "erroneous and wrongful."

Herzl told the Jews that if an incident like the Dreyfus affair could happen in France, considered one of the more enlightened and tolerant countries in Europe, it could happen anywhere. He advocated moving all Jews to a homeland of their own where they wouldn't be subject to the whims of leaders of foreign countries.

Herzl convened the First Zionist Congress in Basel in 1897 and made a historic entry in his diary: "At Basel, I founded the Jewish State." The Congress set up the World Zionist Organization to "create for the Jewish people a home in Palestine secured by public law." At the Second Zionist Congress, also held in Basel, Weizmann was elected to the Congress Steering Committee.

The two individuals who were most closely associated with Zionism, Herzl and Weizmann, were very different people. Herzl was an assimilated Jew who had detailed knowledge neither of Jewish culture nor of the feelings of the people. He had a Messianic quality about him; his position as a outsider attracted many Jews. He was more readily accepted than a Jewish leader from Eastern Europe would have been. In Weizmann's words, "What emerged from the Judenstaat was less a concept than a historic personality."

Herzl convened the Third Zionist Congress in London in 1900. This Congress established the Jewish National Fund, which helped Zionists to buy and develop land in Palestine. He requested support for the movement from Britain and France, and tried to obtain a charter from Abdulhamid II, the Turkish sultan who controlled Palestine within the Ottoman Empire. Unfortunately, Herzl made little progress on either of these two fronts.

Opportunities existed within the movement for members like Chaim Weizmann who thought that progress was being made too slowly. During the winter of 1900-01, Weizmann formed a minority opposition group (the Democratic Faction), which became a force at the 1902 Congress. The Democratic Faction backed people who were willing to immigrate to Palestine and build new settlements.

Weizmann accepted a teaching and research position at Victoria University in Manchester, England, the location of a substantial chemical industry. Weizmann was happy living in England, where a Jew, Benjamin Disraeli, had become Prime Minister in the late nineteenth century during Queen Victoria's reign.

Weizmann wasn't ready to become leader of the Zionist movement after Herzl died. The position was assumed by David Wolffsohn, one of Herzl's inner council, who was considered a placeholder until a stronger leader came along.

In 1905, Weizmann met the British Prime Minister, Arthur Balfour, in Manchester during an election campaign. Balfour, who supported a Jewish homeland in East Africa, expressed an interest in speaking with one of the Zionist leaders who opposed the East Africa plan and was referred to Weizmann. Weizmann was straightforward in his discussions with Balfour. " Balfour asked, "Are there many Jews who think like you?" He was told, "I believe I speak the mind of millions of Jews whom you will never see and who cannot speak for themselves, but with whom I could pave the streets of the country I come from." Balfour commented, "If that is so, you will one day be a force."

In 1907, Weizmann moved closer to assuming the leadership at the Eighth Zionist Congress held in the Netherlands, where he gave an inspirational speech promoting the cause of the "practical" Zionists, the settlers in the Yishuv (the Jews living in Palestine).

In 1907, Weizmann visited Palestine for the first time. Jewish settlers were outnumbered ten to one in a total population of 600,000, comprised of 500,000 Muslims, 60,000 Jews, and 40,000 Christians. He noted: "It's worth a lifetime to glimpse the work of Jewish hands, to see after twenty years of toil, former sand and swamp support flourishing orchards, to see Jewish farmers. I understood many things much better, more clearly; the potentiality of Palestine is immense." Weizmann added: "The air is crystal pure, so pure that you can look back over three thousand years of history." Later, in his memoirs, he observed: "Palestine was one of the most neglected corners of the Turkish Empire."

Weizmann returned to England fired up with the "practical" aspect of Zionism. He tried to convince Baron Edmund Rothschild, the French-Jewish financier, of the importance of establishing a university in Palestine. Rothschild was willing to finance a research institute, but he thought that it was too early to begin a university. A site was selected on Mt. Scopus near the Mount of Olives, but the outbreak of World War I preempted the planning meeting.

In 1915, the British government asked Weizmann to aid the war effort. Britain had a shortage of acetone, an important ingredient of explosives. Weizmann discovered a process to produce acetone by fermenting corn mash. His process was used in Canada, France, India, and the United States.

The Prime Minister asked him what honor he would like to receive for his contributions to the war effort. Prime Minister Lloyd George's War Memoirs noted his response: "'There is nothing I want for myself. I would like you to do something for my people.' That was the fount and origin on the famous [Balfour] declaration about the national home for Jews in Palestine. Dr. Weizmann not only helped us win the war, but made a permanent mark upon the map of the world."

Prior to the World War I armistice, Britain and France met to determine a policy for the Middle East when the war ended. The boundaries of the area discussed were the Mediterranean Sea, the Red Sea, the Arabian Sea, and the Persian Gulf. They signed a secret pact, the Sykes-Picot Agreement, which divided the area into sectors controlled by the Arabs, the British, and the French. The Jews were barely mentioned in the Agreement.

Weizmann, who had become president of the English Zionist Federation in early 1917, was angered by the pact and used all of his persuasive ability on British officials to convince them to back down from the agreements reached.

Weizmann's diplomacy succeeded beyond his dreams. Historian Charles Webster, a war office official, wrote: "With unerring skill, he adapted his arguments to the special circumstances of each statesman. To the British and Americans he could use biblical language and awaken a deep emotional undertone; to other nationalities he more often talked in terms of interest." Weizmann's efforts resulted in the Balfour Declaration, which Webster called "the greatest diplomatic coup of the First World War."

On October 31, 1917, the British cabinet prepared the final draft of the Balfour Declaration. Weizmann had steered the discussions through approximately 2,000 meetings with officials. The Balfour Declaration was a turning point in the Zionist movement and, in fact, the history of the Jewish people. It was not explicit, but it stated the position of the British government, according to biographer Barnet Litvinoff:

> His Majesty's Government view with favor the establishment in Palestine of a national home for the Jewish people, and will use their best endeavors to facilitate the achievement of this object, it being clearly understood that nothing shall be done which may prejudice the civil and religious rights of the existing non-Jewish communities in Palestine, or the rights and political status enjoyed by Jews in any other country.

The issuance of the Declaration ended a difficult time for Weizmann. Before the Declaration, many English Jews didn't support Zionism, because they didn't want their loyalty to England questioned. Others didn't want to offend the Turks, who might retaliate against Jews already living in Palestine. Weizmann had become so frustrated that he offered to resign the presidency of the English Zionist Federation. He was talked out of it by his mentor, Ahad Ha'am, who asked, "To whom do you offer your resignation? Who has appointed you? Fate has appointed you, and only to Fate can you offer your resignation."

On March 8, 1918, Weizmann left England for Palestine, as leader of a British government Zionist commission, to offer advice on the settlement of Jews in Palestine. One month later, General Allenby conquered Jerusalem, which ended 400 years of rule by the Ottoman Empire. In Jerusalem, Weizmann met David Ben-Gurion, who had emigrated from Poland and lived in Palestine since 1906.

Ben-Gurion and his peers in Palestine, who were more militant than Weizmann, weren't satisfied with the vague wording of the Balfour Declaration. They asked Weizmann why he hadn't demanded a Jewish State.

Upon his return to England, Weizmann concentrated his efforts on Zionism. His interests in science became secondary. He maintained this allocation of his time through the early 1920s when the British government made concessions to Arab interests in Palestine. Weizmann became concerned that Britain was wavering in the commitment to Zionism. For that reason, and to seek additional funding for the Zionist movement, Weizmann cultivated support in the United States.

Weizmann's initial difficult relationship with American Jewish leaders, such as Supreme Court Justice Louis Brandeis, encumbered progress toward their mutual goals. Norman Rose, author of a Weizmann biography, speculated that the difficulty between Brandeis and Weizmann was that "Brandeis was the one serious competitor to Weizmann's leadership."

Weizmann considered the United States a principal source of funding for the movement in the 1920s and beyond. Weizmann decided not to work through the Zionist leadership in the United States, but to appeal directly to the people. Biographer Litvinoff described his personal approach: "Weizmann cast a charm over

America, confirming his supremacy in the Jewish world for years to come. He troubled them little with ideology, but he proffered his expectation of a new Jewish world arising in the ancient East as this one had arisen in the modern West. He refused to humble himself, or make Zionism into a charity."

In the summer of 1929, Arab riots in Palestine resulted in over 100 Jewish deaths and considerable destruction of Jewish-owned property. In the early 1930s, Britain restricted the immigration of Jews to Palestine and imposed limitations on the purchase of property by Jews. Weizmann was associated with British support of the Zionist movement for many years, and, disappointed with the reduction of that support, he resigned as president of both the Jewish Agency for Palestine and the World Zionist Organization in 1930.

A more aggressive, if somewhat unrealistic, element then assumed leadership of the Zionist movement. Weizmann believed that the leadership was moving the organization in a direction that would be detrimental to their cause. He released a statement to the press, "I have no understanding of, and no sympathy for, the demand for a Jewish majority in Palestine. Majority does not guarantee security; majority is not necessary for the development of a Jewish civilization and culture. The world will construe this demand only in the sense that we wish to acquire a majority in order to drive out the Arabs."

Many Zionists responded negatively to this statement. He was censured by the World Zionist Organization, and he wasn't asked to resume the presidency of the Organization. It was a bad time for dissension within the Organization. In 1933, Adolf Hitler became the German Chancellor, and discrimination against Jews accelerated in Germany. Two years later, Hitler's anti-Semitic policies became official with the passage of the Nuremberg Laws.

Britain continued to limit the entry of Jews into Palestine. With Weizmann on the sidelines, the Zionist organization didn't have a leader with his stature on the international scene to deal with British government officials. David Ben-Gurion became the leader of the Yishuv in Palestine, but he didn't have Weizmann's international contacts.

At the Zionist Congress in 1935, Weizmann was re-elected to the presidency of both the Jewish Agency for Palestine and the World

Zionist Organization. He built a home in Rehovot, Palestine, around this time.

In the late 1930s, Palestine became an armed camp. Britain assigned an additional 20,000 troops there to maintain order. In 1937, Lord William Peel led a commission to make recommendations about correcting existing conditions. Weizmann reported to the commission: "There are [in Central and Eastern Europe] six million people doomed to be pent up in places where they are not wanted and for whom the world is divided into places where they cannot live and places which they cannot enter." He proposed the creation of a Jewish State as the only practical way of reducing the threat to the freedom and the very existence of European Jews.

Ben-Gurion wrote that Weizmann's testimony before the Peel Commission "was, perhaps, the most profound and penetrating analysis ever given of the plight of the Jewish people and their position in the non-Jewish world, coupled with the strongest and most vigorous claim ever put forward for the immediate creation of the Jewish State as the only deliverance from the danger threatening the Jewish masses."

The Peel Commission initiated the idea of partition and proposed the division of Palestine into an independent Arab State occupying three-quarters of the land area and an independent Jewish State occupying the remaining quarter of the territory. Some sites, such as Jerusalem, would continue under British control since they were religious centers for both Muslims and Jews, as well as Christians. British historian Maurice Edelman observed, "The area offered [to the Jews] was so restricted as to make impossible the emergence of a viable Jewish State."

As World War II approached, Britain backed down from its position of partition. Foremost in the government leaders' thoughts now was the retention and protection of the military bases in the Middle East and their supply routes. Foreign Secretary Anthony Eden established another commission, led by Sir John Woodhead, to review the concept of partition. Zionists referred to this commission as "the Re-Peel Commission." The commission reported that partition of the Holy Land was impractical.

Britain revoked the Balfour Declaration in order to prevent Arabs in the Middle East from aligning with Germany. The government declared that Jewish immigration to Palestine would end in five years, and that an independent Arab state would be established in Palestine in ten years. As Zionist leaders expressed their outrage at these events, the German army entered Poland and the world was at war. By the end of World War II, the six million Jews for whom Weizmann had expressed concern had died; they were either killed outright or died from overwork and malnutrition in Nazi concentration camps.

This restriction of Jewish immigration into Palestine continued after World War II. British authorities allowed only 1,500 a month to enter the country legally. Members of the Zionist movement attempted to bring Jews into Palestine illegally; British authorities in Palestine prevented most of these ships from landing.

Many of these refugees were interned on Cyprus, but most were sent back to their point of origin, which resulted in considerable loss of life. The SS Struma sank off the coast of Turkey, and many of the 750 Jews on board died. Refugees of the SS Patria (198 men, women, and children) committed suicide by blowing up their ship after being denied the right to dock in Palestine.

In 1946, three Yishuv military organizations coordinated their efforts to form the Hebrew Resistance Movement. The Haganah, the main Jewish security force, considered themselves a defensive organization and followed a policy of restraint. The 2,000 members of the Irgun Z'vai Leumi (National Military Organization) were more militant than the Haganah. They didn't restrict themselves to defensive activities, and they took an aggressive stance in dealing with both the Arabs and the British. The Lohamei Herut Israel (Fighters for the Freedom of Israel), known by the acronym Lehi and also as the Stern gang (named for the group's founder), was the most militant of the three organizations.

By mid-1946, Palestine was again an armed camp with 100,000 British troops to maintain order. In June 1946, the British rounded up and detained almost 3,000 Jews suspected of being members of the resistance movement. The movement retaliated by bombing the King David Hotel in Jerusalem, the British administrative center. The bungled bombing killed forty-one Arabs, twenty-eight Britons, and seventeen Jews and was the most controversial event leading up to the establishment of the State of Israel.

At the Zionist Congress in December 1946, Weizmann was heckled by members who had lost faith in his leadership because the foundation of a Jewish State was moving too slowly. Realizing that he no longer had the support of the majority of the members, he resigned from the presidency of the World Zionist Congress. However, even without an official position in the Zionist movement, Weizmann was still considered on the international scene the foremost promoter of Zionism and key representative of world Jewry.

In July 1947, Weizmann was invited to appear before the United Nations Special Committee on Palestine. He promoted the partition of Palestine, and he lobbied strongly for the inclusion of the Negev Desert in the territory the Jews would be assigned in the United Nations plan for partition. Weizmann and other Zionist leaders knew that with irrigation this unproductive wasteland could be made fertile, and it would serve as a buffer with Arab neighbors. Norman Rose wrote that Weizmann's lobbying efforts were "one of the most intricate and diplomatic lobbying exercises in modern diplomatic history."

In October 1947, the *SS Exodus*, a ship carrying 4,500 survivors of concentration camps, was turned away from Palestine. The British government was subjected to much negative world opinion.

In December 1947, Weizmann sailed for England en route to his home in Rehovot. In January, he was told that President Truman wanted to postpone partition and to establish a United Nations trusteeship for Palestine. Weizmann returned immediately to the United States, but President Truman refused to see him. Weizmann was viewed as an individual with no national status.

An intermediary was required, and Harry Truman's old friend from Kansas City, Eddie Jacobsen, volunteered. Eddie had served in Truman's artillery battery in France in World War I and had been his partner in a failed haberdashery venture after the war. Eddie sent a telegram to Truman asking him to see Weizmann. Truman replied that Weizmann had nothing to tell him and that a meeting wouldn't be productive. Eddie flew to Washington to present his request in person. He was accompanied to the oval office by an aide who cautioned him not to speak of Weizmann or of Palestine.

Jacobsen began his conversation with noncontroversial topics and worked his way around to the discussion of one of Truman's heroes, Andrew Jackson. Then Eddie said, "I, too, have a hero, a man I have never met. I am talking about Chaim Weizmann . . . you refuse to see him just because you were insulted by some of our American Jewish leaders. It doesn't sound like you, Harry, because I thought you could take this stuff they have been handing out to you."

It worked. Weizmann met with Truman on March 18, 1948, and told him that whatever actions the Security Council of the United Nations took, the Jewish people would announce the establishment of their State on May 15. Weizmann left the meeting with Truman's promise that the United States would recognize the State of Israel promptly.

During the evening of May 14, Ben-Gurion, as head of the provisional government and of the executive committee of the Jewish Agency, proclaimed the establishment of the State of Israel effective May 15. Truman fulfilled his promise and granted immediate recognition of the new government.

Ben-Gurion, who was to be the provisional Prime Minister (Head of Government) sent a telegram to Weizmann, who was to be the provisional President (Head of State), "On the establishment of the Jewish State, we send our greetings to you, who have done more than any other living man toward its creation. Your stand and help have strengthened all of us. We look forward to the day when we shall see you at the Head of the State in peace."

The fledgling country didn't have time to celebrate its independence. Israel was invaded by Arab armies from Egypt, Iraq, Lebanon, Jordan, and Syria, along with smaller units from Saudi Arabia, Sudan, and Yemen. It is a tribute to the Israeli defense forces that they were able to defend their new country after the abrupt evacuation of British forces on May 14. The fighting continued until an armistice was signed in early 1949.

Weizmann was formally sworn in as the first President of Israel on February 18, 1949. That year he also realized another of his long-term goals, the establishment of the Weizmann Institute of Science in Rehovot. His health began to fail in the early 1950s. His eyesight had been poor for years, but in 1951 he developed glaucoma. He went into a coma on November 9, 1952, and died after suffering two heart attacks.

BRIGHAM YOUNG (1901-1877) Led the Mormons to Salt Lake Valley

"When a furious mob murdered [Mormon founder Joseph] Smith, Young assumed the leadership of the Mormon survivors and redirected their vision toward new goals. Far beyond the Mississippi, in heretofore unsettled territory, lay the Great Basin to which he led the remnants of the Church and its followers. There Young supervised the building of a new society that soon attracted thousands of newcomers from other parts of the Union and from Europe as well."

Oscar Handlin

Brigham Young, the sixth child and third son of John and Abigail Howe Young, was born on June 1, 1801, in Whitingham, Vermont. John Young was a farmer who moved frequently because of increasingly worn-out soil. In 1802, John Young moved his family to Smyrna, New York. John cleared land for farming and built a log dwelling. At an early age, Brigham was introduced to hard work, including logging and driving a team of horses. The family was poor and hired Brigham out to neighbors to earn additional income.

The Youngs were Methodists who originally had been New England Congregationalists. In Brigham's opinion, his parents were "the most strict religionists that lived upon the earth." Brigham held back from joining the Methodist church or any other church. He said a prayer to himself: "Lord, preserve me until I am old enough to have sound judgment, and a discreet mind ripened on a good, solid foundation of common sense." Abigail Young died on June 11, 1815, just after Brigham's fourteenth birthday. He had been close to his mother; in his words, "Of my mother—she that bore me—I can say no better woman lived in the world." Brigham developed into an independent individual with a deliberate manner.

In 1817, John Young married Hannah Dennis Brown, a widow with several children of her own. He broke up his household and moved in with his new wife. Sixteen year old Brigham's father told him, "You now have your time; go and provide for yourself."

Young moved to Auburn, New York, where he was an apprentice in the trades of carpentry, glazing, and painting. In 1823, Young moved to Port Byron, a fast-growing town on the new Erie Canal.

He worked in a furniture repair shop, a wool carding mill, a pail factory, and a boatyard. One of Young's employers observed that he "would do more work in a given time and secure more and better work from his help without trouble than any man they have ever employed."

In 1828, Young moved to Oswego, where he worked on the construction of a large tannery. When the tannery was finished the following year, he moved to Mendon, where his father and several of his sisters had settled. While living in Port Byron, Young had heard "rumors of a new revelation, to the effect of a new Bible written upon golden plates at Palmyra. I was somewhat acquainted with the coming forth of the Book of Mormon through the newspapers [and] many stories and reports circulated as the Book of Mormon was printed and scattered abroad."

In June 1830, Young saw a copy of the Book of Mormon when Samuel Smith, a brother of Joseph Smith, who had found the golden plates on Hill Cumorah, visited Mendon to preach about Mormonism and to sell copies of the "golden Bible."

In January 1830, Young, his brother, Phineas, and his good friend and neighbor, Heber Kimball, traveled to Columbia, Pennsylvania, the location of the nearest Mormon church, to observe Mormons interpreting their religion, prophesying, and speaking in tongues. On April 14, Brigham Young was baptized by Elder Eleazer Miller in the stream behind his home. Young said that before his clothes "were dry on my back [Elder Miller] laid his hands on me and ordained me an Elder, at which I marveled. According to the words of the Savior, I felt a humble, childlike spirit, witnessing unto me that my sins were forgiven." Ordination as an Elder gave Young the authority to preach the gospel. The rest of the family followed him in joining the new religion.

Four things Young liked about Mormonism were its similarities to Puritanism, with its emphasis on common sense; its espousal of "Christian Primitivism," the restoration of Christianity as it existed at the time of Jesus Christ; its authoritarianism, which required unquestioning loyalty to the Mormon prophet Joseph Smith; and its lay priesthood, which provided a path to status and influence.

In the fall of 1832, Young and Heber Kimball traveled to the main Mormon settlement in Kirtland, Ohio, just east of Cleveland, to meet Joseph Smith—founder of the Church of Jesus Christ of

Latter-Day Saints. Upon meeting the charismatic Mormon prophet, Young spoke in tongues and asked the Latter-Day Saints leader's opinion of his gift of tongues. Smith "told them that it was of the pure Adamic language. It is of God, and the time will come when brother Brigham Young will preside over this church."

Young returned to Mendon to preach Mormonism and traveled around upstate New York and Canada baptizing converts. In September 1833, he moved to Kirtland to be near Joseph Smith and the center of Mormon activity. He courted Mary Ann Angell, a former Baptist from Seneca, New York. In February 1834, Young and Mary Ann were married by Sidney Rigdon, an influential Mormon leader. Early the following year, Smith appointed Young one of the Council of Twelve Apostles, modeled on the Apostles of the New Testament, who were responsible for overseeing Mormon churches and missionary activity.

From 1835 through 1837, Young traveled around upstate New York, New England, and Canada spreading the word of Mormonism. On a return visit to Kirtland during this time, he supervised the completion of the Kirtland Temple. Smith encountered difficulties in Kirtland when he attempted to establish his own bank. Because of his indebtedness and his plan to print his own money, Smith was denied a State banking charter. He established the bank anyway; unfortunately, it was adversely affected by the Panic of 1837.

In 1838, Young was drawn into the conflict between Mormons and non-Mormons in Missouri. Non-Mormons were concerned about the Mormons' economic and political power in the region. A series of armed clashes began in Gallatin, Missouri, when non-Mormons attempted to prevent Mormons from voting. Three Mormons were killed at Crooked River, Caldwell County, and seventeen Mormons were killed and fifteen wounded seriously at Haun's Mill, Caldwell County, by an unruly mob of over 200 men.

The Governor of Missouri, Lilburn Boggs, called out the Missouri militia and issued the order that Mormons "must be exterminated or driven from Missouri, if necessary, for the public good." Joseph Smith turned himself in to the authorities, and his brother, Hyrum, and Sidney Rigdon were arrested. Young was the only senior member of the Council of the Twelve Apostles who was not in captivity. The Mormons received only a token payment for their property and, due to threats to their lives, left Missouri for Illinois.

In 1839, Young made his last visit to upstate New York while on his way to a mission that more than doubled church membership in England. He promoted the increase in the number of English Elders and the immigration of English Mormons to the United States. During the next six years, over 4,000 Mormons immigrated to the United States from Great Britain. He also established a Mormon periodical, the *Millennial Star,* in England. Young clearly established a reputation as an efficient administrator and organizer.

Smith escaped from his six-month captivity and established the center of Mormon faith in Nauvoo, Illinois. In July 1841, when Young returned to Nauvoo, he found that it had become a rapidly growing city of 3,000; it would expand to 10,000 by the end of 1841. The Nauvoo Charter gave Mormons comprehensive powers of self-government, although they could not pass any laws contrary to the Illinois and U.S. Constitutions. The mayor and city council formed their own municipal court, and the city controlled its own militia, the Nauvoo Legion.

Young was elected to the Nauvoo city council and was appointed editor of the Nauvoo newspaper, *The Times and Seasons.* His commitment to Mormonism was severely tested in 1841, when Joseph Smith endorsed the practice of polygamy for the Latter-Day Saints. Initially, Young was appalled by the practice. He said that it "was the first time in my life that I had desired the grave." When he expressed his views to Smith, he was told, "Brother Brigham, the Lord will reveal it to you." Young was faced with the dilemma of either practicing polygamy or defying the prophet Joseph Smith. Eventually, he accepted plural marriage.

The practice of polygamy was the greatest source of difficulty for the Mormons, within and outside of the church. Nauvoo was envied as the most prosperous city in Illinois, but its self-government was not easily accepted by non-Mormons. Smith realized that he must look to the Far West as "a place of refuge" where "the devil cannot dig us out." In February 1844, Smith asked the Council of Twelve to send a delegation westward toward California and Oregon to build a temple and to establish a government of their own.

The delegation to the West was delayed by Smith's decision to run for the Presidency of the U.S. in 1844 as an independent candidate. Young and other Mormon leaders did much of the campaigning for the candidate. Smith had problems of his own back in Nauvoo, however. A group of dissidents led by William Law split off from the Latter-Day Saints due to disagreements with Smith's policies, particularly polygamy. Law and his associates established a competing newspaper, the *Nauvoo Expositor*. Smith asked the city council to destroy the press and all copies of the newspaper, a blatant violation of freedom of the press.

Anti-Mormon feeling intensified around Nauvoo, and Smith, his brother, Hyrum, and two other Mormon leaders gave themselves up to county authorities in Carthage. On June 27, 1844, a large, organized mob entered the jail at Carthage, killed Smith and his brother, and wounded another of the Mormon leaders. Young, who was campaigning for Smith in Massachusetts at the time, returned to Nauvoo by a roundabout route to avoid assassination.

Young's only serious rival for the Mormon presidency was Sidney Rigdon. Young's forceful speech, his alignment with the Council of Twelve, and his confidence that the Church would make the right decision made him the clear choice. Anti-Mormon sentiment continued to run high, and Illinois Governor Thomas Ford repealed the Nauvoo charter, which disfranchised both the city police and the Nauvoo Legion. Earlier, he had ordered the Nauvoo Legion to return its State-supplied weapons.

Illinois justice was unable to convict the killers of Joseph Smith and his brother, and anti-Mormon mobs burned barns and crops on farms around Nauvoo. Young realized that they would have to abandon Nauvoo and settle in a frontier sanctuary. Texas was considered a possible site, as were California, Oregon, and Vancouver Island. Young ruled out the latter two because they were involved in ongoing boundary disputes between the United States and Great Britain. He favored the Great Basin of Utah because it was remote and virtually uninhabited by whites.

In February 1846, the main body of settlers left Nauvoo. Young organized twenty-four companies of 100 each and personally selected the leader of each company. Mormons sold most of their property for a fraction of its value. Before leaving Nauvoo, Young was continually threatened with arrest.

The Mormons' trek to the West was the largest and best-organized of all migrations. They spent the first winter on Potawatomi

Indian lands just north of Omaha, Nebraska. Young supervised building 538 log houses and 83 sod houses for 3,483 people. In early 1847, he assumed personal responsibility for the pilot company of 159 pioneers, seventy-two wagons, sixty-six oxen, and ninety-two horses. The company, whose goal was to chart the path to the Great Salt Lake Valley for others to follow, used artificial horizons, a circle of reflection, and sextants.

Initially, they traveled the Oregon Trail along the Platt River, averaging ten miles a day. On the trail, they encountered hostile Pawnees and friendly Sioux Indians. On July 7, 1847, they reached Fort Bridger on the Green River. John C. Fremont's description of the Great Salt Lake region was favorable; however, Jim Bridger, the famous scout, told them that the Indians in the area were unfriendly, and that the area's cold nights would prevent the growth of crops. When they got within fifty miles of the Great Salt Lake (near Ogden, Utah), another scout gave them a favorable report of their destination, including its agricultural potential.

On July 24, 1847, Young saw the Great Salt Lake Valley for the first time, from the mouth of Emigration Canyon: "This is the place." Compared with Nauvoo, the Salt Lake Valley was dry and remote. It was forty-miles long from north to south, twenty-five miles wide, and bounded by majestic snow-capped mountains. Young laid out the city with streets eight rods wide in a perfect grid.

During the winter of 1847-48, Young reorganized the First Presidency of the Church and appointed Heber Kimball First Counselor. Also, he assumed the designation of prophet, seer, and revelator that had been held by Joseph Smith. By the spring of 1848, the settlement had grown from 300 to over 5,000 people.

The first crop was severely reduced by an invasion of crickets, which the settlers could not get rid of. Their prayers were answered when seagulls came from the Great Salt Lake to consume them. Mormons benefited economically during 1849, when wagonloads of gold prospectors passed through on their way to California. Mormons repaired the travelers' harnesses and wagons and sold supplies to them.

During 1849 and 1850, Young sought statehood for Utah and sent two representatives to Washington, D.C., to lobby for it. He did not want territorial status because it would involve federal observers that could limit his control. President Taylor denied the request for statehood; however, upon Taylor's death, President Fillmore granted territorial status to Utah, which was named for the Ute Indians in the region. Young was chosen as Utah's first Territorial Governor, and Mormons were appointed as Associate Justice of the Territory's Supreme Court, U.S. Marshal, and U.S. Attorney.

Young counseled keeping on friendly terms with the Ute Indians in the area. He asked Mormons to "feed them and clothe them . . . never turn them away hungry" and "teach them the art of husbandry." In his opinion, "It was cheaper to feed the Indians than to fight them." From 1850 to 1855, the number of Mormons in the Salt Lake Basin grew from 5,000 to 60,000, mainly from the East but including 15,000 from Great Britain.

In May 1857, President Buchanan sent 2,500 troops to Utah to remove Young as Territorial Governor. As had occurred earlier, anti-Mormon sentiment was rampant, principally due to their practice of polygamy.

Young accepted President Buchanan's appointed Governor, Alfred Cumming, but refused to let federal troops enter Salt Lake City. Young threatened to burn every structure built by the Mormons if the army entered the city. The Mormons vacated the city until July 1858, when peace was made with the federal government. The settlement continued to expand. Young was a good businessman and by the late 1850s had an accumulated wealth between $200,000 and $250,000, earned from lumbering, lumber mills, real estate, and a tannery.

On August 23, 1877, Young became very ill and was diagnosed with cholera. His condition worsened, and he died on August 27 exclaiming "Joseph! Joseph! Joseph!" John Taylor, senior member of the Council of Twelve, became President of the Church in 1880.

Brigham Young provided leadership for the Mormon Church at a critical period in its history, enabling it to become the largest religion founded in the United States. Also, he contributed heavily to the growth of the American frontier and is considered one of the great colonizers in the history of the United States.

BIBLIOGRAPHY

INTRODUCTION

Reivich, Karen, and Andrew Shatte. *The Resilience Factor:*
  7 Keys to Finding Your Inner Strength and Overcoming Life's Hurdles.
  New York: Broadway Books, 2002.

Southwick, Steven M., and Dennis S. Charney. *Resilience:*
  The Science of Mastering Life's Greatest Challenges.
  Cambridge: Cambridge University Press, 2012.

COMPOSERS / ARTISTS / PLAYWRIGHTS —Chapter 1

RICHARD RODGERS

Ewen, David. *Richard Rodgers*. NY: Henry Holt and Company, 1957.

Hyland, William G. *Richard Rodgers*. New Haven: Yale UP, 1998.

Secrest, Meryle. *Somewhere for Me: A Biography of Richard Rodgers.*
  New York: Alfred A. Knopf, 2001.

Taylor, Deems. *Some Enchanted Evenings: The Story of Rodgers*
  and Hammerstein. New York: Harper and Brothers, 1953.

FREDERICK DELIUS

Jahoda, Gloria. *The Road to Samarkand: Frederick Delius.*
  New York: Charles Scribner's Sons, 1969.

Palmer, Christopher. *Delius: Portrait of a Cosmopolitan.*
  London: Duckworth, 1976.

Warlock, Peter (Philip Heseltime). *Frederick Delius.*
  New York: Oxford University Press, 1952.

ANTON CHEKHOV

Laffitte, Sophie. *Chekhov 1860-1904*. NY: Charles Scribner's Sons, 1871.

Tourmanova, Princess Nina Androikova. *Anton Chekhov: The Voice of*
  Twilight Russia. New York: Columbia University Press, 1937.

Untermeyer, Louis. *Makers of the Modern World.*
  New York: Simon & Schuster, 1955.

PIERRE-AUGUSTE RENOIR

Georges-Michel, Michel. *From Renoir to Picasso.*
  Boston: Houghton Mifflin, 1957.

Hanson, Lawrence. *Renoir: The Man, The Painter, and His World*. New
  York: Dodd, Mead, 1968.

Raboff, Ernest Lloyd. *Pierre-August Renoir*. New York: Harper & Row,
  1988.

Renoir, Jean. *Renoir: My Father*. Boston: Little, Brown, 1962.

Rouart, Dennis. *Renoir: Biographical and Critical Study*. Cleveland: World, 1954.

LUDWIG VAN BEETHOVEN

Brower, Harriette. *Story-Lives of Master Musicians*. Philadelphia: Lippincott, 1922.

Burk, John W. *The Life and Works of Beethoven*. New York: Random House, 1943.

Schauffler, Robert Haven. *Beethoven, The Man Who Freed Music*. Garden City: Doubleday Doran, 1929.

Schindler, Anton Felix. *Beethoven As I Knew Him*. Chapel Hill: University of North Carolina Press, 1966.

Sullivan, J. W. N. *Beethoven, His Spiritual Development*. New York: Knopf, 1951.

REFORMERS / ACTIVISTS — Chapter 2

MARTIN LUTHER KING, JR.

Darby, Jean. *Martin Luther King, Jr.* Minneapolis: Lerner, 1990.

Haskins, James. *The Life and Death of Martin Luther King, Jr.* New York: Lothrop, Lee & Shepard, 1977.

Jakoubek, Robert. *Martin Luther King, Jr.* NY: Chelsea House, 1989.

Oates, Stephen B. *Let the Trumpets Sound: The Life of Martin Luther King, Jr.* New York: New American Library, 1982.

Shuker, Nancy. *Martin Luther King*. NY: Chelsea House, 1985.

THOMAS GARRETT

McGowan, James A. *Station Masters on the Underground Railroad: The Life and Letters of Thomas Garrett*. Moylan, Pennsylvania: Whimsie Press, 1977.

Still, William. *The Underground Railroad*. Philadelphia: Porter & Coates, 1872.

SUSAN B. ANTHONY

Anthony, Katherine. *Susan B. Anthony: Her Personal History and Her Era*. New York: Doubleday, 1954.

Cooper, Ilene. *Susan B. Anthony*. New York: Franklin Watts, 1984.

Harper, Ida Husted. *The Life and Work of Susan B. Anthony*. New York: Arno, 1969.

Lutz, Alma. *Susan B. Anthony*. Boston: Beacon, 1959.

Weisberg, Barbara. *Susan B. Anthony*. New York: Chelsea House, 1988.

ELIZABETH CADY STANTON

Clark, Mary Stetson. *Bloomers and Ballots: Elizabeth Cady Stanton and Women's Rights*. New York: Viking, 1972.

Coolidge, Rita. *Women's Rights*. New York: Dutton, 1966.

Griffith, Elizabeth. *In Her Own Right: The Life of Elizabeth Cady Stanton*. London: Oxford University Press, 1984.

Gurko, Miriam. *The Ladies of Seneca Falls*. New York: Macmillan, 1974.

Stanton, Elizabeth Cady. *Eighty Years and More: Reminiscences 1815-1897*. New York: Schocken, 1971.

FREDERICK DOUGLASS

Douglass, Frederick. *Life and Times of Frederick Douglass*. New York: Thomas Y. Crowell, 1966.

Holland, Frederic. *The Colored Orator*. NY: Funk & Wagnalls, 1895.

Huggins, Nathan Irvan. *Slave and Citizen: The Life of Frederick Douglass*. Boston: Little, Brown, 1980.

Miller, Douglas T. *Frederick Douglass and the Fight for Freedom*. New York: Facts on File, 1988.

LUMINARIES / NOTABLES — Chapter 3

SCOTT HAMILTON

Hamilton, Scott. *Landing It: My Life On And Off the Ice*. New York: Kensington Books, 1999.

Hamilton, Scott. *The Great Eight: How To Be Happy*. Nashville: Thomas Nelson, 2008.

HELEN KELLER

Keller, Helen. *The Story of My Life*. New York: Airmont Books, 1965.

Whitman, Alden. "Triumph Out of Tragedy." *New York Times* 2 Jun 1968:1, 75.

PAUL WITTGENSTEIN

Barchilon, John. *The Crown Prince*. New York: Norton, 1984.

Flindell, E. Fred. "Paul Wittgenstein (1897-1961): Patron and Pianist." *The Music Review*. xxxii (1971), 107-124.

ELIZABETH BLACKWELL

Chambers, Peggy. *A Doctor Alone, A Biography of Elizabeth Blackwell: The First Woman Doctor (1821-1910)*. London: Abelard Schuman, 1958.

Ross, Ishbel. *Child of Destiny: The Story of the First Woman Doctor.*
    New York: Harper & Brothers, 1949.

FLORENCE NIGHTINGALE
Boyd, Nancy. "Florence Nightingale." *Three Victorian Women Who
    Changed the World.* New York: Oxford University Press, 1982.
Strachey, Lytton. "Florence Nightingale." *Eminent Victorians.*
    New York: Harcourt Brace Jovanovich, 1918.
Woodham-Smith, Cecil. *Florence Nightingale: (1820-1910).*
    New York: McGraw-Hill, 1951.

RESEARCHERS / CEOs / INVENTORS—Chapter 4

STEPHEN HAWKING
Ferguson, Kitty. *Stephen Hawking: Quest for a Theory of the Universe.*
    New York: Franklin Watts, 1991.
Hawking, Stephen W. *Black Holes and Baby Universes and Other Essays.*
    New York: Bantam, 1993.
White, Michael and John Gribben. *Stephen Hawking: A Life in Science.*
    Minneapolis: Dutton, 1992.

LEE IACOCCA
Abodaher, David. *Iacocca: A Biography.* New York: Macmillan, 1982.
Gordon, Maynard M. *The Iacocca Management Technique.* New York:
    Dodd, Mead, 1985.
Iacocca, Lee, with Sonny Kleinfield. *Talking Straight.* Boston: G. K. Hall,
    1988.
Iacocca, Lee, with William Nowak. *Iacocca, An Autobiography.* New
    York: Bantam, 1984.
Wyden, Peter. *The Unknown Iacocca: An Unauthorized Biography.* New
    York: William Morrow, 1987.

R. H. MACY
Harriman, Margaret Case. *And the Price Is Right.* Cleveland: World,
    1958.
Hendrickson, Robert. *The Grand Emporiums.* NY: Stein and Day, 1979.
Hower, Ralph M. *History of Macy's of New York 1858-1919: Chapters
    in the Evolution of the Department Store.* Cambridge: Harvard
    University Press, 1943.
Hungerford, Edward. *The Romance of a Great Store.* NY: Bantam, 1984.
Trachenberg, Jeffrey A. *The Rain on Macy's Parade.* New York: Times
    Business, 1996.

ISAAC SINGER

Brandon, Ruth. *A Capitalist Romance: Singer and the Sewing Machine.*
Philadelphia: Lippincott, 1977.
Cooper, Grace Rogers. *The Invention of the Sewing Machine.*
Washington, D.C.: Smithsonian Institution, 1968.
Goddard, Dwight. *Eminent Engineers.* New York: Derry-Collard, 1905.

JOHN FITCH

Boyd, Thomas. *Poor John Fitch, Inventor of the Steamboat.* New York:
Putnam's, 1935.
Ferris, J. T. *Romance of Forgotten Men.* NY: Harper & Brothers, 1928.
Flexner, James Thomas. *Steamboats Come True: American Inventors in
Action.* New York: Viking, 1944.
Goddard, Dwight. *Eminent Engineers.* New York: Derry-Collard, 1905.
Westcott, Thompson. *Life of John Fitch, Inventor of the Steamboat.*
Philadelphia: Lippincott, 1857.

STATESMAN / RULERS—Chapter 5

NELSON MANDELA

Hoobler, Dorothy and Thomas. *Nelson and Winnie Mandela.*
New York: Franklin Watts, 1987.
Mandela, Nelson. *Long Walk To Freedom.* Boston: Little, Brown,1994.
Vail, John. *Nelson and Winnie Mandela.* New York: Chelsea House, 1989.

FRANKLIN D. ROOSEVELT

Burns, James McGregor. *Roosevelt: The Lion and the Fox.* New York:
Harcourt, Brace, 1956.
Gould, Jean. *A Good Fight: The Story of F.D.R.'s Conquest of Polio.* New
York: Dodd, Mead, 1960.
Gunther, John. *Roosevelt in Retrospect: A Profile in History.* New York:
Harper, 1950.
Rollins, Jr., Alfred B. *Roosevelt and Howe.* New York: Knopf, 1962.
Sherwood, Robert E. *Roosevelt and Hopkins: An Intimate History.* New
York: Harper, 1948.

WINSTON CHURCHILL

Churchill, Randolph S. *Winston Churchill, Volume II.* Boston: Houghton
Mifflin, 1967.
Cowles, Virginia. *Winston Churchill: The Era and the Man.* New York:
Harper, 1953.
Gilbert, Martin. *Winston S. Churchill.* Boston: Houghton Mifflin, 1971.

James, Robert Rhodes. *Churchill, A Study in Failure, 1900-1939*. New York: World, 1970.
Keller, Mollie. *Winston Churchill*. New York: Franklin Watts, 1984.

ABRAHAM LINCOLN

Borits, Gabor S. *Lincoln's Generals*. New York: NY, Oxford UP, 1994.
Coolidge, Olivia. *The Apprenticeship of Abraham Lincoln*. New York: Charles Scribner's Sons, 1974.
Donald, David Herbert. *Lincoln*. New York: Simon & Schuster, 1995.
Handlin, Oscar and Lillian. *Abraham Lincoln and the Union*. Boston: Little, Brown, 1980.
Oates, Stephen B. *Abraham Lincoln: The Man Behind the Myths*. New York: Harper & Row, 1984.

ROBERT BRUCE

Baker, Nina Brown. *Robert Bruce: King of Scots*. NY: Vanguard, 1948.
Scott, Sir Walter. "History of Scotland." *Tales of a Grandfather*. Boston: Tichnor and Fields, 1861.
Sutcliff, Rosemary. *Heroes and History*. New York: Putnam's, 1965.
Tranter, Nigel. *Robert the Bruce: The Path of the Hero King*. New York: St. Martin's, 1970.
—. *Robert the Bruce: The Steps to the Empty Throne*. London: Hodder and Stoughton, 1969.

SOLDIERS / SAILORS / AIRMEN—Chapter 6

CARL BRASHEAR

Robbins, David. *Men of Honor*. New York: Onyx, 2000.
Stilwell, Paul. *The Reminiscences of Master Chief Carl M. Brashear, U.S. Navy (Retired)*. Annapolis: U.S. Naval Institute, 1998.

DOUGLAS BADER

Brickhill, Paul. *Reach for the Sky: The Story of Douglas Bader, Legless Ace of the Battle of Britain*. New York: Norton, 1954.
Collier, Richard. *Eagle Day: The Battle of Britain, August 6—September 15, 1940*. New York: Dutton, 1966.
Hough, Richard. *The Battle of Britain: The Triumph of R.A.F. Fighter Pilots*. New York: Macmillan, 1971.
Markel, Julia. *Turning Points of World War II: The Battle of Britain*. New York: Franklin Watts, 1984.
Townsend, Peter. *Duel of Eagles*. New York: Simon & Schuster, 1970.

REGINALD MITCHELL

Collier, Basil. A *History of War*. New York: Macmillan, 1974.

Cooke, David C. *The Planes They Flew In World War Two*. New York: Dodd, Mead & Company, 1969.

Cooper, Bryan, and John Batchelor. *Fighter: A History of Fighter Aircraft*. New York: Scribner's, 1973.

Spitfire. Videocassette. Royal Sound Video Productions, 1942. 90 min.

Vader, John. *Spitfire*. New York: Ballantine, 1969.

ULYSSES S. GRANT

Catton, Bruce. *U. S. Grant and the U.S. Military Tradition*. Boston: Little, Brown, 1954.

Grant, Ulysses S. *Personal Memoirs of U. S. Grant*. NY: World, 1952.

Green, Horace. *General Grant's Last Stand: A Biography*. New York: Scribner's, 1936.

Todd, Helen. *A Man Named Grant*. Boston: Houghton Mifflin, 1940.

Woodward, W. E. *Meet General Grant*. New York: Liveright, 1946.

JOHN PAUL JONES

Johnson, Gerald White. *The First Captain: The Story of John Paul Jones*. New York: Coward-McCann, 1947.

Munro, Donald John. *Commodore John Paul Jones, U.S. Navy: A Biography of Our First Great Naval Hero*. New York: William-Frederick, 1954.

Morrison, Samuel Eliot. *John Paul Jones: A Sailor's Biography*. New York: Time, 1959.

Sperry, Armstrong. *John Paul Jones, Fighting Sailor*. New York: Random House, 1953.

Syme, Ronald. *Captain John Paul Jones: America's Fighting Seaman*. New York: Morrow, 1968.

ORGANIZERS / PLANNERS—Chapter 7

STEVE JOBS

Aaseng, Nathan. "Steve Jobs." *Business Builders of Computers* Minneapolis: Oliver, 2000.

Deutschman, Alan. *The Second Coming of Steve Jobs*. New York: Broadway Books, 2000.

Smith, Douglas K., and Robert C. Alexander. *Fumbling the Future*. New York: William Morrow, 1988.

AL NEUHARTH

Neuharth, Al. *Confessions of an S.O.B.* New York: Doubleday, 1989.
Prichard, Peter S. *The Making of McPaper:*
The Inside Story of USA Today. New York: St. Martin's, 1987.

DOROTHY DAY

Coles, Robert. *Dorothy Day: A Radical Devotion.*
Reading, MA: Addison-Wesley, 1987.
Day, Dorothy. *Loaves and Fishes.* Maryknoll, NY: Orbis Books, 1963.
—. *The Long Loneliness: The Autobiography of Dorothy Day.*
San Francisco: Harper Collins, 1952.
Miller, William D. *Dorothy Day: A Biography.*
San Francisco: Harper & Row, 1982.

CHAIM WEIZMANN

Amdur, Richard. *Chaim Weizmann.* New York: Chelsea House, 1988.
Ben-Gurion, David. *Chaim Weizmann—Champion of the Jewish People.*
Jerusalem: Alpha, 1974.
Litvinoff, Barnet. *Weizmann, Last of the Patriarchs.* NY: Putnam's, 1976.
Reinharz, Jehuda. *Chaim Weizmann: The Making of a Zionist Leader.*
New York, Oxford University Press, 1985.
Rose, Norman. *Chaim Weizmann: A Biography.* NY: Sifton-Viking, 1986.

BRIGHAM YOUNG

Bringhurst, Newell G. *Brigham Young and the*
Expanding American Frontier. Boston: Little, Brown, 1986.
Palmer, Richard F. and Karl D. Butler. *Brigham Young,*
The New York Years. Provo, UT: Charles Redd Center for
Western Studies at Brigham Young University, 1982.

GENERAL

Allen, John, ed. *100 Great Lives.* NY: Journal of Living Publishing, 1944.
Bolton, Sarah K. *Famous Men of Science.* New York: Crowell, 1960.
Cohen, Shari. *Coping With Failure.* New York: Rosen, 1988.
Crowther, J. W. *Famous American Men of Science.* NY: Norton, 1937.
Dole, Elizabeth. *Hearts Touched With Fire.* NY: Carole & Graf, 2004.
Hart, Michael A. *The 100: A Ranking of the Most Influential Persons in
History.* New York: Hart, 1978.
Untermeyer, Louis. *Makers of the Modern World.* New York: Simon &
Schuster, 1955.